Critical issues in early childhood education

D0220053

Critical issues in early childhood education

Edited by Nicola Yelland

Open University Press

Open University Press
McGraw-Hill Education
McGraw-Hill House
Shoppenhangers Road
Maidenhead
Berkshire
England
SL6 2QL

email: enquiries@openup.co.uk
world wide web: www.openup.co.uk

and Two Penn Plaza, New York, NY 10121-2289, USA

First published 2005
Reprinted 2006, 2008
Copyright © Nicola Yelland 2005

A catalogue record of this book is available from the British Library

ISBN-10 0 335 21596 3 (pb)   0 335 21597 1 (hb)
ISBN-13 978 0 335 215966 (pb) 978 0 335 215973 (hb)
Library of Congress Cataloging-in-Publication Data
CIP data applied for

Typeset by RefineCatch Limited, Bungay, Suffolk
Printed in the UK by Bell & Bain Ltd, Glasgow

For Keith, Tamsyn, Caja, Gwendoline May and Muriel
who have been critical in my life.

In memory of Sally Lubeck, a remarkable woman,
academic, friend and mother.

Contents

List of contributors

Yarrow Andrew is an early childhood teacher who enjoys the challenges of working in long day care. As a teacher, his main interests are gender and sexuality, children's rights, and challenging adult complacency about what 'child care' should involve. Yarrow has worked in the early childhood field for ten years and still feels he is just beginning to understand children's lives.

Mindy Blaise is currently a Senior Lecturer in New Learning at RMIT University and a Research Fellow at the Centre for Equity and Innovation in Early Childhood Education at Melbourne University. She uses feminist poststructuralism and queer theory in her teaching and researching with teachers and young children to uncover the complexities of classroom life.

Liz Brooker was an early years teacher in London for many years before moving into postgraduate research and teaching at the Institute of Education, University of London. Most of her work has involved an investigation of the ways that education and care systems can contribute to, or combat, the long-term social exclusion of children and young people from disadvantaged groups. Her book, *Starting School: Young Children Learning Cultures* (Open University Press, 2002), which won the Society for Education Studies' annual book award for 2003, was based on a study of four-year-old children as they learned in their homes and in their first year of school. More recently, and currently, she has been researching the experiences of teenage parents and young people who have been 'looked after' by the local authority. Liz now runs a Master's programme in Childhood Studies, focusing on children's rights.

Sheralyn Campbell is an early childhood practitioner-researcher, and Fellow at the University of Melbourne, Centre for Equity and Innovation in Early Childhood. Sheralyn has worked in a variety of children's services as a teacher, policy advisor, manager and mentor. Her PhD research focused on the issues of social justice that were an everyday part of childrens' lives in an inner urban child care centre. Her most recent work is emerging from a small Australian rural child care centre where she continues to focus on the 'politics' of curriculum in early childhood settings. In particular, she is concerned with how feminist poststructural theory can be used in practice to disrupt the meanings of gender, 'race', class and sexualities that constitute inequities within children's worlds.

Gaile S. Cannella is Professor of Education in the Division of Curriculum and Instruction in the College of Education at Arizona State University. She is the author of *Deconstructing Early Childhood Education: Social Justice and Revolution* as well as the 2004 book entitled *Childhood and (Post) Colonization: Power, Education, and Contemporary Practice*. She is also the section editor for Childhood and Cultural Studies in the *Journal of Curriculum Theorizing*. Her professional work focuses on critical qualitative research and cultural studies as related to family, gender, and childhood public policy.

Eileen Honan is a Lecturer in Language and Literacy education at Deakin University, Australia. Eileen's current research interests include creating closer links between the theories and practices of classroom literacy teachers through the use of rhizo-textual analytical techniques, and the introduction of vernacular education in Papua New Guinea. She is co-editor (with Annah Healy) of the collection *Text Next: New Resources for Literacy Learning*.

Richard Johnson's research of late has been related to investigating how the field of cultural studies interpretively impacts children and early childhood/ teacher education programs. Some of this is witnessed in his co-edited book *Resistance and Representation: Rethinking Childhood Education*. A related recent work is his critique of 'no touch' policies in early education in his book, *Hands Off!: The Disappearance of Touch in the Care of Young Children*. Richard's current interests are focused on critiquing traditional, normative practices in the field of early education.

Anna Kilderry is a Research Assistant in the School of Education at RMIT University in Melbourne and her research interests include early childhood curriculum and pre-school teacher education. Previously Anna has been an early childhood teacher, TAFE (technical and further education) teacher and university lecturer in early childhood education. It is through this involvement in early childhood teacher education in the areas of early childhood policy, curriculum and practice that Anna has developed her interest in early childhood teachers' curricula decision-making. Currently Anna is completing her PhD in this area by critically examining how early childhood teachers make their curricula decisions and by considering what influences the teacher when making these decisions.

Jackie Marsh is a Senior Lecturer in Education at the University of Sheffield, UK, where she co-directed, with Elaine Millard, the ESRC Research Seminar Series 'Children's Literacy and Popular Culture' (2002–4). She edited, along with Nigel Hall and Joanne Larson, the *Handbook of Early Childhood Literacy* (Sage, 2003) an international review of research in the field, and is an editor of the *Journal of Early Childhood Literacy*. Jackie is involved in research which examines the role and nature of popular culture and media in early childhood literacy in both in- and out-of-school contexts, and has recently edited a book which explores this area in depth: *Popular Culture, New Media and Digital Technologies* (RoutledgeFalmer, 2004).

Jeanette Rhedding-Jones is Professor in Early Childhood Education at Oslo University College, Norway. Since moving from Australia in 1997 her research has emphasized critical multicultural matters of languages, ethnicities and complexities. She currently leads a research project funded by the Norwegian Research Council entitled 'Gender, complexity and diversity in pedagogical institutions for children aged 0–10'. After being a pre-school teacher-carer and a teacher in early schooling, Jeanette then worked intensively with teachers and student-teachers in Australia to develop new curricula, new ideas and new ways of thinking about professionalism. In 2004 she leads the host committee of the annual international conference Reconceptualizing Early Childhood Education, to be held in Oslo. She is the winner of the 2003 Research and Development Prize across the Faculties at Oslo University College.

Leonie Rowan is Coordinator of the Quality Learning Research Priority Area at Deakin University, Australia. Her research interests relate not only to new literacies and their relationship to new technologies, but also to the ways in which changed and changing social formations demand new and rigorous ways of thinking about and responding to difference in educational settings. She is the author of *Write Me In: Inclusive Texts in the Primary Classroom*, and co-author (with Michele Knobel, Chris Bigum and Colin Lankshear) of *Boys, Literacies and Schooling: The Dangerous Territories of Gender Based Literacy Reforms*.

Sharon Ryan is a Research Associate at the National Institute for Early Education Research and an Assistant Professor at Rutgers, the State University of New Jersey. She has worked as an early childhood and special education teacher, administrator, consultant, and teacher educator. Dr Ryan's research interests are early childhood curriculum and policy, equitable approaches to educating young students, and the potential of alternative theories for reconceptualizing early childhood education in theory, research, and practice. Currently, she is involved in several research projects investigating the implementation of pre-school policy using both qualitative and quantitative methodologies.

Jonathan G. Silin has been a member of the Bank Street College of Education Graduate Faculty since 1992. He is the author of *Sex, Death, and the Education of Children: Our Passion for Ignorance in the Age of AIDS*, co-producer of *Children Talk About AIDS*, co-editor of *Putting the Children First: The Changing Face of*

Newark's Public Schools and editor of Bank Street's Occasional Paper Series. Before earning his doctorate in Curriculum and Teaching from Teachers College, Columbia University, he was a classroom teacher and taught in a variety of early childhood settings.

Jennifer Sumsion is an Associate Professor at Macquarie University. Her research interests focus primarily on pre-service early childhood teacher education and early childhood teachers' identities, work environments, early career experiences and career satisfaction. She has published widely in national and international journals on these topics. Jennifer currently holds an Australian Research Council grant to investigate early childhood teachers' views about the impact of the regulatory environment on their ability to provide quality care. She is also interested in discourses associated with calls to employ more male teachers and has recently completed a report for the New South Wales Department of Community Services entitled '. . . The *"Right"* Men, not Just *More* Men: An Investigation of the Gender Imbalance in the Children's Services Workforce in New South Wales' with Michael Lyons and Andrea Quinn.

Daniel J. Walsh's research seeks to begin to shift early childhood education, both daily practice and the education of teachers, away from an acultural, highly structural and romantic developmentalism to a culturally informed, systemic developmentalism that is attuned to what Lee Cronbach called 'contemporary realities'. He has been involved for the past five years in cross-cultural research looking at early schooling in Japan and the American Midwest. He has published in numerous journals and is the author of two books, *High Risk Children in Schools: Constructing Sustaining Relationships* (Routledge) with Robert Pianta, and *Studying Children in Context: Theories, Methods, and Ethics* with Elizabeth Graue.

Nicola Yelland's research over the last decade has been related to investigating the ways in which children learn with new information technologies in both in- and out-of-school contexts. She is the author of *Early Mathematical Explorations* with Carmel Diezmann and Deborah Butler, and has edited four books, *Gender in Early Childhood* (Routledge), *Innovations in Practice* (NAEYC), *Ghosts in the Machine: Women's Voices in Research with Technology*, and *Critical Issues in Early Childhood* (Open University Press). Nicola works with teachers exploring the ways in which ICT can be incorporated into learning contexts to make them more interesting and motivating for children, so that outcomes are improved. Nicola has worked on numerous Australian Research Council projects related to the use of ICT in educational contexts and has written articles on her research published in international journals.

List of illustrations

List of Tables

List of Figures

1 Against the tide

New ways in early childhood education

Nicola Yelland and Anna Kilderry

At the dawn of the new century it was inevitable to reflect on the state of the world and our lives in them. One of the most obvious manifestations of the change from one century to the next was the apprehension that surrounded the actual event. We were prepared for the ultimate disaster when it was predicted that our daily activities that relied so much on computer networks, would fail, public transport systems would be thrown into chaos and capitalism and commerce would disintegrate as records were lost and business halted. All because at another dawn, that is when computers were created, the systems were made with only two spaces for recording or acknowledging the date and somehow computers might be confused about whether it was 1800 or 1900 instead of 2000. In retrospect, we know that none of this did in fact happen but there was money to be made from promoting Y2K bug salvations. These events and many others epitomized the changes that had occurred in the western world over the course of the century, and in particular, those which have escalated during the past 20 years. Events of the past two decades have served to illustrate how different our lives have become and additionally this reminds us that the world that our children are growing up in is changing at an even faster rate. Such rapid growth was illustrated in Moore's Law (Intel Research, 2004) that the capacity and capabilities of silicon integrated circuits double approximately every two years and mirror the ways in which the content and structure of our lives are constantly multiplying at a tremendous speed.

In such new contexts, issues around globalization have highlighted the need to extend boundaries of existence, together with a recognition of diversity across contexts, cultures, identities, commerce and production. The role of new technologies in everyday activities has reshaped our lifeworlds, so that some jobs have been obliterated and many new styles of living have been created. While we have had to adapt to the changing times, new generations have been inducted into new systems as citizens, workers and consumers. As societies have been characterized by these massive changes and the world at large has in some way become more accessible, and in other ways more elusive, education systems seemed to have maintained their traditional existence. However, it would seem in the structural sense, that the majority of education systems, at least in the western world, have in fact ignored the changes that have been going around them. This has been characterized in a number of ways, including a return to neo-liberal attitudes (e.g. Apple, 2001) and pedagogies influenced by those who think that education systems should be structured and assessed via tests, through measurable outcomes and by strict adherence to standards that are overt and efficient (e.g. United States Department of Education, 2001). For many students and educators, the resultant curriculum and educational experience has been narrowed and reduced to that of prescribed outcomes limited to testing a small range of behaviours that indicate the possession of content and skills more suited to an industrial age. In this educational climate, modernist notions of universality and reason have prevailed and the potential for discovery and moving forward into realms characterized by new learning initiatives is valued only if scientifically tested.

Thus, *grand narratives* (Lyotard, 1984) have prevailed and consequently we hear arguments about 'back to the basics', 'grading kindergarten' and 'no child left behind' to defend testing and stringent accountability measures. Such statements, phrases and policies and their associated practices, whether in the form of adherence to rigid curriculum discipline areas within the school sector, or in the formation of 'child-centred' curricula in the pre-school context, reflect systems that have resisted change. In this way the traditional nature and structure of early childhood education have been sanctified and maintained in these new times. However, it is also apparent that postmodern views are seeping into social and educational thinking whereby many have begun to question the validity and impossibilities of such *grand narratives* and universal truths. Lifeworlds have become complex and thus have required new forms of analyses, descriptions and practice. Harvey (1989) has suggested that postmodernity is characterized by heterogeneity, multiple discourses and recognition of the complexity of diversity and is emancipated by critiques of universal truths and structures. In the rejection of reason, based on empirical evidence, postmodern explanations are often complex and challenging as the analyses and critiques often do not offer solutions or prescriptions for success. As such, postmodern explanations can be problematic for practitioners who want to know, 'what is the best?' for the children in their care. However, in the context of interrogating the educational contexts in which we find ourselves, the use of such perspectives (e.g. poststructuralist, feminist and postcolonial) and techniques (e.g. deconstruction, discourse analysis) has grown in recent times. It is contended here, in this book, that educational contexts, in particular within early childhood education, are evolving to be more relevant to young children's lives and experiences in a variety of ways. This chapter outlines some of the new ways for thinking about early childhood education and provides a rationale as to why the traditional foundations of early childhood education are shifting to make room for new, much needed postmodern perspectives and discourses.

One of the ways this has been happening within the context of early childhood education is via the reconceptualization of the field from a variety of perspectives. This has included critical and postmodern work on changing notions of childhood (e.g. Cannella, 1997; James, Jenks and Prout 1998; Moss, 2002), identities (e.g. Grieshaber and Cannella, 2001), gender and sexuality (e.g. Silin, 1995; Boldt, 2002), and social justice (e.g. Polakow, 1992) to name just a few. Additionally, there has been research into teaching (for example, see Genishi, Ryan, Ochsner and Malter, 2001) and the issues that impact on families of young children (e.g. Grieshaber and Cannella, 2001). What has distinguished this research has been the recognition that we need to engage with difficult, and also hitherto taboo, issues. Many features distinguish this work from previous research in the field, including a move away from discussions that manifested binary contexts, such as pitting *developmentally appropriate* against *inappropriate* and *normal* against *abnormal*. We suggest that new frameworks are needed since we live in complex times and traditional frames do not capture the complexity of lifeworlds experienced today, nor the new ways that are required to adapt to these unfamiliar educational situations. Further, the way that educational settings are viewed is also undergoing changes, with some research acknowledging the sites as being 'multifaceted, multifocal, multicultural sites that survive and thrive on multiplicity and diversity; [and] their survival depends on vigorous discussion, debate, and arguments about their moral and social purposes' (Smyth, 2001, p. 146). In this context, quick solutions may be difficult to achieve but resolutions and practical ways forward are possible although these may not be consistent over time, contexts or cultures.

Early childhood reconceptualists (Block, 1992; Kessler and Swadener, 1992; Silin, 1995; Lubeck, 1996; Cannella, 1997; Tobin, 1997; Grieshaber and Cannella, 2001; Jipson and Johnson, 2001; Soto and Swadener, 2002) have a commitment to bringing about social change and to improving the lives of young children. By taking the next step and changing discourses and educational practice, reconceptualists, via critiques of existing pedagogies, have made significant inroads into early childhood education and the practices inherent in them. These inroads have been created by focusing on the ways in which 'innocent early childhood practices . . . produce inequalities that are mirrored in the broader society' (Genishi et al., 2001, p. 1197) and by taking action against the forces that cause or promote these inequalities. As the critical orientation of such work recognizes the 'complexities, inconsistencies, and ever changing dynamics of teaching and [. . .] acknowledge[s] that their methods can never fully categorize, explicate or elucidate teaching, nor should they' (Ryan et al., 2001, p. 57), this enables early childhood educators to change the educational landscape to be more relevant and inclusive for young children. Some early childhood reconceptualists (see Genishi et al., 2001) are cognisant of the ways in which interpretative studies may provide insights into the complexities of teaching young children but suggest that they do not go far enough to critically question the nature of the practices under study in order to consider the ways in which they impact on issues such as social justice, equity and diversity.

As early childhood education has long been organized and justified on the principles of *developmentally appropriate practice* (DAP), which was founded in the developmental psychology literature from early last century, it has been difficult in practice to think about and understand young children from outside of this knowledge (Prout and James, 1997). One example of a practice that 'grew' out of developmental theory is the 'child-centred curriculum'. It can seem harmless when discussing the main tenets of this practice, but when considered critically, it is apparent that a 'child-centred curriculum' is an adult-dominated arena, heavily developmentally laden with inherent biases and modernist views. Critiques of what it means to be a 'child-centred' practitioner are growing and include scholars such as Dahlberg, Moss and Pence (1999) who suggest that 'child-centred' practice can embody certain modernist views that rely on scientific perspectives of the child whereas postmodern views actually 'decentre' the child within practice. They argue that early childhood educators have choices regarding how they might view children and this can have significant ramifications for practice, since educationally, the child is situated by the adult. Child-centredness and child-centred practices are 'deeply rooted implicit pedagogical knowledge' (Corrie, 1995, p. 4) in early childhood education and are part of the everyday understandings of young children. It is imperative that such assumptions are interrogated so as to unearth the rationale behind its implementation in practice.

Such occurrences in the field have come at a time when governments and bureaucrats have been persuaded that early childhood education, that is, the period from birth to 8 years of age, is increasingly being recognized as fundamental to the lives of young children and their families. Expediently, for political success or otherwise, research reports have contended that attitudes and performance in the early childhood years can have an important impact on educational outcomes in the later years of schooling and, as a result, policy-makers are keen that they should be seen to be providing an effective start to learning. Resources and discussion have thus been redirected to this end of the education spectrum and consequently the importance of the early years and the topics and issues concerning young children not only have a high profile but are also being considered as essential to all subsequent outcomes and interactions. This has meant that in higher education early childhood programmes are in great demand and resources are being directed to innovative programmes which can demonstrate a capacity to prepare early childhood educators that are capable of dealing with the challenges inherent to educating young children in the twenty-first century. This situation is made more com-plex by the demands of life in the information age and changing societal expectations and views. For example, theories of learning and socialization intrinsic to much early childhood educational literature were conceptualized in vastly different social and economic contexts. These views, that inherently contain modernist thinking, are maintained even though the world has moved into the twenty-first century. Justifications for maintaining the status quo continue, and it is our contention that such outdated practices and atti-tudes need to be challenged. To provide another example, DAP has privileged certain ways of being and knowing that do not recognize the diverse qualities of children and their families in a global context. In doing so, it has the effect of alienating the qualities of diversity, qualities that should be celebrated. Further, it suggests that there is a universal state that we should all be striving for which is based on western ways of doing and knowing. In recent times these contentions have been challenged and early childhood education is coming to be known for its openness to new ideas and for the multidiscipli-nary nature of the sector that has facilitated the process of reconceptualiza-tion. The terrain of early childhood has been remodelled significantly over the past decade and contemporary and alternative views and perspectives are beginning to have an impact on practices and pedagogies. It must be said that even though the DAP view also wants the best for children, this develop-mental paradigm can be uncompromising at times and has assisted in the perpetuation of white middle-class views of the world and the ways in which they may be universally achieved in the field. Developmental psychology, and the structuralist approach inherent to it, have privileged theories such as that of Piaget (e.g. Piaget, 1953). These theories have suggested that young children pass through universal stages of development determined according to their chronological age, and that learning takes place as the result of interacting with materials and is experiential in its nature. The fact that interactions with materials and experimenting are a part of learning is not being disputed here, nor is child development theory as *one* informant for practice. Instead, the issue being deliberated is the all-encompassing effect that developmental the-ory has on early childhood education and the dominance of the psychological paradigm governing, informing and determining early childhood curriculum and practice (Goffin and Wilson, 2001). For example, the impact of Piaget's work in early childhood education has been immense, and incredible, when we consider that Piaget did not regard himself as an educationalist, nor indeed as a developmental psychologist. It has been contended that Piaget made an important contribution to epistemological beliefs (theory of knowledge) in the field, in particular in relation to the ways in which a young child develops and learns in specific instances and under certain conditions. However, there are reasons to be critical of Piagetian theory being readily applied to the early childhood educational context. The first issue lies with the fact that Piaget's developmental theories were incomplete (Ausubel, 1967; Sullivan, 1967; Lawton and Hooper, 1978), were not tested and some critics go so far as to criticize Piagetian theories as being no more than mere 'observations' (Sullivan, 1967). The second issue is the uncritical extrapolation of Piaget's theories into early childhood educational contexts. It is here that educators often justify their curriculum and programme based on Piaget's stages and statements on learning, assuming that they are stem from reliable and valid sources (Sullivan, 1967). When discussing the transference of psychological theories to educational settings, Ausubel said that extrapolation can be a problem and even be harmful, when

> it is premature, uncritical, or unselective; that is when the findings or theories that are being applied from the parent discipline are themselves inadequately validated or lacking in theoretical cogency, when the relevance of basic-science knowledge for the actual problems encountered in the applied field is far-fetched or tenuous, or when no account is taken of the supplementary research of an engineering nature that is necessary before basic science generalizations can cope with the added complexities posed by the practical objectives of the applied discipline. Unfortunately, however, it is precisely the latter kind of extrapolation that has prevailed thus far in education.
>
> (1967, p. iii)

Individual issues and theories should be critically examined before they are eagerly applied in the educational sense. Otherwise education ends up with arbitrary, irrelevant curricula parameters and pedagogies that dictate whether a child is 'ready' for education and which often views children in a deficit model as 'egocentric' and 'pre-logical' (Piaget, 1968). If developmental theories govern early childhood pedagogies (for example, by questioning if the child is developmentally ready), and early childhood content within a curriculum (for example, by describing the type of experiences that are deemed to be suitable for pre-operational or pre-conceptual children), they will have far-reaching effects on the shape of early childhood education. Specific aspects of Piaget's theories, for example, the notion that the child is an active learner and needs to use their senses for learning in infancy, can make pedagogical sense to early childhood educators planning for effective learning. These are not the issues contested here. We maintain that the removal of Piaget's theory, as well as other developmental theories, from their position of *primacy* in the field will enable new ways engaging with learning in the early childhood years.

Recently, there have been notable initiatives and research conducted from postmodern perspectives that are beginning to have an impact on early childhood education. For example, Dahlberg et al. (1999) have discussed the reconstruction of early childhood education from outside developmental perspectives, Moss (2002) has argued for early childhood to be positioned within a broader domain and Soto and Swadener (2002) suggest new liberating discourses and pedagogical spaces as a basis for theorizing in the field. Newly emerging paradigms are now evident, but they do require some further nourishment and consideration. Members of the early childhood education community need to sustain and grow this platform of ideas, critiques and theories. Consequently, questions will arise in practice that will be centred on issues such as: How can we successfully navigate change in contemporary times? In what ways can we create contexts for learning that are relevant to young children and their families? And, What are the critical issues or educational discussion that need to occur in this new climate?

It is apparent that in contemporary times the skills of early childhood educators are broadening and are being reconceptualized from practitioners who do *what is said to be right*, to practitioners who ask, *In what ways can we create effective learning environments?* The new aspects of practitioners' discourse are a result of living in more complex and uncertain times which have led to the emergence of multifaceted questions and issues regarding the ethical considerations of practice, the cultural ramifications of practice, and the consideration of equity in education. Maintaining currency and relevance in the early childhood sector requires a continual engagement with critical issues, as well as finding new ways to adapt to changing educational circumstances. Early childhood educators must look beyond the boundaries of the field, and ask questions about their practice. By conceptualizing, postulating and recognizing critical issues in early childhood education, educators can create new understandings about these significant educational issues in changing times.

This volume aims to add to the exciting and challenging exchanges by theorizing about critical issues in early childhood practices and pedagogies that require consideration at this time, for change to occur so that the field may move forward. This may frequently feel like swimming against the tide, but in reconceptualizing the significant issues, and by expanding the boundaries of theory and practice, we will engage in discussions that we hope will do the following:

- create more equitable early childhood teaching and learning practices;
- provide deeper understandings about early childhood education theories, especially perspectives that take into account the lifeworlds of young children in new times;
- encourage new teaching and learning practices that meet the needs of being a lifelong learner and citizen of the twenty-first century;
- facilitate the exploration of contemporary understandings about the shared relationships with other educational sectors, that also struggle

with creating relevant, engaging and learner-focused curricula for contemporary times.

In doing so, we pose the following questions:

- What are some of the long held beliefs in early childhood education, that need to be challenged?
- What can postmodern perspectives offer to early childhood educators?
- How can early childhood educators deal with the complex issues that arise in the lives of young children?

This book explores critical issues in early childhood education in a broad range of contexts. The issues to be examined are not only *critical* in terms of being *fundamental* to early childhood education but they are also *critical* in that they present ideas and utilize frameworks, which are *not traditional* in the sector. In fact, they often deal with issues that have been considered as taboo, or interrogate ideas with methodologies that are postmodern in perspective which can challenge the comfort zone of early childhood educators. Such issues and methodologies are increasingly being sought out by teacher educators, parents, teachers and community members, who find that developmental perspectives do not satisfactorily explain and assist them in their interactions with young children and their families.

It is envisaged that this book can assist the early childhood sector to actively revisit, reposition and redefine early childhood teaching, and to deconstruct, transform and interrogate early childhood pedagogy by offering new frameworks, discourses and visions. One of the main advantages of an edited book is that it presents a range of views, in this case from eminent early childhood authors from Australia, the United States, the United Kingdom and Norway, who research and theorize from varied perspectives.

Overview of the book

The critical discussion of salient early childhood issues is reflected in the chapters that comprise this book and it endeavours to challenge and confront educators with a wide range of topics. The chapters provide early childhood educators with a forum in which to engage with contemporary ideas and practices from alternative and often, contrasting perspectives than those that have been traditionally associated with the education of young children. The perspectives will provide opportunities to critique aspects of the sector that many early childhood educators have accepted as being beyond question, as well as act as catalysts for further contemporary interrogations and investigations. In this educational age, instead of being influenced solely by the psychological perspective, early childhood education now benefits from the ideas that have emerged from other disciplines such as anthropology, cultural studies, sociology, and philosophy. This is enriching the capacity of early childhood educators to respond to the new demands of contemporary times with pedagogies and practices that are suited to the changing needs and interests of young children and their families. The structure of the book has been organized so that the critical issues are broadly situated in three fundamental areas in early childhood education:

1   Contemporary views of early childhood *education* and *teaching.*
2   Rethinking early childhood *practices.*
3   The emergence of *new technologies and multi-literacies.*

Part 1 of the book outlines some contemporary views of early childhood education and the ramifications for teaching and learning contexts. In separate chapters, Cannella and Walsh begin by exploring two alternative views of how we might deal with the issue of Developmentally Appropriate Practice (DAP). Both views have support in the early childhood field, and readers will take their own position when reading them. One of the aims in collating this book was to present *diverse viewpoints*, so that readers can discuss the positions and issues being interrogated and make their own evaluations. This exchange of different views enables readers not only to clarify their own position, but to think about, and perhaps even adapt, aspects from a contrasting perspective to their own views. Not all conceptualizing about curriculum issues requires the abolishment of ideas. For example, child development theories aim to promote nurturing and caring environments, and these are concepts to aspire to (Genishi et al., 2001). However, we also need to consider the ways in which certain cultural, gendered, socio-economic and political issues, that are all critical aspects of pedagogy, might be ignored in this context. It is such issues that are unravelled here by the authors in Part I.

In Chapter 2, Cannella puts forward the notion that early childhood reconceptualists and developmentalists should work together to create new discourses for early childhood education. Such discourses will recognize both the sociopolitical and historical contexts of the field. Cannella suggests moving toward a *critical early childhood*, one where educators ask vital questions and critically advocate for the care and education of young children. Daniel Walsh, in Chapter 3, takes the view that developmental theory remains necessary for early childhood education, but recognizes that it does not provide all the knowledge that may be required about the development and education of young children. He refers to Piaget as the *patron saint* of early childhood education and discusses the important role that cultural psychology can play within early childhood education. In considering some of the complex issues that face early childhood teachers, Blaise and Andrew, in Chapter 4, use queer theory and feminist poststructuralism to confront gender and sexuality in early childhood teaching practice. They point out how, despite having good intentions, early childhood educators not only can ignore the complexities of gender and sexuality in early childhood settings, but also unknowingly strengthen the existing power dynamics that operate in these educational environments. In Chapter 5, Sumsion uses poststructural perspectives to theorize about children's understandings of a male early childhood teacher. She carefully analyses children's portrayals of their male early childhood teacher and attempts to understand the ways that the children position the teacher by examining the apparent underpinning discourses that are evidenced in her data. The issues of silence and voice are raised in Silin's Chapter 6. He attentively traces the importance of the unspoken word, and considers how powerful language can be when embodying people's expressions and ideas and explores what this can mean for early childhood education. The way that the issues of silence and voice are portrayed in Silin's chapter encourages early childhood educators to think very differently about language and voice and the associated pedagogical implications.

In Part 2, the rethinking of early childhood practices, Ryan in Chapter 7 interrogates the nature of child-centred pedagogy, which has been the mantra of early childhood programmes for so long. Ryan considers how child-centred pedagogical discourses can limit children's agency and identities as learners and contends that children's play is not necessarily a neutral space. In Chapter 8, Brooker also engages with a discussion about child-centred pedagogy. She argues that her study found some of the ways in which children from non-white, middle-class families can be educationally disadvantaged since they do not share the same home life experiences and values as white middle-class children and families, values that are highly regarded in schools. Brooker's examination of the ways that culturally different home experiences can frame the students' school experience makes us think very carefully about how we position children so early on in their formal educational life, particularly within a play-based pedagogy.

In Chapter 9 Rhedding-Jones explores various conceptualizations of *diversity* and questions the practical and discursive positioning of early childhood education in relation to the wider discourse of diversity. Using various scenarios, from day care contexts across two continents, Rhedding-Jones makes a strong case for exploring and critiquing the notion of diversity. Equity and children's access to learning is the topic of Campbell's Chapter 10, where she puts children's tactics and the teacher's practice under review. Campbell puts forward some critical examples of how power is enacted in early childhood classrooms and provides some strategies on how to engage with an anti-discriminatory approach to teaching. In Chapter 11, Johnson explores the (mis)representations of identity in early childhood classroom play props by using a critical theoretical stance as a way to move away from a familiar view to a more critical one. By disrupting multicultural pretend play props, and by (re)reading landscapes, Johnson shows how visual culture can impact on our educational practice and even protect normalized notions of children and childhood.

In Part 3, the authors, Marsh, Rowan and Honan and Yelland, focus on the emergence of new literacies and technologies and their impact on the lives of young children. In Chapter 12, Marsh explores the communicative practices of pre-school children in multi-modal textual times. She highlights the dominance of print-based models of literacy in formal educational settings and contrasts this to that of their home lives where young children are exposed to, or 'saturated', in different types of media experiences. In Chapter 13, Rowan and Honan report on how early childhood educators can become both *literally* and *literarily* lost in searching for a meaningful literacy agenda in these changing times. They argue that particular forms of literacy are privileged over others and how complex it can be for early years teachers to navigate their way through all the conflicting information surrounding literacy in school contexts. In Chapter 14, Yelland examines the ways in which information and communication technologies (ICT) have changed our lives and discusses the ways in which they have the potential to influence new learning in schools. Using mathematics and numeracy as an example, she suggests that we might consider both mathematical activities and numeracy from a different standpoint and offers two ways to do this in a new model of numeracies and a way of viewing mathematical tasks that might facilitate rethinking the opportunities we provide for establishing a skills base for children to become numerate in the twenty-first century.

The chapters in this book aim to assist both graduate and undergraduate early childhood students, educators, teacher educators and other early childhood professionals to engage in dialogue about significant issues affecting early childhood education in contemporary times. The contents of this book were designed to highlight the complexity of the issues that we, as early childhood educators, encounter on a daily basis and the ways in which such issues are changing the ways we live our daily lives. One of the aims of education is to prepare citizens for the 'real world', and the 'real worlds' of today are multifaceted and often the issues that arise are not easily solved but instead need to have multiple readings and interpretations. Theories, both old and new, require critical appraisal and it is hoped that readers will create their own ways to distinguish what tenets are valuable to their own educational contexts. What we hope for, is that by foregrounding the various perspectives and issues raised in this book, we will stimulate productive discussions that may ultimately extend the ways in which early childhood education is viewed and practiced and we encourage you to enjoy the invigorating feeling of swimming against the tide.

References

Apple, M. (2001) *Educating the Right Way*. New York: Routledge.

Ausubel, D. (1967) Foreword, in E. V. Sullivan (ed.) *Piaget and the School Curriculum: A Critical Appraisal* (Bulletin No. 2 ed.). Ontario: The Ontario Institute for Studies in Education.

Block, M.N. (1992) Critical perspectives on the historical relationship between child development and early childhood educational research, in S. Kessler and B.B. Swadener (eds) *Reconceptualizing the Early Childhood Curriculum: Beginning the Dialogue* (pp. 3–20). New York: Teachers College Press.

Boldt, G.M. (2002) Toward a reconceptualization of gender and power in an elementary classroom, *Current Issues in Comparative Education*, 5(1). http.//www.tc.Columbia.edu/cice/articles/gls151.htm (accessed 10 June 2004).

Cannella, G.S. (1997) *Deconstructing Early Childhood Education: Social Justice and Revolution*. New York: Peter Lang.

Corrie, L. (1995) Vertical integration: teachers' knowledge and teachers voice, *Australian Journal of Early Childhood*, 20(3): 1–5.

Dahlberg, G., Moss, P. and Pence, A. (1999) *Beyond Quality in Early Childhood Education and Care: Postmodern Perspectives*. London: RoutledgeFalmer.

Genishi, C., Ryan, S., Ochsner, M. and Malter, M. (2001) Teaching in early childhood education: understanding practices through research and theory, in V. Richardson (ed.) *Handbook of Research on Teaching* (4th edn) (pp. 1175–1210). Washington, DC: American Educational Research Association.

Goffin, S.G. and Wilson, C. (2001) *Curriculum Models and Early Childhood Education: Appraising the Relationship* (2nd edn). Upper Saddle River, NJ: Prentice Hall.

Grieshaber, S. and Cannella, G.S. (2001) *Embracing Identities in Early Childhood Education: Diversity and Possibilities*. New York: Teachers College Press.

Harvey, D. (1989) *The Condition of Postmodernity: An Enquiry into the Origins of Cultural Change*. Oxford: Basil Blackwell.

Intel Research (2004) *Moore's Law*. http:www.intel.com/research/silicon/mooreslaw.htm (accessed 16 June 2004).

James, A., Jenks, C. and Prout, A. (1998) *Theorizing Childhood*. New York: Teachers College Press.

Jipson, J. and Johnson, R.T. (2001) *Resistance and Representation: Rethinking Childhood Education*. New York: Peter Lang.

Kessler, S.A. and Swadener, B.B. (1992) *Reconceptualizing the Early Childhood Curriculum: Beginning the Dialogue*. New York: Teachers College Press.

Lawton, J. and Hooper, F. (1978) Piagetian theory and early childhood education: a critical analysis, in L. Siegal and C. Brainerd (eds) *Alternatives to Piaget: Critical Essays on the Theory* (pp. 169–99). New York: Academic Press.

Lubeck, S. (1996) Deconstructing 'child development knowledge' and 'teacher preparation', *Early Childhood Research Quarterly*, 11: 147–67.

Lyotard, J-F. (1984) *The Postmodern Condition: A Report on Knowledge*. Manchester: Manchester University Press.

Moss, P. (2002) Time to say farewell to 'Early Childhood'? *Contemporary Issues in Early Childhood*, 3(3): 435–8.

Piaget, J. (1953) *The Origin of Intelligence in the Child*. London: Routledge and Kegan Paul.

Piaget, J. (1968) *Six Psychological Studies*. New York: Vintage Books.

Polakow, V. (1992) *The Erosion of Childhood*. Chicago: University of Chicago Press.

Prout, A. and James, A. (1997) A new paradigm for the sociology of childhood? Provenance, promise and problems, in A. James and A. Prout (eds) *Constructing and Reconstructing Childhood: Contemporary Issues in the Sociological Study of Childhood* (2nd edn). London: The Falmer Press.

Ryan, S., Ochsner, M. and Genishi, C. (2001) Miss Nelson is missing! Teacher sightings in research on teaching, in S. Grieshaber and G.S. Cannella (eds) *Embracing Identities in Early Childhood Education: Diversity and Possibilities* (pp. 45–59). New York: Teachers College Press.

Silin, J.G. (1995) *Sex, Death, and the Education of Children: Our Passion for Ignorance in the Age of AIDS*. New York: Teachers College Press.

Smyth, J. (2001) *Critical Politics of Teachers' Work: An Australian Perspective*. New York: Peter Lang.

Soto, L.D. and Swadener, B.B. (2002) Toward liberatory early childhood theory, research and praxis: decolonializing a field, *Contemporary Issues in Early Childhood*, 3(1): 38–66.

Sullivan, E.V. (1967) *Piaget and the School Curriculum: A Critical Appraisal* (Bulletin No. 2 ed.). Ontario: The Ontario Institute for Studies in Education.

Tobin, J.J. (1997) *Making a Place for Pleasure in Early Childhood Education*. New Haven, CT: Yale University Press.

United States Department of Education (2001) *No Child Left Behind. Executive Summary*. http://www.ed.gov/nclb/overview/intro/execsumm.html (accessed 12 May 2004).

PART 1
Contemporary Views of Early Childhood Education and Teaching

2 Reconceptualizing the field (of early care and education)

If 'western' child development is a problem, then what do we do?

Gaile S. Cannella

> We must learn to be vulnerable enough to allow our world to turn upside down in order to allow the realities of others to edge themselves into our consciousness.
>
> (Delpit, 1993, p. 139)

In 1997, I began the book *Deconstructing Early Childhood Education: Social Justice and Revolution* with the above quote from Lisa Delpit. At that time, I believed that the *bona fide* devotion to those who are younger sincerely exhibited by early childhood educators and researchers would open the door to that vulnerability. I continue to believe that the concern for those who are younger is honest and very well intended. I trusted, and still believe, to a somewhat lesser degree, however, that the genuine concern for younger human beings would (or could) lead to a willingness to turn one's world (and beliefs) upside down. Much of the work in the field since 1990, and certainly since 2000, challenges truth orientations, turns the 'world upside down', and reexamines notions of diversity, equity, and power in the conceptualization of child, family, and notions of care and education, as well as constructions of professional expertise. Early childhood educators and researchers in the international community have engaged in deconstructions of dominant notions of 'child'. Further, these critiques represent the range of thinking that includes postmodern, feminist, poststructural, and even postcolonial perspectives and lead to reconceptualizations of knowledges and possibilities for all of us (whether labeled young or old, adult or child).

Yet, this work continues to represent only a small percentage of the disseminated scholarship and academic constructions of practice within the field. Some academics in early childhood education and related fields have chosen to ignore and dismiss the perspectives as radical and uncaring without even attempting to develop a conscious awareness of the life positions from which such views might emerge.[1] In my earlier writing, I certainly underestimated the disciplinary and regulatory powers embedded within truth-oriented

Enlightenment/Modernist discourses that would exhibit control over what could be contemplated by individuals and the profession in general. We are all familiar with these dominant discourses that indeed seem to control the mainstream of early childhood education. Most prominent are: child development, scientific knowledge, redemption themes that would 'save third-world/disadvantaged/at risk' children, or accreditation and accountability. I did not realize that so many scholars would respond with comments like: 'If we don't use child development as our knowledge base, then what do we use?', 'How do we know children?' and the most common 'Don't throw the baby out with the bath water.' As already demonstrated by a number of scholars and diverse forms of life experience, 'Child development (or any type of psychological learning theory) is NOT the baby', unless we believe that human beings are limited to our socially embedded 'scientific' constructions of them. As a field, we have continued to ignore the ways that younger human beings have been fully functioning members of diverse cultures and societies for thousands of years without the so-called 'benefit' of Western child development knowledge. Further, as a field, whether behaviorally or developmentally oriented, we have not faced the possibility that belief in developmental progress, scientific knowledge, and an unquestioned assumption that we can 'know' the minds and physical nature of 'others' is monocultural (Lincoln and Cannella, 2004), ethnocentric, and even phallocentric (de Lauretis, 1987; Walkerdine, 1988; Walkerdine et al., 1989; Boyden, 1990; Joseph et al., 1990; Burman, 1994).

I understand that most who continue to support the various forms of developmental psychology, and this includes socio-cognitive, culturally grounded interpretations, are deeply committed to the welfare of 'children' and do not believe that modernist science is ethnocentric. However, I also suggest that we are all so embedded within our own claims to truth (and their related discourses) that we 'forget' that those truths are most likely human constructions (Nietzsche, 1887/1969; Ferguson, 1993), generated within a time and context that supported particular beliefs about the world; our beliefs in natural predetermined truths (as examples, child development knowledge or science as construct) are so embedded that we 'forget that we made them up, then we forget that we forgot' (Fendler, 1998, p. 61).

I was especially reminded of this forgetfulness at the American Educational Research Association Conference in San Diego (2004) in a discussion about the future of the field of early childhood education. Although some participants attempted to focus on the political complexities in the field, others were uncomfortable and could only repeat the dominant claims that children need adults who interact with them in engaging ways. This argument ultimately constitutes a kind of reinscription of middle-class, white, Western theories of learning that, by implication, blame the teacher and child for lack of success. Most audience members did not indicate that they were familiar with the range of reconceptualist work over the past 15–20 years. Further, although many sociopolitical questions were asked, the responses revealed an apolitical truth-oriented stance. On the whole, reconceptualist terminologies were dismissed and again referred to as representing talk, but not action. Most were either silent or displayed a total lack of awareness of the direct critical actions that are taken by reconceptualist early childhood researchers and educators on a daily basis; these actions have been practically oriented toward basic issues in education and child care such as teacher education program development, a curriculum for young children, community politics and public policy, nonviolent protest, and even the reconceptualization and transformation of research practices. Terms like 'postmodernism', 'poststructuralism', 'pedogogical revolution', and 'critical theory' seem to generate avoidance in those professionals who fear the loss of the expert status created for them by virtue of developmental and psychological learning theories. The power of the 'expert' has previously served to legitimate their assumed 'right' to speak 'truth' for, and about, the lives and learning of those who are younger. One can only hope that many in the audience who remained silent were/are actually aware of reconceptualist work and attempts to construct a transformative, action-oriented field of critical voices.

For a number of years now, many of us in the United States (e.g. Bloch, 1987; Silin, 1987; Kessler and Swadener, 1992; Tobin, 1995, 1997; Kaomea, 2003; Cannella and Viruru, 2004) and around the world (e.g. Yelland, 1998; MacNaughton, 2000; Grieshaber, 2001; Hultqvist and Dahlberg, 2001; MacNaughton, 2001; Bloch et al., 2004) have challenged these dominant discourses related to the notion of 'child', whether deterministic constructions of progress, universalist developmental psychologies, or general scientific conceptualizations of human beings as knowable through scientific truth. The arguments have critiqued modernist Western assumptions about the world (including children and interpretations of them), focused on diversity and ways of being in the world that have been silenced, challenged the construction of authoritative structuralist expertise that would judge others, and drawn attention to the historical, contextual, and even political, power-oriented nature of generating knowledge that is legitimated in the name of science and labeled as 'best practice'. This work, which could be labeled as cultural, feminist, critical, and at times postmodern, opens doors leading to new spaces and positions from which fields like early childhood education can be reconceptualized. Knowledges, purposes, and even communications and collaborations with others can be rethought and reconstituted. Such scholarship constructs avenues from which diverse human contexts can more easily be accepted and addressed, exposes the range of human possibilities that can be appreciated and supported, and unmasks the webs of power that emerge as human beings survive and function together. Conceptually, the possibilities for supporting diverse knowledges, facilitating new actions and practices, and fostering various ways of living/being with and learning from each other are limitless.

Although reconceptualist perspectives and scholarship offer increased possibilities and opportunities for those who are younger, and for all of us, we are also contemporarily located at a point in time in which critical reconceptualist research has revealed a public discourse that has historically and without shame used 'children' to further political agendas. These particular agendas have not improved/will not improve life conditions for those who are younger and actually increase conditions that result in oppression and control. In the contemporary world context, and most often led by the United States, this public discourse has strengthened its hold on the public imaginary (Barone, 2003; Cannella and Viruru, 2004) and used the 'welfare of children' to foster hyper-capitalism (an interpretation of all forms of knowledge through capitalist economics) and patriarchy (including an unquestioned, foundational sexism). These discourses legitimate imperialist judgment over others, and reinscribe racism, heteronormativity, and ethnocentrism.

To illustrate this point, even though both child developmentalist and reconceptualist scholars have challenged the appropriateness of testing to determine cognitive ability, albeit for different reasons, the general public has begun to accept the notion as if valid and accurately representative of human functioning. Today, children around the world are being tested and judged more than ever, and multinational businesses (e.g. marketing test instruments, selling scoring services, providing tutors and training, selling materials for test preparation) are gaining power in a hyper-capitalist environment that accepts the notion that 'money can be made' by constructing, measuring and judging individual (and group) strengths and weaknesses (Kohn, 1999; Sacks, 1999; Ayers, 2000; Meier, 2000). Developmentalists have challenged the cognitive, social, and emotional appropriateness of such judgments for working with young children; reconceptualists have problematized the universalist, deterministic truth orientations that are assumed within the testing construct and unmasked the ways that judgmental practices create power for particular groups of people over others. However, neither group has been heard in a way that would halt the daily suffering of those who are younger as they are made to sit quietly with their pencil and paper, and judged as 'lacking' or 'superior', while particular adults get richer and reconstitute their own capitalist, or 'expertise'-oriented, positions of power.

Reconceptualist work has fostered the recognition of the historical, political, and complex nature of the knowledges that we use and the contexts in which we find ourselves. I believe that reconceptualists and developmentalists should join together to take this work further, to generate new discourses and to construct actions that actually challenge the power that has been created over children which has led to their being constructed and labeled as ignorant, innocent, and without agency beyond their own developmental explorations. Apparent also is that such power reigns over the field of early childhood education (as a gendered field that always focuses more on people than financial gain), and over those traditionally oppressed groups whose voices have been silenced in the 'name of saving their children' (e.g. the poor, people of color, groups whose dominant language is not English). The purposes of this chapter are therefore: (1) to provide a summary of the reconceptualist scholarship in early childhood education (and related fields) that can lead to the construction of and appreciation for diverse possibilities and ways of interpreting and experiencing the world; and (2) to propose themes that are needed for the reconceptualization of the field in our contemporary global context in which new forms of disciplinary and regulatory power are being generated over all of us, adult and child alike. I invite developmentalist and reconceptualist early childhood researchers and educators, as well as those who would at all costs avoid labeling themselves as either, to join in the creation of a contemporary field that recognizes the sociopolitical and historical contexts in which we function as we also join with younger human beings and their families in the never-ending struggle for social and economic justice, equality, and the nonjudgmental appreciation of all human beings.

Reconceptualist scholarship: generating points of critical consciousness for the field of early childhood education

Reconceptualist scholarship is grounded in the range of philosophies, political movements, diverse forms of scholarship, and educational applications that have in recent history challenged monocultural ways of being and believing. This foundation, although always open to critique and contestation, draws attention to the social political context(s) and complexities that generate and perpetuate our material circumstances and beliefs about the world. To understand reconceptualist scholarship in early childhood education, one must first be cognizant of that grounding. This work directly impacts the scholarship that is/has been conducted in early childhood education, but also offers specific knowledges, perspectives, and ways of interpreting the world that are directly (without being filtered through the field of early childhood education) related to the everyday lives of those who are younger.

Challenges to universalist truths and monocultural being

The critical analysis and deconstruction of dominant knowledges did not, of course, begin with the field of early childhood education. Our work contains the ideas, writing, and identities of others. As examples, Foucault (1977) argued that there is no single author; Derrida proposed that there are no original sources (1981; Pinar et al., 1995). Long before early childhood reconceptualists began to focus on critical issues in the field, broad-based challenges to dominant knowledges and resultant power had been mounted both outside and within the field of education in general.

Philosophical perspectives

Most are aware of the range of philosophical views that have countered beliefs in certainty, views like poststructuralism or postmodernism (Lyotard, 1993; Cannella and Bailey, 1999). Grand narratives that assume the existence of universal truths applicable to all human beings have been deconstructed and exposed as privileging particular ways of being while disqualifying others. Whether through critiques of western linearity, challenges to the Christian discourse of salvation, deconstructions of Marxist or capitalist economic grand narratives, or problematizations of Piagetian structuralism, the belief that human existence conforms to a predetermined reality that is to be discovered or revealed and then applied to everyone has been soundly refuted. Further, the underlying assumptions and privileged belief structures that have benefited particular groups over others have been criticized in an age in which diversity and difference are increasingly recognized by individuals and groups who join in the struggle that would celebrate multiple knowledges and ways of interpreting the world. Regarding those who are younger (as for all of us), these philosophical challenges result in a perspective from which 'what we think we know' must be questioned. Taken-for-granted beliefs are no longer accepted, beliefs like: 'science' as revealing the 'truth' about human beings (whether labeled child or adult); adults (as experts) possessing knowledge of and judgmental power over children; human change as representing growth, development, and, if optimalized, further representing progress. From within these philosophical perspectives, beliefs about human beings (including those who are younger) must be questioned.

Material life circumstances

Further, from material, physical locations that some would define as marginalized and oppressed, groups of people who have experienced the unequal distribution of power in their everyday lives have increasingly chosen to speak about their own materiality, to voice the experiences of their own concrete real-world positions. From these various locations have emerged new discourses that (in addition to revealing the problems with the oppressive imposition of a universalized western gendered thought on everyone) open doors to ways of thinking and being that generate possibilities for all of us. The results are fields like: cultural studies that shatter the boundaries of traditional disciplinary thought (Hall, 1981, 1999; Morley and Chen, 1996; Surber, 1998); women's studies and the various feminist perspectives that expose the diverse experiences of the largest marginalized group in the world (hooks, 1984, 2000;

Collins, 1990; Lerner, 1993; Grosz, 1994); queer theory and gender studies that challenge notions about what is 'normal' and who has assumed the power to define normality (Crimp, 1988; Fuss, 1991; Butler, 1990, 1993; Sedgwick, 1993); and postcolonial/subaltern studies that uncover, not only the continued effects of past physical occupations (such as economic ruin, cooptation of resources, and institutional imposition), but also the invasive long-term effects of constructing particular groups of people as savage, ignorant, and not civilized (Bhabha, 1990; Said, 1978, 1993, 1996; Spivak, 1988, 1999; Young, 2001).

The importance of these positions that represent daily life and material experience can be more specifically illustrated. As examples, in some locations, cultural studies began by examining the lived daily experiences that revolve around socio-economic status often referred to as 'class', introducing notions like the social construction and embeddedness of human historical relations and life conditions (Thompson, 1963); cultural studies has grown to include ethnic and multicultural studies as well as the examination of popular culture. This work is directly related to the lives of younger human beings as they live in a myriad of ways and conditions, whether in poverty or wealth (and the complex material conditions that result), as members of particular racial, language, ethnic, and gender groups, and as individuals who are intimately involved in popular culture as creators (e.g. language, counter-culture), consumers, or recipients (e.g. movies, toys, dress, and the less obvious like religious impositions or capitalist competition to create parenting fads and training, educational content and materials that can be sold, or other forms of saleable products) (Cannella and Viruru, 1999; Cannella and Kincheloe, 2002). The range of feminist perspectives, although differing on specifics, generally attempts to realize social justice for women, to insure equity, equality, and control over one's own life, and to eliminate sexism. Again, directly related to the lives of younger human beings are not only the messages that are given to children through curriculum content and teacher expectations and behaviors, but the daily communications received about women (in the home, school, community, nation, and world), whether those women are treated with respect as equals and also view themselves as such (whether through parent conversation and behavior, equitable reward for women in work situations, the equal representation of women and diversity of ideas in all aspects of the community, and even institutional gender equity). Through the continuous deconstruction of 'regimes of the normal', queer theory and gender studies physically challenge unquestioned beliefs that particular ways of living one's life, or understanding self and others, are more appropriate, normal, or acceptable than others. Constructions like 'identity' that assume a fixed and rational normal being or notions like 'development' that have privileged prediction and predetermination are consequently rethought. Notions of normalcy in childhood, or maturity/immaturity in human change, are recognized as actually limiting possibilities for those who are younger and creating power for those who define what is 'normal' (usually those who are labeled adults).

As a final example, postcolonial studies points to the construction of particular groups of people (usually people of color) as the 'other' for the direct purpose of exploiting those groups. Knowledges have been/are denied as realms of power are created that serve the agendas of the colonizer, a colonizer who may function by imposing direct force, but who has more often chosen to inscribe desires that would create the servant into the intellectual and moral image of the master. The concept of time, the definition for human, the will to literacy, and even the moral dispensation of liberty and democracy are just a few examples of the discourses that create that image. Younger human beings (especially in the United States) are being taught that they are superior to Others (whether as Americans, as those who are wealthy, as those with white skin, as those who practice the religion that will save their souls, or as those who are intellectually smarter and more developed). Whether through purposeful power agenda or subconscious illusion, these messages of superiority are inscribed and reinscribed. Accepting the notion that one's beliefs, knowledges, abilities, religious practices, and so on, are superior to Others is a dangerous condition that can lead to continued marginalizing of particular groups (for example, children of color in schools and neighborhoods) and to worldwide conflict as children who have been taught that they are either superior or inferior later live (or fight) in the world together as adults (Cannella and Viruru, 2004).

Civil rights movements and legal activism

In the middle of the twentieth century, people in a variety of locations around the world chose to take physical actions (e.g. various forms of civil disobedience) and to use legal mechanisms to demand that all citizens be heard and treated with equity and civil respect. These grassroots movements stood for a range of issues and circumstances – from equity for farm workers to activism by student groups, environmentalists, and indigenous peoples, to a focus on civil rights for racial equality, to women's rights and social activism. Multiple voices and knowledges were heard (Evans, 1979; Morris, 1984). The explosion of civil rights created an openness to cultural issues more broadly, the potential for understanding regarding societal expectations and support in general (e.g. social provision, forms of social democracy, diverse forms of parenting, even diversity of curriculum content knowledges in schools). These movements and their successes created an even more receptive environment for diverse philosophical orientations concerning reality and appreciation for the voices of the marginalized (Lincoln and Cannella, 2004).

However, particularly in the United States, the hard-fought battles for civil liberties and the acknowledgement of diverse voices met with resistance from groups who were threatened by the loss of power. These groups are often labeled the 'conservative right' and the 'religious right' and are characterized as representing extremist moral, economic, and intellectual beliefs that would be imposed on all humanity. Such groups, many especially maddened by the increased recognition of women's diverse voices, joined with a growing business lobby that challenged regulations for environmental protection and moved to create a legislative environment in which corporate capitalism would become synonymous with democracy. Large corporations and right-wing ideologues would benefit, more than individuals or groups of people, from this collaborative push for legislative actions (Herman, 1981; Dowie, 1995; Berry, 1997). During the past 30 years, the battle has been waged: as 'culture wars'; as backlashes against women; as support for a small number of the poor and people of color, while most at the lower end of the economic ladder lost ground; as the reinscription of religious patriarchy; as multi-national capitalism, imposed as if necessary for liberty and democratic processes. These experiences and our current circumstances, of course, directly impact the lives of younger human beings. Contemporary child care and educational practices have been influenced by the successes of movements for civil liberties but forcefully countered by patriarchal, religious extremist, capitalist power organizations and institutions. For example, in the USA, the focus in schools is on accountability, punishing those who do not perform, and on a monocultural view of knowledge – generally patriarchal, right-wing, controlling, and established using methods that would support capitalism (e.g. the range of testing, scoring, and tutoring companies). Although children could learn much if experiencing a value structure and curriculum understandings that focused on critical civil liberties and public activism, we have not as a broad educational community chosen to use methods such as critical pedagogical (Lankshear and McLaren, 1993; Freire, 1993, 1994, 1998; McLaren, 2000) understandings of literacy and other content. Rather, we teach reading as functional practice, as a mechanical process. Recently when a mother of two children stated, 'I'd rather my children learn to live social justice rather than how to read if I must make a choice,' a well-known early childhood educator responded to her, 'Don't you want your child to learn to read?' Most researchers and practitioners do not appear to even recognize that we are not using what we've learned about civil liberties, political activism, and legal action with children. We are accepting one way of understanding the world in the name of accountability without question. As educators, many of us are accepting knowledges, curricular practices, and teaching methodologies as if they had no political impact. We are not demanding that everyone have a voice or acknowledging the complexities of education that can perpetuate privilege and lead to further social injustice. We are not determining whose lives, knowledges, skills, and views of the world are privileged and whose are silenced/ignored in the societal and educational choices being made.

Critical educational praxis

As implied in the above discussion that illustrates our refusal to employ educational methods that would reconceptualize and transform our work with children, challenges to universalist truth and monocultural perspectives have also come from a variety of locations from within the field of education (in addition to the field of early childhood education). Work in educational foundations has recognized the existence and importance of multiple histories and multi-voiced narratives regarding educational experience and foundational belief structures. Further, this work acknowledges the role of contexts, politics, and power in both societal conditions and educational practice (Spring, 1972, 2004; Giroux and McLaren, 1989; Apple, 1993; Giroux, 1993; Sleeter, 1996). The field of curriculum theory is an excellent example of challenges to grand narratives that result in the reconceptualizing of purposes, agendas, content, and the role of education as transformative practice. Curriculum theory has emerged as a diversified field that replaced a preoccupation with curriculum development and design with notions of understanding that admit to social, political and cultural embeddedness – acknowledging curriculum as gendered texts, as political texts, as religious texts, as racial text, to name a few (Pinar et al., 1995). The field is now hybrid, a field that – although generally practiced in educational institutions – always addresses 'issues of representation as well as issues of unequal distribution of material resources and power outside the school door' (McCarthy, 1993, p. 291).

Finally, critical pedagogy or 'pedagogy of revolution' (McLaren, 2000), as illustrated by the methods of critical literacy practiced by Paulo Freire, provides one alternative for a transformative educational methodology that acknowledges the problems with universalist truth orientations. Although legitimately critiqued by feminists and others as continuing to include western male forms of liberation, critical pedagogy does generate one possibility for the reconceptualization of practice with younger human beings of all ages. Critical pedagogy would always include the following pivotal points:

- acts of knowing as grounded in one's own being;
- historical and cultural world viewed as transformable through human actions;
- learner connections between his/her own life conditions and history;
- learners open to new constructions of reality that are generated through 'a collective, shared, social enterprise in which the voices of all participants must be heard' (McLaren, 2000, p. 163);
- learners as experiencing their own potency as human subjects who explore and critique generative themes (phases of critical literacy); and
- recognizing the myths of dominant discourses and taking transformative action (Lankshear and McLaren, 1993).

In the field of education generally and related to critical pedagogy specifically, the seeds for reconceptualizing work in all educational environments have been sown; we are now given the responsibility for supporting and valuing those potentially transformative grains.

Crossing disciplinary boundaries in the recognition of sociopolitical contexts and reconceptualization

Most early childhood educators point to the multidisciplinary nature of the field. While contemporary dominant discourses appear most influenced by psychology (a field that has been soundly critiqued through both philosophical and material challenges to deterministic truth orientations), historically early childhood education emerged from a variety of fields that included sociology and, to a lesser degree, anthropology. Contemporarily, scholarship that crosses disciplinary fields and recognizes our societal and cultural embeddedness has introduced perspectives and ways of understanding the world that are directly applicable to the lives of younger human beings and those who are profoundly concerned about them. This work illustrates in a variety of ways the ever present sociopolitical context through which beliefs and knowledges are constructed and either inscribed or disqualified.

The following are illustrative examples of this sociopolitical embeddedness and the ways in which cross-disciplinary work is directly applicable to the reconceptualization of early childhood education. As a social history of family life, Phillippe Ariès (1962) demonstrated how the image of the child and concepts such as race, class, and family were actually constructed as a reaction to, and as attempts to control, difference. The work of Valerie Walkerdine (1988) in *The Mastery of Reason: Cognitive Development and the Production of Rationality* illustrates the ways in which Piaget was influenced by individualistic Enlightenment patriarchy, as well as the belief that democratic governance was necessary for world survival. While most of us are drawn to the concern for democratic practices, we cannot deny that cognitive developmental theory privileges both the individual as construct (rather than group orientations) and forms of reasoning that are stereotypically male, as well as a deterministic stance that would assume to know the mind of the child (or anyone else). Extensive work by Stephanie Coontz (1992) provides a well-documented counter to the public discourse on family that generally assumes one correct form. She problematizes notions of traditional family values, demonstrating the ways that myths are created as if they are unquestionable truths to achieve particular political ends. Examples of these myths are the discourse that elevates the nuclear family as the ideal, or that the development of 'self-esteem' has always required a nonworking mother who savored the child's first steps. Further, Coontz illustrates that there have always been diverse forms of childrearing. In *Mother Infant Bonding: A Scientific Fiction*, Diane Eyer (1992) traces the history of the myth of bonding, demonstrating our societal tendencies to both accept 'scientific' research as if unquestionable and our even stronger tendency toward mother blaming and control. In the seminal work, *Deconstructing Developmental Psychology*, Erica Burman (1994) unveils the gendered and Western cultural assumptions that are embedded in developmental psychology. Discussing everything from behaviorism to child-centeredness, from Bowlby to Piaget, Burman illustrates how particular groups of people (i.e. women, the poor, people of color) have been/are discredited, labeled as incompetent, and controlled from within the mask of 'developmental psychology'. From the field of sociology, Allison James, Chris Jenks, and Alan Prout (1998) explore the historical, political, and cultural dimensions of the construction of childhood (see also, James and Prout, 1990).

Finally, work that has not always been directly applied to early childhood education has for many years at least partially challenged major truth orientations of both developmental psychology and early childhood education. An example of this work is Barbara Rogoff's (1991) comparison of Piagetian and Vygotskian theories in *Apprentice in Thinking: Cognitive Development in Social Context*. Rogoff discusses Vygotskian (1962, 1978) socio-cognitive theory as a description of human development in which growth trajectories are determined by the values, knowledges, and even survival needs of a particular culture at a particular point in history. Vygotskian socio-cognitive perspectives actually opened the door in developmental psychology quite some time ago to the notion that there is not one form of human development and that development is a cultural phenomenon. However, Vygotsky also proposed that knowledge and the tools for learning (perhaps learning itself) are cultural constructions; methodologies like child-centeredness are considered forms of learning that may fit with particular cultural values and not others. Reconceptualist scholarship has, in a sense, broadened this perspective by introducing notions that recognize the potential cultural embeddedness of all of our concepts – perhaps taking Vygotskian notions to a different plane. Just as Vygotsky proposed that developmental change is multidirectional and cultural, reconceptualists argue that the concept of 'development' itself is a cultural (mainly western and male) construction and that notions of development and learning theories are problematic in that they assume we can know 'Others scientifically', creating a form of imperialist, deterministic expertise and power for those who claim to possess that scientific knowledge.

The above points and examples illustrate the very social and even political foundations/agendas that underlie the various beliefs that are perpetuated in particular contexts, cultures, and histories. Reconceptualist work has demonstrated that 'what we think we know' about children, families, human change, education, and a multitude of other issues is very dependent on the value structures and biases of those who have been given, or who have taken, the 'right' to speak, to theorize, or to claim the truth about others. This multitude of reconceptualist work begs that we always ask the questions: What were the hidden (or not so hidden) agendas tied to the emergence of particular knowledges? Or actions? Under what circumstances did particular beliefs emerge? How have we forgotten the ways in which our 'truths' have been constructed? Who has been/is helped? Hurt? Privileged? Disqualified?

Critical dispositions in early childhood education

Over the past 15 or so years, volumes of reconceptualist work have also been directly generated in the field of early childhood education. This scholarship has included such a range of perspectives that a 'critical disposition' has now emerged that can serve as a lens from which to unmask hidden assumptions and agendas (that serve a multidimensional will to power) as well as open doors for new possibilities for interactions and collaborations with younger human beings, their families and communities, and with each other. This work is extensive and sheds light on contemporary political practices that are infused throughout all components of the field. This critical disposition (and the scholarship that explains it) can be used to construct partnerships across the field of early childhood education as positions from which to take action regarding contemporary public policies (that benefit no one and may even cause harm), and to eventually reconceptualize the field as a whole.

An overview of this work is important to fully understand the unlimited possibilities for partnership and transformation. Some of the earliest work can be represented by a volume entitled *Critical Perspectives on Early Childhood Education*, edited by Lois Weis, Philip Altbach, Gail Kelly, and Hugh Petrie (1991). This volume covers the range of critical reconceptualist possibilities in the field by including such issues as gendering in preschool classrooms by Bronwyn Davies, a critique of the two-tiered system of early childhood education in the USA by Julia Wrigley, and the comparison of family support and social provision in countries around the world by Sally Lubeck. Challenges to the traditional scientific and professional foundations and knowledge bases of early childhood education can be found in the work of Marianne Bloch (1987, 1992) and Jonathan Silin (1987). At the same time, Shirley Kessler and Beth Blue Swadener, in an edited volume, called for the reconceptualizing of early childhood curriculum as a democratic practice (1992). This text presents perspectives such as feminist curriculum practices (Janice Jipson), the deconstruction of the discourse of care (Valerie Polakow), and the politics of early childhood language education (Lourdes Diaz Soto), to name just a few.

During the 1990s and in recent years, a vast literature has been created that specifically addresses previously hidden/disqualified issues that directly relate to the education of young children. This literature ranges from specific classroom practices and professionalism, to identity and sexuality for both teachers and those who are younger, to early childhood cultural and family studies, to public policy, politics, and the reconceptualization of the field in general. Because of the interdisciplinary, boundary-crossing nature of reconceptualist work, much of the scholarship does not fit easily into one category. The following, although not all inclusive, are illustrations of that work.

Classroom practice, the purposes of early education in general, and teacher professional behavior have been reconceptualized in the work of such scholars as Hauser and Marrero (1998) who investigated the operation of equity in a first grade classroom, Bailey (1997) as she examined the imposition of early childhood curriculum on the bodies of young children, or Ritchie (2001) in the exploration and implementation of a collectivist, Aotearoa Te Whäriki curriculum for young children. Over a period of years, Leavitt (1994, 1995) demonstrated ways that societal regulatory practices directly influence daily childcare practices and impose regulatory power over children and childcare professionals. Further, Silin (1995) explored the denial of social issues and daily life experiences exhibited by teachers in general in their attempts to 'protect' children from the world outside the classroom. All of this work demonstrates the need for a critical disposition that would continuously examine what we 'think we know' about children, teaching, society, and even ourselves. This disposition would recognize the existence of power as infused, as located within the knowledges and methods that we choose, and as potentially dangerous. Probably most importantly, beliefs about the capabilities of those who are younger would be continually challenged and open to new possibilities.

Reconceptualization of beliefs about childhood identities, and even teacher identities, as illustrated through gender studies in early childhood education, is an excellent example of the broadening of the field away from normalizing, narrow constructions of individual and sexual child identities. Following the work of Davies (1989, 1993) and Walkerdine (1981), a range of Australian scholars have both challenged dominant constructions of maleness and femaleness and illustrated ways in which gendered forms of control are reinforced in classrooms. This has been illustrated in computer work by Alloway (1995), block play by Danby and Baker (1998), male control of general play situations by MacNaughton (1995), and acceptance of male aggression by Reid (1999). Further, the 'missing', even denied, aspects of childhood and teacher identities and resultant educational/care practices are brought to light by the authors in *Making a Place for Pleasure in Early Childhood Education* (Tobin, 1997). The various chapters illustrate the ways that our narrow expectations for sexual outcomes treat children and teachers as if without human desire and as fixed, predetermined identities. As examples, Boldt (1997) explores the ways that behavior that is not heteronormative is treated as needing correction (for the child's future happiness) and King (1997) autobiographically discusses the denial of gay teaching identities in the classroom. The poststructural, feminist, queer, and even hybrid recognition that identities are shattered, changing, and contextual has been illustrated in a variety of ways by early childhood scholars with direct classroom practices implicated and new ways of functioning illustrated. As examples, Tobin suggests that we should doubt 'well-intended interventions' (1997, p. 32) that would be assumed to lead to particular outcomes and destabilize what we think we know about childhood – acknowledging our limits can actually be an act of freedom for both children and adults. Hughes and MacNaughton (2001) even propose that children be encouraged to examine different ways of being gendered and the politicization of their identities through various discourses, cultural products, and expectations.

Early childhood reconceptualists have used the work of the various scholars in cultural studies, and created their own literature, to demonstrate the historical, cultural, and social embeddedness of beliefs about childhood specifically, and the various experiences that are so often intellectually tied to 'childhood' such as concepts like family, welfare/care, and education. Cultural studies of childhood include the work of Adler (2001) who examines identity and Asian-American children, Viruru (2001) who explores early childhood education from a subaltern perspective, introducing components of postcolonial theory to naturalistic inquiry, Silin (2003) who demonstrates the ways that real lived narratives blur any dichotomous separations of adult/child, parent/offspring, and others.

Early childhood cultural studies has most recently become increasingly critical, acknowledging the potential interweaving of power and politics into discourses and actions that are inscribed and that are conversely reconstituting themselves within the field – as well as outside. This acknowledgement, perhaps more than any other, has generated perspectives and reconceptualizations that can change the face and nature of the field. This rethinking places at the forefront the recognition that all aspects of the field are inextricably tied to values agendas (and resultant political actions or status quo-producing inactions), power, and public policy. Dahlberg's work provides an excellent example as she and others problematize dominant ideas in the field of early childhood education like the notion of 'quality' (Dahlberg et al., 1999), proposing that early childhood institutions be constituted as 'forums in civil society [that] provide opportunity for *constructing a new public discourse about early childhood* itself, an important part of what might be called a "politics of childhood" ' (1999, p. 77). This political discourse must recognize global and local conditions, the domination of the field by the United States, and the changing nature of the world around all of us. More recent work focuses on global change and the ways that childhood is constructed, constituted, and governed from within particular perspectives, belief structures, and technologies (Hultqvist and Dahlberg, 2001). Popkewitz and Bloch (2001) demonstrate the ways that educational reform actually reinscribes already dominant political agendas by simply renaming old forms of oppression; this renaming is illustrated in their examination of the exclusionary properties of notions of 'social inclusion' as giving the impression that new views of the 'child' and the 'family' are being generated.

Finally, the political and even colonialist nature of the research practices that have led to the construction of the field of early childhood education is being discussed. Kaomea (2001, 2003) calls attention to the conflicts faced by indigenous early childhood educators who attempt to work in, and perhaps tear down, the master's house (e.g. the dominant knowledges and perspectives in the field that privilege particular groups of people). Cannella and Viruru (2004) attempt to acknowledge a postcolonial and marginalized perspective, the recognition that many of those who are both younger and older have not been included, and have even been disqualified, by much of the work in the field. We call for a field that (1) continually challenges the construction of power for one group over another; (2) places at the forefront an anti-oppressive stance; and (3) reinforces transformative actions that celebrate activist (rather than docile) bodies, for children, their teachers, and everyone.

In addition to the possibilities generated through critical reconceptualist work, the contemporary, immediate need for such a reconceptualized field is clearly demonstrated through recent events in the United States. Legislative mandates such as *No Child Left Behind* (2001) and the US National Research Council report on *Scientific Research in Education* (2002) demonstrate the ways that our beliefs about 'child', 'family', and 'education/care practices' are not separate from sociopolitical agendas. We now live in a time when we risk the imposition of very narrow, patriarchal, and even colonialist views of child, family, education, and public policy (Cannella and Lincoln, 2004b). Reconceptualist, developmentalist, and all other early childhood educators who are truly concerned about children, their families, their teachers, and their communities must join together to take action.

Creating a contemporary collaboration: moving toward a critical early childhood education

The various professionals in the field of early childhood education can join together to take immediate political action regarding the material and political conditions in which the field is functioning and as directly related to the everyday lives of children. First, we can explore, learn about, and accept diverse forms of knowledge from the children and communities within which we work. Until we appreciate the physical bodies, experiences, and knowledges of the traditionally marginalized, our concerns for children will never be realized. Second, we should develop practices in care and education settings that are critical in nature, that continuously ask the questions: Whose knowledge is being taught? Who decided that the knowledge was important? What happens to individuals and groups within the use of this knowledge or these methods? How are various individuals and peoples being represented? Who is being helped? And who is hurt? Finally, we should work toward a field of early childhood education that contributes to a new 'critical public social science' (Cannella and Lincoln, 2004a, p. 298) – a field that publicly challenges the 'will to truth' that would claim power for one group over others and fosters continual public, open discussion – a field that recognizes our embeddedness in the social and the political and is willing to engage in continual critique and critical advocacy – a field that acknowledges our role in the perpetuation of the status quo and the continued need to turn upside down our beliefs and biases 'in order to allow the realities of others to edge themselves into our consciousness' (Delpit, 1993, 139).

Note

1   Parents, teachers, and community workers who represent nondominant life experiences seem to embrace epistemological views that naturally challenge truth-oriented forms of science. I believe that we must consider why education and childcare practices in diverse cultural settings have NOT usually, unless attempting to satisfy NAEYC accreditation standards, followed Western psychological conceptualizations of child. Practices have more likely represented cultural, historically contextual, socially familiar, even political power orientations and survival expectations that dominate human beings in a particular time and context. As a white, middle-class, educated American woman during the twentieth century, I can say that I felt liberated and validated by the constructivist perspectives and teaching methods that have emerged from neo-Piagetian theory. However, I did not ask questions like: Do I like these teaching methods because I have learned to be materialist and value exploration? Do some groups (e.g. gender, cultural, socio-economic) benefit from such forms of teaching more than others? Do I have the right to call myself an expert in the learning of 'others'?

References

Adler, S.M. (2001) Racial and ethnic identity formation of Midwestern Asian-American children, *Contemporary Issues in Early Childhood*, 2(3): 265–94.

Alloway, N. (1995) *Foundation Stones: The Construction of Gender in Early Childhood*. Carlton, Vic: Curriculum Corporation.

Apple, M. (1993) *Official Knowledge: Democratic Education in a Conservative Age*. New York: Routledge.

Ariès, P. (1962) *Centuries of Childhood: A Social History of Family Life.* Trans. by R. Baldick. New York: Vintage Books.

Ayers, W. (2000) The standards fraud, in J. Cohen and J. Rogers (eds) *Will Standards Save Public Education?* Boston: Beacon Press.

Bailey, C. (1997) In search of the queer body: implications for research and curriculum in early childhood education. Paper presented at the meeting of the American Educational Research Association, Chicago, IL.

Barone, T. (2003) Challenging the educational imaginary: issues of form, substance, and quality in film-based research, *Qualitative Inquiry,* 9(2): 202–17.

Berry, J. (1997) *The Interest Group Society.* New York: Longman.

Bhabha, H.K. (1990) The other question: difference, discrimination, and the discourse of colonialism, in R. Ferguson (ed.) *Out There: Marginalization and Contemporary Cultures* (pp. 71–89). Cambridge, MA: MIT Press.

Bhabha, H.K. (1994) *The Location of Culture.* London: Routledge.

Bloch, M.N. (1987) Becoming scientific and professional: An historical perspective on the aims and effects of early education, in T.S. Popkewitz (ed.) *The Formation of School Subjects* (pp. 25–62). Basingstoke: Falmer.

Bloch, M.N., Holmlund, K., Moqvist, I. and Popkewitz, T. (2004) *Governing Children, Families and Education: Restructuring the Welfare State.* New York: Palgrave Macmillan.

Boldt, G. (1997) Sexist and heterosexist responses to gender bending, in J. Tobin (ed.) *Making a Place for Pleasure in Early Childhood Education* (pp. 188–213). New Haven, CT: Yale University Press.

Boyden, J. (1990) Childhood and the policy makers: a comparative perspective on the globalization of childhood, in A. James and A. Prout (eds) *Constructing and Reconstructing Childhood: Contemporary Issues in the Sociological Study of Childhood.* Basingstoke: Falmer.

Burman, E. (1994) *Deconstructing Developmental Psychology.* New York: Routledge.

Butler, J. (1990) *Gender Trouble.* London: Routledge.

Butler, J. (1993) *Bodies that Matter.* London: Routledge.

Cannella, G.S. (1997) *Deconstructing Early Childhood Education: Social Justice and Revolution.* New York: Peter Lang.

Cannella, G.S. and Bailey, C. (1999) Postmodern research in early childhood education, in S. Reifel (ed.) *Advances in Early Education and Day Care,* vol. 10 (pp. 3–39). New York: JAI Press.

Cannella, G.S. and Kincheloe, J.L. (eds) (2002) *Kidworld: Childhood Studies, Global Perspectives, and Education.* New York: Peter Lang.

Cannella, G.S. and Lincoln, Y. (2004a) Claiming a critical public social science: reconceptualizing and redeploying research, *Qualitative Inquiry,* 10(2): 298–309.

Cannella, G.S. and Lincoln, Y. (2004b) Dangerous discourses II: comprehending and countering the redeployment of discourses (and resources) in the generation of liberatory inquiry, *Qualitative Inquiry,* 10(2): 168–274.

Cannella, G.S. and Viruru, R. (1999) Generating possibilities for the construction of childhood studies, *Journal of Curriculum Theorizing*, 15(1): 13–22.

Cannella, G.S. and Viruru, R. (2004) *Childhood and Postcolonization: Power, Education, and Contemporary Practice*. New York: RoutledgeFalmer.

Collins, P.H. (1990) *Black Feminist Thought: Knowledge, Consciousness and the Politics of Empowerment*. New York: Routledge.

Coontz, S. (1992) *The Way We Never Were: American Families and the Nostalgia Trap*. New York: Basic Books.

Crimp, D. (1988) *AIDS: Cultural Analysis, Cultural Activism*. Cambridge, MA: MIT Press.

Dahlberg, G., Moss, P. and Pence, A. (1999) *Beyond Quality in Early Childhood Education and Care: Postmodern Perspectives*. London: Falmer.

Danby, S. and Baker, C. (1998) How to be masculine in the block area, *Childhood* 5(12): 151–75.

Davies, B. (1989) *Frogs and Snails and Feminist Tales: Preschool Children and Gender*. Sydney: Allen and Unwin.

Davies, B. (1993) *Shards of Glass*. Sydney: Allen and Unwin.

de Lauretis, T. (1987) *Technologies of Gender: Essays on Theory, Film, and Fiction*. Bloomington, IN: Indiana University Press.

Delpit, L. (1993) The silenced dialogue: power and pedagogy in educating other people's children, in L. Weis and M. Fine (eds) *Beyond Silenced Voices: Class, Race, and Gender in United States Schools* (pp. 119–39). Albany, NY: SUNY Press.

Derrida, J. (1981) *Dissemination*. Trans. B. Johnson. Chicago: University of Chicago Press.

Diaz Soto, L. (ed.) (1995) *The Politics of Early Childhood education*. New York: Peter Lang.

Dowie, M. (1995) *Losing Ground*. Boston: MIT Press.

Evans, S. (1979) *Personal Politics*. New York: Knopf.

Eyer, D.E. (1992) *Mother Infant Bonding: A Scientific Fiction*. New Haven, CT: Yale University Press.

Fendler, L. (1998) What is it impossible to think? A genealogy of the educated subject, in T. Popkewitz and M. Brennan (eds) *Foucault's Challenge: Discourse, Knowledge, and Power in Education* (pp. 39–63). New York: Teachers College Press.

Ferguson, K.E. (1993) *The Man Question: Visions of Subjectivity in Feminist Theory*. Berkeley, CA: University of California Press.

Foucault, M. (1977) What is an author? In D.F. Bouchard (ed.) *Language, Counter-Memory, Practice* (pp. 113–38). Ithaca, NY: Cornell University Press.

Freire, P. (1993) *Pedagogy of the Oppressed*. New York: Continuum.

Freire, P. (1994) *Pedagogy of Hope: Reliving Pedagogy of the Oppressed*. New York: Continuum.

Freire, P. (1998) *Pedagogy of Freedom: Ethics, Democracy, and Civic Courage*. Boulder, CO: Rowman and Littlefield.

Fuss, D. (ed.) (1991) *Inside/Out: Lesbian Theories, Gay Theories*. New York: Routledge.

Giroux, H. (1993) *Living Dangerously: Multiculturalism and the Politics of Difference*. New York: Peter Land.

Giroux, H. and Mclaren, P. (1989) *Critical Pedagogy, the State, and Cultural Struggle*. Albany, NY: State University of New York Press.

Grieshaber, S. (2001) Advocacy and early childhood educators: identity and cultural conflicts, in S. Grieshaber and G.S. Cannella (eds) *Embracing Identities in Early Childhood Education* (pp. 60–72). New York: Teachers College Press.

Grosz, E. (1994) *Volatile Bodies: Towards a Corporeal Feminism*. Bloomington, IN: Indiana University Press.

Hall, S. (1981) *Culture, Ideology, and Social Process*. London: Open University Press.

Hall, S. (1999) Cultural studies and its theoretical legacies, in S. During (ed.) *The Cultural Studies Reader* (pp. 97–112). New York: Routledge.

Hauser, M.E. and Jipson, J.A. (eds) (1998) *Intersections: Feminism/Early Childhoods*. New York: Peter Lang.

Hauser, M.E. and Marrero, E. (1998) Challenging curricular conventions: is it feminist pedagogy if you don't call it that? In M.E. Hauser and J.A. Jipson (eds) *Intersections: Feminisms/Early Childhood* (pp. 161–76). New York: Peter Lang.

Herman, E.S. (1981) *Corporate Control, Corporate Power*. New York: Cambridge University Press.

hooks, b. (1984) *Feminist Theory from Margin to Center*. Boston: South End Press.

hooks, b. (2000) *Feminism is for Everybody: Passionate Politics*. Cambridge, MA: Southend Press.

Hughes, P. and MacNaughton, G. (2001) Fractured or manufactured: gendered identities and culture in the early years, in S. Grieshaber and G.S. Cannella (eds) *Embracing Identities in Early Childhood Education: Diversity and Possibilities* (pp. 114–29). New York: Teachers College Press.

Hultqvist, K. and Dahlberg, G. (eds) (2001) *Governing the Child in the New Millennium*. New York: RoutledgeFalmer.

James, A., Jenks, C. and Prout, A. (1998) *Theorizing Childhood*. New York: Teachers College Press.

James, A. and Prout, A. (1990) *Constructing and Reconstructing Childhood*. Basingstoke: Falmer Press.

Johnson, R.T. (2000a) *Hands off! The Disappearance of Touch in the Care of Children*. New York: Peter Lang.

Johnson, R.T. (2000b) Colonialism and cargo cults in early childhood education: does Reggio Emilia really exist? *Contemporary Issues in Early Childhood*, 1(1): 61–78.

Joseph, G., Reddy, V. and Searle-Chatterjee, M. (1990) Eurocentrism in the social sciences, *Race and Class*, 31(4): 1–26.

Kaomea, J.L. (2003) Reading erasures and making the familiar strange: defamiliarizing methods for research in formerly colonized and historically oppressed communities, *Educational Researcher*, 32(2): 14–26.

Kaomea, J.L. (2001) Dilemmas of an indigenous academic: a Native Hawaiian story, *Contemporary Issues in Early Childhood*, 2(1): 67–82.

Kessler, S. and Swadener, B.B. (1992) *Reconceptualizing the Early Childhood Curriculum: Beginning the Dialogue*. New York: Teachers College Press.

King, J.R. (1997) Keeping it quiet: gay teachers in the primary grades, in J. Tobin (ed.) *Making a Place for Pleasure in Early Childhood Education* (pp. 235–50). New Haven, CT: Yale University Press.

Kohn, A. (1999) *The Schools Our Children Deserve: Moving Beyond Traditional Classrooms and Tougher Standards*. Boston: Houghton Mifflin.

Lankshear, C. and McLaren, P. (1993) Introduction, in C. Lankshear and P. McLaren (eds) *Critical Literacy: Politics, Praxis, and the Postmodern* (pp. 1–56). Albany, NY: State University of New York Press.

Leavitt, R. (1994) *Power and Emotion in Infant-Toddler Day Care*. Albany, NY: State University of New York Press.

Leavitt, R. (1995) Infant day care research: limitations and possibilities, in S. Reifel (ed.) *Advances in Early Education and Day Care* (vol. 7): *Social Contexts of Early Development and Education* (pp. 155–78). Greenwich, CT: JAI Press, Inc.

Lerner, G. (1993) *The Creation of Feminist Consciousness: From the Middle Ages to Eighteen-Seventy*. New York: Oxford University Press.

Lincoln, Y.S. and Cannella, G.S. (2004) Qualitative research, power, and the radical right, *Qualitative Inquiry*, (10)(2): 175–201.

Lyotard, J-F. (1993) *The Postmodern Explained*. Minneapolis: The University of Minnesota Press.

MacNaughton, G. (1995) A post-structural analysis of learning in early childhood settings, in M. Fleer (ed.) *DAPcentrism: Challenging Developmentally Appropriate Practice* (pp. 25–54). Watson, ACT: Australian Early Childhood Association.

MacNaughton, G. (2001) *Rethinking Gender in Early Childhood Education*. London: Paul Chapman Education Publishing.

McCarthy, C. (1993) After the canon: knowledge and ideological representation in the multicultural discourse on curriculum reform, in C. McCarthy and W. Crichlow (eds) *Race, Ideitity and Representation in Education* (pp. 289–305). New York: Routledge.

McLaren, P. (2000) *Che Guevara, Paulo Freire, and the Pedagogy of Revolution*. Boulder, CO: Rowman and Littlefield Publishers.

Meier, D. (2000) Educating a democracy, in J. Cohen and J. Rogers (eds) *Will Standards Save Public Education?* (pp. 3–34). Boston: Beacon Press.

Morley, D. and Chen, K. (eds) (1996) *Stuart Hall: Critical Dialogues in Cultural Studies*. London: Routledge.

Morris, A. (1984) *The Origins of the Civil Rights Movement: Black Communities Organizing for Change*. New York: The Free Press.

National Research Council (2002) *Scientific Research in Education* (Committee on Scientific Principles for Educational Research, R.J. Shavelson and L. Towne, (eds), Center for Education, Division of Behavioral and Social Sciences and Education). Washington, DC: National Academy Press.

Nietzsche, F. ([1887] 1969) *On the Genealogy of Morals*. Trans. W. Kaufmann. New York: Vintage Books.

No Child Left Behind Act of 2001, Pub. L. No. 107–110, 115 Stat. 1425 (2002). http://www.ed.gov/policy/elsec/leg/eseal02/107–110.pdf (accessed 4 November 2003).

Pinar, W., Reynolds, W., Slattery, P. and Taubman, P. (1995) *Understanding Curriculum: An Introduction to the Study of Historical and Contemporary Curriculum Discourses*. New York: Peter Lang.

Popkewitz, T. and Bloch, M. (2001) Fabricating the child and family: the practice of reason as the politics of social inclusion and exclusion, *Journal of Curriculum Theorizing*, 17(3): 63–84.

Reid, J. (1999) Little women/little men: gender, violence and embodiment in an early childhood classroom, in B. Kamler (ed.) *Constructing Gender and Difference: Critical Perspectives on Early Childhood* (pp. 167–89). Creskill, NJ: Hampton Press.

Ritchie, J. (2001) Reflections on collectivism in early childhood teaching in Aoteraroa/New Zealand, in S. Grieshaber and G.S. Cannella (eds) *Embracing Identities in Early Childhood Education: Diversity and Possibilities* (pp. 133–47). New York: Teachers College Press.

Rogoff, B. (1991) *Apprenticeship in Thinking: Cognitive Development in Social Context*. New York: Oxford University Press.

Sacks, P. (1999) *Standardized Minds: The High Price of America's Testing Culture and What We Can Do to Change It*. Cambridge, MA: Perseus Books.

Said, E. (1978) *Orientalism*. London: Routledge and Kegan Paul.

Said, E. (1993) *Culture and Imperialism*. London: Chatto and Windus.

Said, E. (1996) Orientalism, in P. Mongia (ed.) *Contemporary Postcolonial Theory: A Reader* (pp. 205–25). London: Arnold.

Sedgwick, E.K. (1993) *Tendencies*. Durham, NC: Duke University Press.

Silin, J. (1987) The early childhood educator's knowledge base: a reconsideration, in L.G. Katz (ed.) *Current Topics in Early Childhood Education* (pp. 17–31). Norwood, NJ: Ablex.

Silin, J. (1995) *Sex, Death and the Education of Children: Our Passion for Ignorance in the Age of AIDS*. New York: Teachers College Press.

Silin, J. (2003) The future in question, *Journal of Curriculum Theorizing*, (19)(2): 9–24.

Sleeter, C.E. (1996) *Multicultural Education as Social Activism*. Albany, NY: State University of New York Press.

Spivak, G.C. (1988) Can the subaltern speak? In C. Nelson and L. Grossberg (eds) *Marxism and the Interpretation of Culture*. Urbana, IL: University of Illinois Press.

Spivak, G.C. (1999) *A Critique of Postcolonial Reason: Toward a History of the Vanishing Present*. Cambridge, MA: Harvard University Press.

Spring, J. (1972) *Education and the Rise of the Corporate State*. Boston: Beacon Press.

Spring, J. (2004) *How Educational Ideologies are Shaping Global Society*. Mahwah, NJ: Lawrence Erlbaum Associates.

Surber, J.P. (1998) *Culture and Critique: An Introduction to the Critical Discourses of Cultural Studies*. Boulder, CO: Westview Press.

Thompson, E.P. (1963) *The Making of the English Working Class*. New York: Pantheon.

Tobin, J. (1995) Post-structural research in early childhood education, in J.A. Hatch (ed.) *Qualitative Research in Early Childhood Settings* (pp. 223–43). Westport, CT: Praeger.

Tobin, J. (ed.) (1997) *Making a Place for Pleasure in Early Childhood Education*. New Haven, CT: Yale University Press.

Viruru, R. (2001) *Early Childhood Education: Postcolonial Perspectives from India*. New Delhi: Sage.

Viruru, R. and Cannella, G.S. (2001) Postcolonial ethnography, young children, and voice, in S. Grieshaber and G.S. Cannella (eds) *Embracing Identities in Early Childhood Education: Diversity and Possibilities* (pp. 158–72). New York: Teachers College Press.

Vygotsky, L.S. (1962) *Language and Thought*. Cambridge, MA: MIT Press.

Vygotsky, L.S. (1978) *Mind in Society: The Development of Higher Psychological Processes*. Cambridge, MA: Harvard University Press.

Walkerdine, V. (1981) Sex, power and pedagogy, *Screen Education*, 38: 14–21.

Walkerdine, V. (1988) *The Mastery of Reason: Cognitive Development and the Production of Rationality*. London: Routledge.

Walkerdine, V. and the Girls and Mathematics Unit (1989) *Counting Girls Out*. London: Virago.

Weis, L., Altbach, P., Kelly, G. and Petrie, H. (eds) (1991) *Critical Perspectives on Early Childhood Education*. Albany, NY: State University of New York Press.

Yelland, N. (ed.) (1998) *Gender in Early Childhood*. New York: Routledge.

Young, R.J.C. (2001) *Postcolonialism: An Historical Introduction*. Oxford: Blackwell Publishers.

3 Developmental theory and early childhood education
Necessary but not sufficient

Daniel J. Walsh

Over the years I have become frustrated by the strident emphasis on developmental theory in early childhood education (hereafter, the field), as though little else is necessary for working with young children. Hearing people in the field describe themselves and others as 'developmental', as though they had reached a higher plane troubled me. However important understanding children's development and learning is, early schooling, in its many forms, requires other understandings as well. In this chapter *schooling* refers to the broad range of contemporary early childhood programs that exist for children both in the USA and internationally.

I have wondered whether many self-described 'developmentalists' are actually interested in early schooling and children, or if they simply viewed it as a convenient 'subject pool' for studies. Much research that goes on in 'university lab' preschools often has little to do with schooling. University preschools in the USA are indeed convenient places to find subjects – parents have already signed consent forms and the schools are designed for researchers with observation booths and laboratory rooms for ease of access. In fact, when nursery schools, funded by the Rockefeller Foundation, began in Home Economics units at major universities in the 1920s, they were not used for teacher training or for research on early schooling. They provided young women with experiences deemed necessary for good mothers and provided psychologists with a readily available subject pool of young children to study. The early childhood programs that grew up around these university nursery schools focused on children's development with little attention to the context within which children were developing.

These frustrations notwithstanding, I argue in this chapter for the importance of developmental theory for those who work with young children. In my view, abandoning developmental theory would be seriously short-sighted. My argument is straightforward. Because the dominant developmental perspective in the field is based on outmoded theory that has not stood up to empirical testing, we can and should replace it with contemporary developmental theory which considers contextual factors, such as culture. Further, we should *rethink* developmental theory and its relationship to early schooling.

In this chapter, I begin with a brief historical overview. I then explain why the dominant developmental perspectives in the field are no longer useful. Finally, I argue that contemporary developmental theory has much to offer the field.

Background

The idea that children go through sequential, predictable stages has been around for hundreds of years. For example, Martin Luther ([1532] 1967, p. 98) wrote, 'My [son] Hans is about to enter upon his seventh year, which is always climacteric, that is, a time of change. People always change every seventh year.'

Stage theory infused the field from its beginnings: Comenius compared children to plants and argued that schooling should fit children's nature. Later Pestalozzi and Froebel developed these themes further. Froebel spoke of 'the divine laws of development' and divided childhood into *early childhood* (birth through age 8 – a definition that continues today) and *later childhood*. In early childhood, children's intellectual capability was limited compared to later childhood. Pestalozzi developed the *Laws of Human Unfolding*.

The theme, that young children are developmentally different from older children and adults, has remained central in the field's history. Because it was thought that young children differ developmentally, it necessarily followed that they learn differently from older children and adults. Consequently, it was thought that schooling for young children should differ from schooling for older children and adults (Chung and Walsh, 2000). Weber, describing kindergarten training at the end of the nineteenth century, noted, 'It was argued that teachers working with young children needed an extensive understanding of human development. Indeed, [G. Stanley] Hall maintained the need for psychological knowledge "increased inversely with the age of the student" ' (1969, p. 120). Given this romantic and maturationist view of children developing through predictable and sequential stages, not surprisingly, those developmentalists most important to the field have been stage theorists and include Freud, Gesell, Erikson, and most notably, Piaget.

Sigmund Freud first came to the USA in 1909. G. Stanley Hall invited him to give a series of lectures at Clark University. Wanting to ensure a large audience, Hall brought in many 'kindergartners' (as kindergarten teachers were then called) who were working in his Child Study project. The kindergartners were fascinated by Freud's emphasis on the emotions. Consequently emotional development became a strong theme in the field, especially during the growth of nursery schools in the 1920s, when the field shifted its identity from kindergarten, now part of the elementary school, to the nursery school.

This focus on development, rather than on other areas of schooling, for example, curriculum, instruction, and assessment, has remained dominant in the field. In many universities, early childhood education is located in departments with names like Human Development and Family Studies. In contemporary discourse, *developmental* has become a stamp of approval with the implication that a good early childhood program is developmental.

'What we've known all along'

A most curious phenomenon was the rapidity with which the field embraced Piagetian theory. Piaget became a 'patron saint' to the field in a way that Gesell, Freud, and Ericson, though respected, did not. Everyone believed in and read about Piaget, even if few actually read his original works. My question is, How did such a complex theory become so popular? Anyone who doubts its complexity, is directed to Piaget's 'Piaget's theory' (1970). Even established scholars have confessed their confusion about aspects of it. For example, Gelman (1979), long a leading Piagetian, has admitted that she never understood what Piaget meant by 'reflexive abstraction', which is an important construct in the theory.

So what was the appeal of Piaget's theory for early childhood education? Let me suggest three reasons. First, Piaget gave scientific vindication to what the field had always believed – that young children are different, that they are cognitively limited, and that they go through predictable sequential stages. Second, as Donaldson (1978) pointed out, Piaget's *findings*, that is what children do in his tasks, remain remarkably stable. Ask a child to compare tall thin beakers with short fat ones, and she will perform as Piaget predicted. This predictability continues to capture the field's attention. Third, Piaget wisely refused to draw practical implications of his theory for education, thus allowing many, often competing, versions of Piagetian practice to emerge. As Murray remarked, 'Piagetian developmental theory is sufficiently imprecise . . . that any innovation that makes a major provision for the self-initiated and self-regulated activity of the pupil can be justified in [it]' (1979, p. 34). As a result, the field was able to fashion a comfortable discourse on development that mixed Piagetian theory with the dominant romantic maturationism of the first half of the century (Walsh, 1991).

Even more curious is the fact that the field continues to retain Piagetian theory long after developmental psychologists realized its shortcomings. However stable his *findings*, Piaget's *claims*, that is, his interpretation of the findings, have not withstood empirical testing. In 1978 Donaldson wrote *Children's Minds* and Gelman and Baillergeon in 1983 constructed 'A Review of

Some Piagetian Concepts'. Both persuasively demonstrated serious weaknesses in Piagetian theory and stage theory in general. These, and other critiques that followed, should have marked the end of Piaget's influence, but, strangely, the field ignored them. As a result, the dominant developmental perspective in the field is based on outmoded theory – stage theory, in general, and Piagetian theory, in particular – that is no longer tenable.

Contemporary developmentalism

The 'three grand systems' (Damon, 1998, p. xv) of the twentieth century – Piaget, psychoanalysis, and learning theory – described development in universal terms. These theoretical systems viewed development as lawful and, with minor adjustments, the same for everyone, everywhere, across time. The grand systems focused on biology and evolution, viewed development as an individual process, and ignored culture (Bruner, 1996). Developmentalists attended to those periods of human development most marked by change – infancy, early childhood, and adolescence. The contemporary discourse of *developmentally appropriate practice* (see Bredekamp and Copple, 1997), which assumes that practice, or at least the worthiness of practice, can be determined by knowledge of children's development, reflects the universalism of the grand systems.

These grand systems are no longer viable. Damon, analyzing the successive editions of the *The Handbook of Child Psychology* (1946, 1954, 1970, 1983) wrote, 'The grand old theories were breaking down. Piaget was still represented by his 1970 piece, but his influence was on the wane throughout the other chapters. Learning theory and psychoanalysis were scarcely mentioned' (1998, p. xv). The most recent edition of the *Handbook* (1998) gives the grand theories respectful historical attention, but they have been replaced by approaches that are more systemic (e.g., Lerner, 1998) and cultural (e.g., Shweder et al., 1998).

For example, Lerner describes a systems perspective on development as:

> These mechanistic and atomistic views of the past have been replaced by theoretical models that stress the dynamic synthesis of multiple layers of analysis, a perspective having its roots in systems theories of biological development . . . In other words, development, understood as a property of systemic change in the multiple and integrated levels of organization (ranging from biology to culture and history) comprising human life and its ecology, or, in other words, a *developmental systems perspective*, is an overarching conceptual frame associated with contemporary theoretical models in the field of human development.
> (1998, p. 2)

Elder et al. gave salient examples of developmental theorists exhibiting remarkable 'blindness to social history and context' (1993, p. 6). Describing Terman's longitudinal study of 'gifted' children born between 1904 and 1917, they noted that 'Terman's study almost succeeded in not collecting any systematic information on the sample's depression experiences, and it paid very little attention to the home front and overseas experiences of wartime Americans' (1993, p. 6). Similarly Hollingshead's *Elmtown's Youth* 'did not take into account the Great Depression experience of his subjects, the consequences of which might include father unemployment and severe income loss, in turn leading to adverse changes in family roles and increase family tensions' (1949, p. 7).

Contemporary developmentalists are interested not in 'structure, function, or content *per se*, but in change, in the processes through which change occurs, and thus in the means through which structures transform and functions evolve over the course of human life' (Lerner, 1998, p. 1). The contemporary focus is on a complex human being, whose development is neither an internal nor an individual process. Lerner noted,

> A developmental systems perspective involves the study of active people providing a source, across the life span, of their individual developmental trajectories; this development occurs through the dynamic interactions people experience with the specific characteristics of the changing contexts within which they are embedded.
>
> (1998, p. 16)

It is contended here that cultural psychology (e.g., Bruner, 1996; Cole, 1996; Shweder et al., 1998) is the systems model most applicable to early childhood education. Cultural psychology views culture as the most significant system within which people develop. An essential assumption of cultural psychology is that descriptions and explanations of development require explicit and careful attention to the culture and to the specific situation where development occurs. Bruner explained:

> The truths of theories of development are relative to the cultural contexts in which they are applied. The plasticity of the human genome is such that there is no unique way in which it is realized, no way that is independent of opportunities provided by the culture into which an individual is born ... Man is not free of either his genome or his culture ... To say, then, that a theory of development is 'culture free' is to make not a wrong claim, but an absurd one.
>
> (1986, p. 135)

From a cultural perspective, culture is neither an independent variable nor an overlay on some universal process (Miller, 1998; Shweder et al., 1998). Culture cannot be controlled for, as though development is essentially universal but marked by minor cultural and other variations, as Shweder et al. explained:

> [I]t is evident that culture does not surround or cover the 'universal' child. Rather, culture is necessary for development—it completes the child. Culture provides the script for "how to be" and for how to participate as a member in good standing in one's cultural community and in particular social contexts. Simultaneously, a cultural psychology perspective recognizes that children are active constituents of their own cultures and that changes in individuals initiate changes in their relations with others and thus in their immediate cultural settings.
>
> (1998, p. 896)

Culture is both the context *within* which the child develops and the context *into* which the child develops. Development is best understood as the process of growing into a culture, of becoming a member of specific groups, in specific cultural and historical contexts. Children are systems developing within systems (Pianta and Walsh, 1996). A cultural developmentalism is interested not in how children develop generally, were that possible, but in the ways in which children at a given time and in specific situations, like early schooling, become, for example, Japanese or Portuguese or the Midwestern version of an American. As Shweder et al. stipulated:

> The wager of cultural psychology is that relatively few components of human mental equipment are so inherent, hard wired, or fundamental that their developmental pathway is fixed in advance and cannot be transformed or altered through cultural participation. The bet is that much of human mental functioning is an emergent property that results from symbolically mediated experiences with the behavioral practices and historically accumulated ideas and understandings (meanings) of particular cultural communities.
>
> (1998, p. 867)

Conclusion

I have argued that contemporary developmental theory is critical to pedagogical theory, for young children, in fact, for people of all ages. I believe that educators who ignore contemporary developmental theory do so not so much at their own risk but at the risk of children.

I remain critical of an over-emphasis on developmental theory. Certainly pedagogical practice or theory cannot and should not be based *solely* on developmental theory. I do note that arguments that suggest that developmental theory can suggest the *how* of pedagogy but not the *what* oversimplify matters. Research on infants and young children (e.g., Karmiloff-Smith, 1991; Gallistel and Gelman, 1992; Wynn, 1992) has established that young children come into the world predisposed to learn some things more than others. This research has strong implications for early schooling.

The challenge is that contemporary developmental theory is complex and does not allow for the predictable sequential stages so long held sacred in the field. It does not allow for charts that describe how 3-year-olds act compared to 3.6-year-olds. It requires close attention to context – the larger cultural context, and the immediate local context of the preschool classroom and the beliefs and expectations that there await the child.

Basically, I am arguing for the need to base practice on scientific knowledge. Scientific knowledge is always tentative and ever changing. Unfortunately, the field has long favored orthodoxy over science. In my view, arguments that suggest we should abandon a developmental perspective completely simply substitute one limited perspective, and one narrow orthodoxy, for another. Certainly, we need to keep developmental theory in perspective. Early schooling is a complex endeavor and requires the insights of a range of theoretical perspectives.

I believe the field needs a vital, useful contemporary developmental theory that moves it beyond the limitations of the perspectives that dominate the field today. Working with young children requires being able to begin to see them in all their possibilities and potentials. It requires being able to understand how they learn and grow in different contexts. This seeing and understanding cannot be done without effective developmental theory.

The implications of cultural psychology for schooling are being developed. Bruner (1996) provided an excellent start. But clearly this perspective requires us to move beyond the individualistic and ahistorical view of children that dominated the twentieth century. It requires seeing development as a function not only of biology and evolution, but also, and importantly, of culture and situation (Bruner, 1996). A cultural psychology holds great promise for extending the possibilities and potentials of the young children in our care.

References

Bredekamp, S. and Copple, C. (1997) *Developmentally Appropriate Practice in Early Childhood Programs Serving Children from Birth through Age 8* (2nd edn). Washington, DC: National Association for the Education of Young Children.

Bruner, J.S. (1986) *Actual Minds, Possible Worlds*. Cambridge, MA: Harvard University Press.

Bruner, J.S. (1996) *The Culture of Education*. Cambridge, MA: Harvard University Press.

Chung, S. and Walsh, D.J. (2000) Unpacking 'child-centeredness': a history of meanings, *Journal of Curriculum Studies*, 32: 215–34.

Cole, M. (1996) *Cultural Psychology: A Once and Future Discipline*. Cambridge, MA: Harvard University Press.

Damon, W. (1998) Preface, in *Handbook of Child Psychology* (5th edn), in W. Damon and R.M. Lerner (eds) *Handbook of Child Psychology*. Vol. 1. *Theoretical Models of Human Development* (pp. xi–xvii). New York: John Wiley and Sons.

Donaldson, M. (1978) *Children's Minds*. New York: W. W. Norton.

Elder, G.H., Modell, J. and Parke, R. (1993) Studying children in a changing world, in G.H. Elder, J. Modell and R. Parke (eds) *Children in Time and Place: Developmental and Historical Insights* (pp. 3–21). New York: Cambridge University Press.

Gallistel, R. and Gelman, R. (1992) Preverbal and verbal counting and computation, *Cognition*, 44: 43–74.

Gelman, R. (1979) Preschool thought, *American Psychologist*, 34: 900–5.

Gelman, R. and Baillargeon, R. (1983) A review of some Piagetian concepts, in P. H. Mussen (ed.) *Handbook of Child Psychology*. vol. III, *Cognitive Development* (pp. 167–230). New York: John Wiley and Sons, Ltd.

Karmiloff-Smith, A. (1991) Beyond modularity: innate constraints and developmental change, in S. Carey and R. Gelman (eds) *The Epigenesis of Mind: Essays on Biology and Cognition*. Hillsdale, NJ: Erlbaum.

Lerner, R.M. (1998) Theories of human development: contemporary perspectives, in W. Damon and R.M. Lerner (eds) *Handbook of Child Psychology*. Vol. 1. *Theoretical Models of Human Development* (5th edn, pp. 1–24). New York: John Wiley and Sons, Ltd.

Luther, M.L. ([1532] 1967) Every seventh year brings a change (from 'Table talk collected by Conrad Cordatus'), in T. Tappert (ed.) *Luther's Works*, Vol. 54 (p. 190). Philadelphia, PA: Fortress Press.

Miller, P.J. (1998) The cultural psychology of development: one mind, many mentalities. Paper presented at the Social Development Consortium, University of Illinois at Urbana-Champaign, February.

Murray, F.B. (1979) The generation of educational practice from developmental theory, *Educational Psychologist*, 14: 30–43.

Piaget, J. (1970) Piaget's theory, in P.H. Mussen (ed.) *Carmichael's Manual of Child Psychology* (3rd edn, pp. 703–32). New York: John Wiley and Sons, Ltd.

Pianta, R.C. and Walsh, D.J. (1996) *High-Risk Children in Schools: Constructing Sustaining Relationships*. New York: Routledge.

Shweder, R.A., Goodnow, J., Hatano, G., LeVine, R.A., Markus, H. and Miller, P. (1998) The cultural psychology of development: one mind, many mentalities, in W. Damon and R.M. Lerner (eds) *Handbook of Child Psychology*: Vol. 1.

Theoretical Models of Human Development (5th edn, pp. 865–937). New York: John Wiley and Sons, Ltd.

Walsh, D.J. (1991) Reconstructing the discourse on developmental appropriateness: a developmental perspective, *Early Education and Development*, 2: 109–19.

Weber, E. (1969) *The Kindergarten: Its Encounter with Educational Thought in America.* New York: Teachers College Press.

Wynn, K. (1992) Addition and subtraction by human infants, *Nature*, 358: 749–50.

4 How 'bad' can it be?

Troubling gender, sexuality, and early childhood teaching

Mindy Blaise and Yarrow Andrew

Mindy: *The aim of this chapter is to tell how Yarrow, a male preschool teacher in an Australian rural community child care centre and I, a female early childhood teacher educator practicing in the United States at a large research university, used queer theory and feminist poststructuralism to challenge gender and sexuality in our teaching practices. The field of early childhood tends to avoid examining gender in a critical way and its relationship to teaching, learning, and identities. Instead we convey a simple and unproblematic notion of children's 'gender role development'. Therefore, we decided to conceptualize a wider project of analyzing the complexities of teaching and learning, taking into account the genderedness of children and teachers. When enacting pedagogies intended to confront and disrupt gender inequities in our classrooms, we took up Tobin's challenge of 'queering up both traditional and progressive notions of gender identity and sexuality' (1997, p. 31). During this collaborative project, we critically analyzed our 'good' and 'bad' teaching actions, and in doing so were building on the work of Ryan et al. (2001) by attempting to provide new, provocative, and some might argue, more complex images of early childhood teaching for our students.*

Our work together is about the ways in which we have been 'bad' teachers, who rejected the notion that developmentalism and developmentally appropriate practices provide us with what we need to know in order to interact with young children. Instead, we believe that gender is a critical factor in what we do, and we make it the center of our practice. Not only did we use queer theory and feminist poststructuralism to critically examine 'safe' and developmentally appropriate practices to confront our fears of moving beyond the fictional image of the 'good' early childhood teacher, but these alternative perspectives also informed us about the ways in which Yarrow and I conceptualized sexuality and gender. For example, instead of seeing young children as asexual, innocent bundles of joy, who unproblematically move through a set of predetermined developmental stages, we believe that children are sexual, and capable of finding pleasure through their gendered selves. For us, gender is understood as a social, political, and cultural construction in which children take an active part (Davies, 2003). We believe that the social construction of gender and sexuality is not only complicated, but also political and risky. From our experiences of working with young children, we believe that they know about gender discourses and gender norms, and how to use them to construct femininities and masculinities in their everyday lives. These complicated and political understandings of gender and sexuality influence who Yarrow and I are as educators, and how we teach young children and future early childhood teachers.

This chapter discusses a small part of our ongoing work together, highlighting how we attempted to challenge sexuality and gender in our classrooms by being 'bad' teachers and how this collaborative project informed our practices in the early childhood and university classrooms. We attempted to expand the image of the early childhood teacher to include someone who keeps pushing themselves to be 'bad', engaging in 'risky' teaching, and feeling uncomfortable, rather than simply accepting the limits and safety of conventional early childhood practice and knowledge.

Yarrow: When Mindy and I began this study, we did not know how our students would respond. What we believe is that as a discipline, despite the rhetoric of child-centredness, we work hard at constructing children in certain ways. These ways tend to reinforce the existing power dynamics between adults and children. We believed that some of these 'safe' practices were limiting the liberatory possibilities in our classrooms. By being 'bad', we wanted to try and undermine these power dynamics, in both the preschool and university classrooms. The ways in which the field of early childhood constructs children are not designed to help them be successful human beings (they will have to wait many years for that privilege), but rather are designed to constrain them within the mould of being a child at a particular age and stage. Developmental theory has done its best to set benchmark standards for what a child should be doing and capable of at any given age, and these standards seem to ignore the complexities of gender and sexuality and the ways in which children might deviate from or subvert such suggested norms.

Being 'bad' teachers, to us, is about letting go of these notions, and finding out what a classroom might look like if we did so. This was not easy. Mindy and I are both products of a system, and are very used to working within it. However, working in different areas of the field, that is a child care centre and a university, we were each able to provide for the other an alternative viewpoint about gender and teaching, which provided opportunities to question each other's usual teaching practices.

One of the areas in which a child's desires for themselves and our desires on their behalf differ most markedly, is in terms of sexuality. And while being 'bad' has relevance to all aspects of our practice, it can be seen most clearly in areas like sexuality, where being a good early childhood teacher or teacher educator seems to mean separating sexuality from gender, ignoring sexuality almost entirely, and not seeing the equity issues within gender and sexuality.

Mindy: *At the university, I work hard at troubling teaching and learning in the early childhood courses that I teach. Working from a queer and feminist poststructuralist perspective means that gender, and its social, historical, cultural, and political construction, are always placed at the center of my practice. Sexuality is addressed directly, as I question heterosexuality as a norm, and the ways in which children and teachers use these understandings to maintain and reinforce gender inequity. One of the most obvious ways that these perspectives influence my teaching is in the topics that I choose to include and omit in the early childhood methods courses that I teach. For example, while teaching the early childhood course entitled 'Guiding Young Children', I chose to focus on identities, discourse, and relationships instead of spending the majority of weeks discussing developmentally appropriate practices or the developmental domains of young children. I have found that raising issues about gender and sexuality with preservice teachers is difficult, especially when they resist thinking about teaching, learning, and young children in more critical and political ways (for a more thorough discussion see Blaise, 2003). My work with Yarrow has helped me sort out some of the pedagogical dilemmas I faced while troubling gender in my practice.*

Our project began as we shared with each other some of the issues we were encountering around sexuality and gender in our early childhood settings. I was complicating notions of gender with preservice early childhood teachers and Yarrow was uncovering children's sexual knowledge and questioning their ideas of gender. Slowly we began documenting our classroom practices and posing real-life gender dilemmas with each other. I say slowly, because I remember after Yarrow shared a particularly provocative classroom event with me, I asked, 'Are you documenting any of this stuff? Like using a tape recorder? You are talking about things that are too important to forget or miss' and he replied, 'What? Are you crazy? I don't get paid enough to do research in the classroom and I don't have time.' Fortunately though, about three months later, he asked, 'Hey, do you have a tape recorder I can borrow? I can't keep track of everything that the kids are saying.'

As Yarrow began systematically documenting these gender events happening in his classroom, I started incorporating them into the content of the early childhood course I was teaching. As our research took on a more formal feeling, I began noticing the dramatic ways that it was informing my own practice. First, this data provided me with real examples from a preschool classroom to share with my class. Preservice teachers were able to see that it just wasn't Mindy talking about all of these uncomfortable things, but there was a real teacher, doing things differently in the classroom, being 'bad', and actually questioning children about their understandings of gender and sexuality. Second, it challenged me to rethink my role as an early childhood teacher educator, reminding me that troubling gender and thinking beyond child development was a necessary part of my practice, especially if I believed in teaching for equity.

Yarrow: A moment that became pivotal in our study was a discussion that I had with my preschool class about 'The Sex Game', a game that had been initiated by a small group of children from seemingly out of nowhere. Coming back from a lunch break, one of my fellow staff members took me aside and told me that some children had started playing a game that I might need to have a look at (as you can tell, adults are always worried about sex!). My first sighting of the game was that afternoon, when I saw four children playing what looked to an outside observer like a chasing game, except that one of the rules when you caught someone was that you had to drag them to the ground (laughing all the while) and pretend to kiss them. When I asked a group of children what they were playing, they looked at each other, as if to say, 'How honest should we be?', and after looking at each other again, one child said, 'The Sex Game'. My only question at the time was whether everyone was comfortable playing it, and as they agreed that they were, I left it at that. One of our usual rules as a group is that no one should be made to play a game they don't want to play. It is the children's responsibility to ensure that someone's decision *not* to play is respected. This seemed like a good rule to have for 'The Sex Game' too, and had the added advantage of normalizing this game as just another game.

As I thought about it, though, I realized that this could be an opportunity to talk with the children about some of their understandings about sex. I wanted us to have this discussion, because, from the outset, the children assumed that the teachers would want to shut it down, or restrict them from playing it. From my first question about it, where they looked at each other complicitly, it was clear that they knew that some knowledge should not be shared with adults, because adults just cannot cope! I hoped we could shift that assumption.

At a quiet point in the afternoon, we sat down as a group, and I asked them about 'The Sex Game'.

'The Sex Game'

26/6/02
Yarrow: How do you play 'The Sex Game'?
Samuel: You touch them, you hide them, you sex them.
Yarrow: Why do you hide?
Samuel: Because people will stop you!
Yarrow: Why?
Joel: Because sexing is bad for kids.

I then ask the wider group whether they think 'sexing' is bad or good. There is some glancing at each other, and varying opinions, but most say it is good.

Yarrow: When did 'The Sex Game' start?
Clare: This week.
Yarrow: How do you sex someone?

Joel: Kissing bits, kissing on the lips . . .

Various voices: . . . ears, eyes, nose, teeth!

Samuel: Some girls run around in the nuddy and when they catch the boys they [the girls] take their [the boys'] clothes off.

Jake: Yeah, they take their knickers off.

Jodi: Boys don't have knickers, they have jocks.

[much laughter]

Yarrow: Is it a pretend game? I don't see anyone running around naked.

Most answer that it is pretend, though one child says it is real.

Yarrow: Who made it up?

Joel: Samuel did!

Yarrow: Samuel, where did you learn this game?

Samuel: [looks down, and says quietly] From Julia, a big girl.

A little later, while walking back to our normal room:

Maya: Sex is a rude word, but it's funny.

As a teacher, I understand that most people expect that I will avoid talking about sex, either because young children are too naïve to bring up such a taboo topic or I would be too uncomfortable with it. There was a certain amount of anxiety that I felt as I facilitated the discussion with the children. Yet at the same time I felt vindicated, because their spontaneous responses showed that they had been waiting for an opportunity to talk about this subject.

What they did reveal, even in this short discussion, was how much they already know about sex. For example, they knew that sex was about lying down, getting naked, kissing, and power. They also understood some of the rules, or culture, of sex – that it is regarded as private and secret.

Mindy: *When I presented 'The Sex Game' and Yarrow's conversation to preservice teachers, they understood children's talk and actions quite differently. For example, they saw these children as innocent and rationalized that they didn't really 'know' what they were talking about. Preservice teachers wanted more information about these children that would explain why they were interested in sex and playing an inappropriate game. They kept asking, 'Now, how old are these kids again?' and 'What kinds of families did they come from?' I overheard one preservice teacher commenting to her small group of peers, 'But, this didn't happen **here**, right? It was in Australia.' As a class, they were concerned that these children must have been exposed to inappropriate behaviors at home, pointing out that the children who instigated 'The Sex Game' were boys and they probably were not good students.*

Yarrow: A common way that adults dismiss children's sexuality is the idea that sex knowledge is unnatural for young children, and it must have come from a corrupted child. It's easy for me to fall into this trap too. I could have read this as being Julia's fault, and that this is why my group of pre-schoolers were talking about sex. But as I watched them participate, both in the discussion and in the game itself, I could see that they were all enthusiastically bringing their knowledge of sex into this new play scenario. If this were just a story about one child having gained precocious knowledge about sex, then I would expect the other children either to be uninterested, puzzled, or possibly curious. Instead this is a subject that they were all *already* excited about, and when the subject was raised, they all wanted to speak at once. I needed no classroom management skills for this discussion, because they were all keen to listen and share what they knew, as they leaned forward with their bodies and had their eyes opened wide, to join in the conversation better.

Mindy: *While sharing Yarrow's stories about 'The Sex Game' with my class, I was beginning to realize that preservice teachers were resistant to these images of young children, teaching, and learning. Their shocked facial expressions, opened mouths, shaking of heads in disgust, and crossed arms made me question if they were ready for this kind of information. Yarrow was not doing his job. They believed that a 'good' early childhood teacher would have immediately stopped this game or better yet, prevented the game and talk from ever occurring in the classroom. I started to question if this information was appropriate. Maybe we should have been discussing the merits of developmentally appropriate practice and how child development can be used for observing and planning. This is the knowledge that preservice teachers expected and wanted, not questioning and rethinking their beliefs and ideas about young children and teaching.*

   I wondered if preservice teachers were unable to move beyond simplistic notions of biological and socialization models of gender and sexuality? And, if so, would they be willing to see young children as actually having sexual knowledge or the ability to use their sexual knowledge to actively construct themselves and others as gendered beings? At this point, I had to make a pedagogical decision. Do I simply let it go, hoping that these complicated and troubling images of young children and teaching might magically make a difference in preservice teachers' understandings about their role as teachers or do I continue providing more complicated notions of how we become gendered and what it means to be an early childhood teacher? What risks were involved by choosing to confront preservice teachers about children, learning, and teaching? That is, what are the gains and losses of being a 'bad' teacher educator? Can I afford to do this kind of teaching? How can I afford not to?

   My ongoing conversations with Yarrow about these issues, particularly how and why he was confronting gender in his practice, helped me realize that troubling gender in the classroom with young children and preservice teachers is a necessary part of my teaching. If I don't present these ideas, who will? As the semester progressed, I found that instead of backing down about these troubling issues, I became more explicit about how alternative theoretical perspectives, such as queer theory and feminist poststructuralism, help raise new questions about teaching and learning. I gave myself permission to be a 'bad' teacher as I challenged the class to think about how they will address gender and sexuality in their practice and to envision what kind of teacher they want to be.

Yarrow: Because discourses of heterosexuality are so dominant in the lives of these children, same-sex attraction remains almost unthinkable for them. When both the girls and the boys know and conform to their prescribed roles in a game, there seems to be no predicament. It only becomes apparent when someone refuses to play by the rules. For example, one girl, Clare, found it hard to join 'The Sex Game'. Her dilemma is that she normally plays with and identifies with the boys, and gets included as such. But here, the girls were making the rules, and to them, Clare was wanting to be on the wrong side, meaning that the girls would have to chase and kiss her. I believe in Clare's right to transgress gender boundaries and therefore I chose to intervene.

> *21/8/02*
> Yarrow: Clare wants to be chased.
> Jodi: [emphatically] But we've got to kiss her!!
> Yarrow: I'm sure Clare doesn't want to be kissed either!

Contained within Jodi's statement is the clear implication that girls cannot kiss girls. I knew this, and often find myself explaining to the children that same-sex attraction is possible. In this case I chose to let the children assume that I was unaware of the rules of heterosexuality, and pretended that the issue was not about girls kissing girls, but that Clare just didn't understand that when you are on the boys' team you had to pretend not to like being kissed. By doing so, I was able to suggest a more direct resolution to the issue, that maybe there wasn't an issue at all. And as it happened, this seemed to be enough, because Clare was able to join the game alongside the boys.

This incident with Clare remains a vivid reminder of what is opened up when I choose to 'allow' these games in my classroom. Choosing to be involved remains a risky activity for me as a teacher, particularly as a male in the field. Parents, through their fears about sexuality, want me to police these games and suppress them. By talking about this game with the children, I became a participant. I was not only condoning the games, but in some way encouraging them as well. I know that I am always at risk of accusations of sexualizing these children inappropriately. Consequently, I try and counteract my fears by being aware of how much all these children seem to desire an outlet for their questions and thoughts about sex.

Mindy: *As Yarrow and I continue to confront these discourses in our classrooms, we realize that simply moving beyond child development is risky in a range of ways. This kind of teaching is risky because it disrupts the image of the 'good' early childhood teacher, positioning us as 'bad'. We are a field that is identified as nice ladies who don't talk about these things with children! It's risky for Yarrow, not just because he is a male early childhood teacher, but because the parents that he works with certainly don't want or expect him to raise and encourage these issues with their innocent children. It's risky for me, because I'm pushing child development to the side and refusing to give preservice teachers 'the facts' about good teaching, and therefore could be regarded as not doing my job.*

However, we do believe that it is important for all of us to work on liberating that 'bad' teacher within ourselves, and that we need to be more prepared to take risks or live on the edge in our practice. We are not convinced that the careful approach benefits children. If we want the children in our classrooms to experience a more equitable world, we have to be prepared to be controversial in the process. We need to encourage early childhood teachers to get uncomfortable and shift their thinking to a range of issues considered 'taboo' for young children, such as sex play, religion, racism, poverty, or death. We might begin this task by rethinking the content that we teach in our early childhood teacher preparation programs. What do preservice teachers gain from an education based exclusively on child development? What if traditional child development courses were replaced by subjects that focused on post-modern perspectives, identities, gender, or images of teaching and learning? In the university classroom, this might mean pushing my feelings of safety aside as I recognize when preservice teachers are resisting alternative ways of understanding children, and then raising their awareness about these reactions, attempting to get them to discover why they are feeling uncomfortable. This strategy might create opportunities for preservice teachers to gain a better understanding of their own values and beliefs and how they will influence practice.

Yarrow: We need to encourage early childhood teachers to be uncomfortable and shift their thinking about gender, sexuality, teaching, and learning. Instead of shutting down games and play that might make us uncomfortable, we should push ourselves to discuss such taboo subjects as sex play, same-sex relationships, religion, death, as they emerge in the classroom. This implies creating a classroom environment that allows such topics to surface. For example, children will sometimes draw attention to a teacher's body by referring to their breasts or penis. This has usually embarrassed teachers, who tend to ignore such comments. Perhaps we should instead use them as springboards for discussing with children their knowledge and interest of such topics, or our own discomfort.

Mindy: *Finally, if we believe in the importance of providing children with the tools to understand their experiences with gender and sexuality, then we cannot remain* *silent in either the early childhood or university classrooms. Rather than children needing to be constructed as 'bad' for talking about difficult subjects like sex and sexuality, we need to be prepared to be 'bad' too, and engage in these important conversations with children and preservice teachers. This will mean that the field of early childhood needs to find ways to support those teachers who are willing to take chances, as they challenge early childhood norms, and begin the hard and problematic work of constructing and enacting new images of what it means to be an early childhood teacher. We believe that one way we can support 'bad' teachers is by sharing stories of risky teaching with each other in various contexts that may include the staff room, university courses, professional conferences, or in publications. Such discussions have no prescribed agendas except honesty and frankness from both teachers and children.*

References

Blaise, M. (2003) Getting 'unstuck': complicating gender in early childhood. Paper presented at the American Educational Research Association Annual Meeting, Chicago, Illinois, 21–25 April 2003.

Davies, B. (2003) *Frogs, Snails and Feminist Tales: Preschool Children and Gender*. (Rev. edn). Creskill, NJ: Hampton Press, Inc.

Ryan, S., Ochsner, M. and Genishi, C. (2001) Miss Nelson is missing!: Teacher sightings in research on teaching, in S. Grieshaber and G.S. Cannella (eds) *Embracing Identities in Early Childhood Education: Diversity and Possibilities* (pp. 45–59). New York: Teachers College Press.

Tobin, J.J. (1997) *Making a Place for Pleasure in Early Childhood Education*. New Haven, CT: Yale University Press.

5 Preschool children's portrayals of their male teacher

A poststructuralist analysis

Jennifer Sumsion

Introduction

This chapter draws on poststructuralist understandings to analyse children's portrayals of their male preschool teacher and to examine the discourses underpinning their portrayals. The study reported in the chapter had aimed to generate data that could contribute to informing policy decisions about whether efforts should be made to recruit more men into the children's services workforce. As the data revealed, however, gender-related discourses were overshadowed by regulatory discourses. The prominence of regulatory discourses raises unsettling questions about how children might perceive their teachers and construct their experiences of their early childhood settings.

Increasingly, early childhood educators and researchers are recognizing the importance of listening to children's voices if they are to gain insights into their experiences of early childhood settings. Recent studies have sought children's views of what they like and dislike about the services they attend (Evans and Fuller, 1998; Farrell et al., 2002); their opinions of their teachers' practices (Daniels et al., 2001); and their perceptions of the opportunities they have to influence decisions within services (Sheridan and Samuelsson, 2001). Such studies reinforce that children are competent social actors capable of reporting on and engaging in discussion about their experiences and perspectives (O'Kane, 2000). Seeking children's views about issues that affect them, then, seems essential for informed decision-making within early childhood settings, and about children's services, more generally.

My intention in the study reported in this chapter was to work with children to generate data that could inform policy about the gender make-up of the early childhood workforce. Debates about whether efforts should be made to recruit more men to early childhood education are well rehearsed (see, for example, Cameron and Moss, 1998; Sumsion, 2000a; MacNaughton and Newman, 2001) but rarely, if at all, do they draw on young children's experiences and views of male teachers. I wanted to begin to address that omission by investigating how children portrayed their male preschool teacher.

In contrast to some earlier studies of young children's perceptions of their teachers (e.g., Armstrong and Sugawara, 1989; Smith et al., 1989; Summers et al., 1991; Klein, 1998; Diamond and Cooper, 2000), this study aimed to theorize children's responses, rather than simply report them. As Mayall (1999) argues, the views or standpoint of the typically less powerful, in this case young children, provide an opportunity to interrogate and critique frequently taken-for-granted truths – and to envisage other possibilities. For this reason, I wanted to go beyond reporting children's voices to consider the discourses in which they were embedded. In doing so, I found it helpful to draw on poststructuralist perspectives.

Theorizing discourse

Following MacNaughton (1998) and others who draw on the work of Foucault, I use the term *discourse* to refer to the categories we use to make sense of and to engage with our social world; in other words, 'our way of naming things and talking about them' (Dahlberg et al., 1999, p. 31). Discourses signify what we consider normal and desirable (MacNaughton, 1998). They reflect particular ways of 'thinking, feeling, believing, valuing, and acting' (Gee, 1996, p. 131) and stipulate 'what can be said and done, by whom and when' (Ryan et al., 2001, citing Burman, 1994 and Hicks, 1995–96). As such, they legitimize and proscribe certain ways of operating in the world.

Poststructuralists contend that discourses are culturally and historically specific and that each discourse represents only one 'possible way of giving meaning to reality' (MacNaughton, 2000, p. 51). At any one time, there is a limited array of often competing discourses in circulation, some of which become more powerful than others (ibid.). Our choice of discourses is limited to those we perceive available to us. Theorizing discourses in this way, I believe, enabled me to hear and to value individual children's voices while locating their portrayals of their teacher within a larger cultural-historical and social context.

The children and their context

The study involved 63 children who attended a 40-place community-based Australian preschool. These children chose to participate in the study after informed consent had been obtained from the parents of all children in the preschool. They accounted for 79 per cent of the children taught by Bill (a pseudonym), the male teacher-director and the only male staff member, during a two-year period. The children ranged in age from 3 years and 9 months to 5 years and 8 months, with a mean of 4 years and 11 months. The gender composition of the sample (57 per cent boys, 43 per cent girls) reflected the unusually high proportion of boys in Bill's group in one particular year.

The preschool was located in an affluent Sydney suburb and provided a 9a.m.–3p.m. programme for children aged from 3 to 5 years. The older children attended three days per week and the younger children two days. Almost all children were from two-parent families and spoke English as their first language. As these demographics are not representative of young children generally, caution is needed when considering the relevance of the findings to other settings. Similarly, structural differences between preschools and child care centres[1] may mean that caution is required when generalizing across service types.

The preschool was highly regarded within the community, and since Bill's appointment, some two years prior to the commencement of the study, enrolment waiting lists had grown substantially. Parents and staff welcomed his warm and relaxed manner, the positive relationships he readily established with them, his commitment to the service and the energy he invested in his work. In casual conversations, they referred frequently to the successful camping weekends away he organized for families and staff and his transformation of the outdoors area into an attractive garden-like setting that offered many possibilities for imaginative play.

According to Bill, his efforts to infuse conventionally 'masculine' interests into the programme were also well received by children, staff and families. He described, for example, how he had driven his car into the preschool, put it up on jacks, taken the wheels off and pulled the brakes apart and the extensive discussion that these activities had generated. In Bill's view, it was important for children to see both men and women undertaking a wide range of roles and activities so that they could begin to develop an appreciation of the options available to them. Apart from his strong interest in demonstrating that men, like women, can care for and nurture young children, Bill considered that he was a typical early childhood teacher with a commitment to child-centred practice.[2] For some time, he had been involved in an ongoing study about men in children's services. When he invited me to extend that study by talking with the children whom he taught, I accepted with delight.

Portraying bill

The children's portrayals of Bill consisted of their drawings of him and their explanations of their drawings and their responses during conversational interviews. Guiding questions underpinning our conversations included, *Can you tell me about your drawing? What does Bill do at preschool? Is there anything that you especially like to do with Bill? Do you think Bill is a good teacher? Why/why not?* Because children generally chose to be interviewed in outside locations where there was considerable competition from environmental sounds, I relied on note-taking rather than audio-taping to record details of our conversations.

The drawings and accompanying text reporting the children's explanations and interview responses were filed in a display folder that the children and I referred to as 'our book about Bill'. The folder was freely available for them to peruse, and many chose to revisit their contributions. When re-readings elicited further comments about Bill, these were added to the original text, with the children's permission.

Analysing children's portrayals of Bill

I began analysing the children's portrayals of Bill by reading and rereading the children's drawings and accompanying text to identify recurring themes. I then turned to tools emerging from poststructuralist understandings to deconstruct these themes and to identify and illuminate the discourses in which they were embedded. Because I had set out to gain insight into children's perceptions of male teachers, I focused initially on gender.

Drawing on feminist poststructuralist perspectives that see gender as socially constructed and continually negotiated, rather than a biologically determined binary divide (Yelland and Grieshaber, 1998; MacNaughton, 2000), I looked for instances in which children's drawings, descriptions, or narratives about Bill seemed to do the following:

- position him in ways that conformed to or challenged traditionally gendered views;
- indicate whether the children were engaged in dualistic gender category maintenance work (Davies, 1989); and/or
- provide insights into the versions of masculinity the children permitted and portrayed.

As it turned out, however, gender discourses were not nearly as salient in the children's portrayals of Bill as those associated with regulation. To analyse these discourses, I turned to Gore's (1995, 1998) typology of regulatory techniques derived from Foucault's (1977) theorizing about disciplinary power. These techniques include, but are not limited to the following:

- regulation by rules or restriction (including the use of sanctions, rewards or punishment);

- surveillance (closely observing, watching, supervising, threatening to watch);
- normalization (invoking, requiring, setting or conforming to a standard, defining the normal; using evaluative processes and judgements to define in what ways and to what extent individuals conform to, or depart from, what is considered normal);
- exclusion (the converse of normalization, establishing the boundaries of what is considered normal; pathologizing what is outside these boundaries; sometimes sanctioning or removing that which is not considered normal);
- distribution (dividing into parts, partitioning space; arranging bodies in space).

(Adapted from Gore, 1995, p. 103)

This typology constituted a useful lens for further reading and rereading of the data. Analysis of the remaining salient themes – work, play, caring and teaching – was informed by poststructuralist sensitivity to binary oppositions.

In their portrayals of Bill, children drew on overlapping rather than discrete discourses. In many cases, multiple discourses were evident in a single portrayal, although without exception, children spoke of him with warmth, affection, and respect. As Figure 5.1 illustrates, just under half the children drew on gender discourses, the original focus of the study. In contrast, three-quarters referred to regulation, while approximately one-third of children referred to work and an equal number to play. Discourses associated with caring were evident in one-fifth of responses while references to teaching were made in two-thirds of responses.

In the remainder of the chapter, I deconstruct these discourses and begin to consider possible implications for early childhood teachers and settings. Because there seemed relatively few explicit links between discourses of gender and regulation, I examine these separately. As discourses of work and play, on the other hand, appeared to be connected, as did those of caring and teaching, I refer to these pairings as clusters in the discussion that follows.

Discourses of gender

As Figure 5.1 shows, gender discourses were evident in 47 per cent of portrayals. In 11 per cent of all portrayals, children used discourses that reflected highly conventional views of masculinity and gender relationships. I classified these discourses as *strongly traditional*. They included images of Bill engaging in activities such as surfing, motor bike riding, playing soccer, and mowing the lawn, many of which took place beyond the preschool context. They focused on attributes associated with normative masculinity, such as adventurousness,

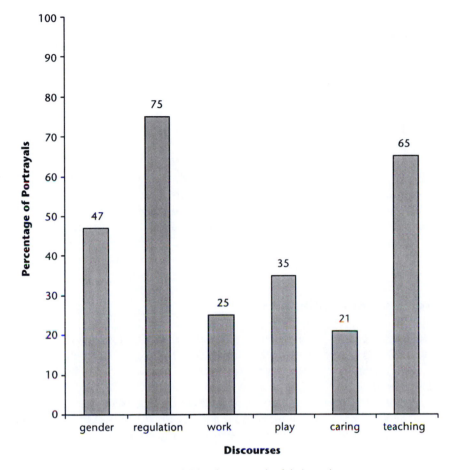

Figure 5.1 Discourses evident in children's portrayals of their teacher.

fearlessness, physical strength, stamina and dexterity, outdoor responsibilities and an affinity for the outdoors. Boys who portrayed Bill in strongly tradition-ally gendered ways also emphasized male camaraderie based on shared interests traditionally perceived as masculine, such as wrestling, block play, construction toys, and enjoyment of the outdoors. The absence of women or girls suggested that these boys may have seen gender as a mutually exclusive binary construct with boundaries that require strict policing.

More commonly, children's portrayals of Bill reflected a mix of con-ventional views of masculinity and gender relationships, with some gender-neutral elements. These gender discourses, which I labelled *somewhat traditional*, were evident in 30 per cent of all portrayals of Bill. Although these children permitted some slippage from traditional versions of masculinity, they set limits on the extent to which they tolerated departure from normative masculinity. For example, one boy (5 years, 7 months) explained how Bill engaged in a range of gender-neutral teaching activities but in his drawing portrayed Bill playing soccer with him.

Only 6 per cent of all portrayals of Bill reflected *non-traditional* gender discourses. These portrayals actively sanctioned qualities and interests not generally associated with conventional masculinity. One boy (4 years, 9 months) focused on his close relationship with Bill (Figure 5.2). This child's emphasis on mutual emotional support and interdependency as the basis of the relationship, as he saw it, was qualitatively different from the other boys' portrayals of male camaraderie based on shared, conventional male interests and grounded in more traditional gender discourses.

In general, however, the gender discourses used by the children seemed more likely to reproduce dominant cultural values about gender than to challenge them. Collectively, though, the gender discourses in children's portrayals of Bill were overshadowed by those associated with regulation.

Discourses of regulation

Regulatory discourses were evident in 75 per cent of children's portrayals. It seemed that, to these children, regulation was an integral part of preschool life and an important responsibility of their teacher. Their portrayals reflected several regulatory techniques identified by Gore (1995, 1998), including regulation by rules and restrictions, surveillance, normalization, and exclusion. Children's experiences of each of these techniques are described below. As the extracts illustrate, these techniques were frequently overlapping, rather than discrete.

Rules and restrictions

Children were acutely aware of the rules and restrictions governing their lives within the preschool. They referred most often to those that regulated their bodies by delineating what was expected, condoned or forbidden, and emphasized Bill's role in enforcing these rules and restrictions:

> He doesn't let people run inside and he doesn't let them roll around inside. (boy, 5 years, 5 months)

> He makes sure that no kids push little kids down. He makes sure that nobody pushes me. (girl, 5 years, 6 months)

> He tells the kids naughty things that they can't do. (boy, 3 years, 9 months)

I follow him because sometimes I'm shy. He's sad that I'm going to big school. Sometimes he wants to come to big school and visit me because he won't see me. Sometimes I get a bit scared so I ask Bill to help. (boy, 4 years, 9 months)

Figure 5.2 Non-traditional gender discourses.

He tells people to stop doing things that they are not supposed to do. He tells everyone to stop fighting. He tells them to play. (boy, 5 years, 7 months)

In addition, children referred frequently to rules and restrictions designating their use of time and space; in other words, what they were to do and when and where they were to do it:

He tells kids when it is time to talk. (boy, 3 years, 9 months)

When it's inside time, he tells everyone to go inside. (boy, 5 years, 7 months)

He tells us when it's fruit time and lunch time. He tells us when we can get up from rest time. (girl, 5 years, 6 months)

Children also described some of the implicit rules underpinning rituals that governed how events in the preschool day were to be managed:

He puts music on when it's rest time. (boy, 5 years, 5 months)

He does news. He doesn't tell news. He sits there and he says, 'Where did you get that from?' (boy, 4 years, 6 months)

The children recognized that Bill used a range of surveillance techniques to monitor their compliance to these rules, restrictions and rituals.

Surveillance

Children conveyed a sense of Bill constantly watching the unfolding of events in the preschool. Sometimes, they referred to surveillance on a global level, as Figure 5.3 illustrates.

Some children attributed Bill's surveillance of them to his concern for their physical safety:

He likes to look at the kinds of bugs we find outside, just in case they are poisonous. (boy, 5 years, 5 months)

More commonly, they portrayed Bill watching specifically for potential transgressions of rules and restrictions. They explained that he targeted children with a history of transgressing these rules and restrictions:

Bill is looking around and watching. He likes to look around. (girl, 5 years, 4 months)

Figure 5.3   Surveillance.

When we go outside he watches us less [in case] we are very bad. (boy, 4 years, 5 months)

He keeps an eye on G because she always pushes us. (girl, 5 years)

Children also referred to Bill's surveillance of the products they produced:

He likes to look at our drawings and paintings. He likes to look at what we make [with the construction toys]. He likes to look at things we do in the sand. (boy, 4 years, 7 months)

He watches us and when we finish our painting he says 'lovely'. (boy, 4 years, 5 months)

Typically, these products were then publicly displayed, thus enabling ongoing monitoring:

He likes hanging everything up. He puts up some of our paintings.

> When we print things at the computer, he puts them on the wall.
> When we do drawings, he hangs them on the wall. (girl, 4 years, 11
> months)

Collectively, then, children's portrayals conveyed an image of Bill as an omni-
present figure in the preschool.

Normalization

The responses that the children made indicated that they seemed to connect
to Bill's constant surveillance of them to his intervention with measures
to encourage their conformity to 'normal' and 'desirable' behaviour.
They described a range of normalizing techniques. Some involved direct
intervention:

> If M and E are mean to me, I'll go over to Bill and he asks M and E if I
> can play with them, and they always say 'yes'. (girl, 5 years, 5 months)

Children knew that compliance was rewarded. Sometimes rewards were
indirect, such as securing Bill's approval:

> He always gets happy when people do good things. (boy, 5 years
> 7 months)

At other times, they were more tangible, with early release from rest time a
much-cited example:

> He likes to call out the good resters and they go and do something.
> (girl, 5 years, 2 months)

Children understood that if they failed to comply with these measures to
normalize their behaviour, they faced the possibility of exclusion.

Exclusion

There were many references to Bill excluding children who did not adhere to
the rules and restrictions of the preschool. Exclusion could mean temporary
banishment from favour:

> Bill gets angry at people who don't listen to him. (boy, 5 years,
> 5 months)

It could also involve bodily removal from the context in which expectations of normalized behaviour had been flouted, as well as the redistribution of children elsewhere within the preschool:

> He talks to the boys if they are throwing sand at us girls. He will say 'Stop doing it. Go and sit down.' (girl, 5 years, 5 months)

> If we don't be very good when we sleep, he makes us go next to another person. (boy, 4 years 7 months)

> We get a chance. But if we're bad again we have to sit at the table. (boy, 4 years 5 months)

As with other regulatory techniques, children seemed to accept processes of exclusion as a natural part of preschool life.

Distribution

According to the children, Bill not only redistributed them following their transgressions but also as a preventative measure to reduce the likelihood of breaches of rules and restrictions. They implied that he used this technique to try to prevent the formation of particular groupings of children that could prove 'dangerous' or 'undesirable'. As one child said succinctly:

> He keeps us away from G. (girl, 5 years)

Like children, materials and resources were carefully distributed to encourage desired behaviour. Once again, children emphasized Bill's role as regulator:

> He sets all the stuff out on all the tables. He puts the toys out. He tells us what to do when we don't know what to do. (boy, 4 years, 2 months)

In short, the children's portrayals showed Bill exercising a great deal of authority and regulatory power through a range of regulatory techniques. They saw this power as productive (Foucault, 1980; Gore, 1995, 1998), rather than repressive, and a source of stability and security. In the words of one child:

> He makes sure everyone keep safe. He makes sure everything goes the right way. (girl, 5 years, 6 months)

Children not only recognized these regulatory techniques; they, too, made use of them. Some children, for example, seemed quick to categorize children whom they perceived did not conform to what was permissible as 'other', and to see non-conformity as a basis for exclusion. This tendency was particularly evident in the several references to the non-conforming child, 'G'. Other children took pleasure in subverting regulatory power. One child joked about how he managed to circumvent Bill's surveillance:

> I like sitting behind his chair so he can't see me and he thinks I'm not there. (boy, 5 years, 6 months)

In general, however, children's resistance to these techniques of regulatory power seemed minimal. To these children, they seemed a natural and accepted part of everyday preschool life.

Discourses of work and play

A third cluster of discourses evident in children's portrayals of Bill were associated work and play. In 25 per cent of children's portrayals, children referred to Bill as working while 35 per cent portrayed him engaging in play. Their portrayals implied that they may have seen work and play as binary opposites. To some children, work seemed to occupy a large chunk of Bill's day:

> One of his favourite things is working. (boy, 5 years, 6 months)

> He works all the time. He goes to the office and works. (boy, 5 years, 7 months)

They seemed unsure about the precise purpose of this work, perhaps because it was undertaken mostly in his office, a space from which they were excluded. References to the nature of his work were therefore somewhat vague:

> He does jobs. (boy, 4 years)

> He does writing. (girl, 4 years, 3 months)

> He works at the computer (girl, 4 years, 8 months)

> He talks on the telephone (boy, 4 years, 7 months)

But, essentially, they constructed work as an adult activity that distanced Bill from them. In contrast, they portrayed his participation in play as a way of reducing the physical and social distance between Bill and the children, as Figure 5.4 illustrates.

He's playing with the children. He's throwing the ball to the children and they are throwing it to their friends. I'm bouncing it to Bill and he's bouncing it to M and she's bouncing it to E. (girl, 5 years, 5 months)

Figure 5.4   Play as a means of lessening distance between children and teachers.

Children alluded to two aspects that contributed to lessening this distance. First, play provided opportunities for reciprocity:

> He plays with me lots of times and I play with him. (boy, 4 years, 9 months)

Second, play seemed to engender a playfulness in Bill that temporarily released him from adult responsibilities and constraints. Figure 5.5 conveys some sense of this playfulness and its liberating effect.

When children described Bill playing, they made no concurrent reference to any use of regulatory power. It seemed to them that when he engaged in play, he relinquished his customary attachment to techniques such as surveillance, normalization, and exclusion. His engagement in play seemed to unsettle the traditional adult–child binary and was welcomed by these children.

While references to regulation were absent from children's discourses of play, gender discourses were frequently interwoven. Boys' portrayals of Bill's participation in play, in particular, generally drew on discourses that reflected gender-stereotyped interests, and a valuing of physical strength and male camaraderie that reinforced traditional gender power relations:

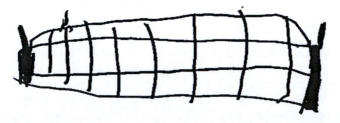

Bill is jumping on the trampoline. He wants to touch the sky. (boy, 4 years, 11 months)

Figure 5.5 Play as liberation.

> I like playing games with him. I like wrestling with him when he's got my hat. (boy, 5 years, 7 months)

> I build blocks with him. And I like playing games with him and dressing up as Superman. (boy, 5 years, 8 months)

In contrast, the fourth and final cluster of discourses evident in children's portrayals seemed relatively gender-neutral. These discourses were associated with caring and teaching.

Discourses of caring and teaching

Unlike the binary discourses work and play, the discourses of caring and teaching in children's portrayals, on initial reading, suggested a continuum. References to caring, or more typically, helping, appeared in 21 per cent of all portrayals. For the most part, children perceived that Bill cared for them by helping them to do what they had difficulty doing for themselves:

> I can't write my name so he writes my name for me. (girl, 3 years, 11 months)

> If the kids have trouble putting on shoes after rest time, he helps them. (girl, 4 years, 5 months)

> He reads stories in the book corner to the kids because the kids don't really read the words. (girl, 5 years, 2 months)

In other words, Bill's caring helped to compensate for their inadequacies.

In a small number of portrayals, the focus became more one of Bill assisting children to acquire skills. These children referred, in equal measure, to helping and teaching:

> He teaches us lots of things. He teaches us to dance. When we do the 'around and around' song, when we get crooked he helps us to get out of being crooked. (boy, 4 years, 5 months)

> He helps us learn to read. He says, 'Can you spell HGLL?', and then we have to read it. (boy, 5 years, 6 months)

> He helps us learn stuff – good paintings and really hard puzzles. He teaches us to make chains and patterns. He teaches us to read. (boy, 5 years, 8 months)

Explicit references to teaching were made in 65 per cent of all portrayals. They mostly reflected a transmission view of teaching and learning and positioned Bill as possessor of knowledge and adult expert:

> He shows me what to do on the computer. And he teaches us how to write our names and I know how to write my name because he showed me. (girl, 5 years, 2 months)

> He's great because teaches us all different things. He teaches us about gravity and the moon. And he even teaches us about dinosaur bones. (girl, 5 years, 5 months)

Despite their varying emphasis on helping and teaching, almost all portrayals in which these discourses were evident seemed to involve children's constructions of themselves as 'not yet able' (Cannella, 1997, p. 151), rather than as agentic learners, capable of critical inquiry and knowledge construction. They conveyed an image of children as passive receivers and reproducers, 'awaiting receipt of adult knowledge and enrichment' (Dahlberg et al., 1999, p. 50). In positioning themselves as less capable than adults and in need of their guidance, the discourses of caring and teaching taken up by the children reflected and reinforced perceptions of an adult-child binary.

Did the children consider Bill a good teacher?

All children considered Bill a good teacher, although 25 per cent seemed to find it difficult to explain why. The remaining children were almost equally divided in the reasons they gave. One quarter thought Bill a good teacher because he taught them new skills or knowledge. The same proportion referred to his personal qualities such as his sense of humour and fun, enthusiasm, kindness and helpfulness, while 21 per cent thought him a good teacher because of use of his regulatory power and the predictability and security that provided. His gender was not cited as a reason.

With the exception of gender, the children's responses to this question were generally consistent with the range of discourses they employed when portraying Bill, although their weighting differed. This consistency suggests that children, like adults, have an investment in and a commitment to the discourses they take up (MacNaughton, 1998). It also foreshadows the challenges involved in disrupting dominant discourses.

What Might We Learn from This Study?

This study has drawn on poststructuralist perspectives to make visible children's perceptions of their male preschool teacher and the discourses within which they have constructed him. Like previous studies of children's perceptions of their early childhood teachers, the children in this study portrayed their teacher in a variety of caring, teaching, play- and work-related, and regulatory roles. The extent to which they focused on these respective roles, however, differed considerably from findings reported previously.

For example, these children referred to their teacher's involvement in work in 25 per cent of portrayals, compared to only 8 per cent in Summers et al. (1991) and 4.7 per cent in Smith et al. (1989). Interestingly, other studies reviewed did not include work as a category, perhaps because it did not feature to any extent in children's responses. It is interesting to speculate about whether there was more emphasis on work in the current study because Bill was male, and work is often traditionally seen as a male role, or whether it simply reflects the intensification of teacher-directors' administrative loads.

The most noteworthy difference between the findings of this study and those of previous studies, however, was the pervasiveness of children's references to their teacher's regulatory roles (75 per cent). In earlier studies, these roles were far less prominent, with the proportion of children referring to them ranging from 31 per cent in one setting studied by Klein (1998) to 12.6 per cent in Smith et al.'s (1989) study. Again, questions arise as to whether these differences were primarily a reflection of children's perceptions of Bill's teaching style (which seemed informal and relaxed), their possibly stereotyped expectations about masculinity and the explicit exercise of power, or the conceptual tools and theoretical perspectives guiding the analysis of the data. With a small study of this kind, a conclusive answer remains elusive.

Another key difference between the findings of this study and those of many previous studies stems from the use of gender enactment as a category of analysis. In 41 per cent of portrayals, children represented Bill enacting gender in ways that were consistent with traditional gender expectations. For these children, it seemed that one of Bill's roles was to maintain normative ways of performing masculinity. Gender enactment has not been a prominent focus in previous studies of children's perceptions of their teachers.

What meaning, then, might early childhood educators, researchers and policy-makers draw from these findings? In the following discussion, I focus first on gender given that my initial intention in undertaking the study was to generate empirical data that might inform policy decision-making about the gender imbalance in the early childhood workforce. However, in the absence of either an equivalent 'control group' of children taught by a female teacher, or the opportunity to investigate the responses of the children in this study to a female teacher, it is difficult to make strong assertions about the possible effects of the gender imbalance.

Nevertheless, it seems reasonable to conclude that the paucity of non-traditional gender discourses and images in children's portrayals of Bill suggest that they did not perceive him as challenging or disrupting dominant and normative ways of enacting gender. These findings, therefore, do not support claims that the involvement of more men in early childhood education would necessarily challenge children's stereotyped views about gender. Nor do they support claims, on the other hand, that young children seek or need a male presence to counter the so-called feminized culture of early childhood settings. In 53 per cent of children's portrayals gender simply was not salient. These findings caution against taking at face value arguments in the often vociferous debate about the effects and implications of gender make-up in the children's services workforce. They also reinforce the need for further empirical data that takes into account the perspectives of children themselves.

Far more prominent in the children's portrayals of Bill were discourses of regulation, and it is these, in particular, that I want to focus on in the remainder of this discussion. Others, too, have highlighted the prevalence of surveillance and regulation and processes by which power is enacted in early childhood settings (see, for example, Leavitt, 1994; Holligan, 2000). After documenting the use of regulatory power in three Scottish nursery schools, Holligan wondered 'how oppressive it might feel as a child being watched continually, even if as adults we do it with the best of intentions' (2000, p. 145). Interestingly, the children in the current study did not appear to be concerned about Bill's surveillance of them and his use of other regulatory techniques. Admittedly, if they had, they may not have wanted to share those concerns with an unfamiliar adult. It seems likely, however, that these middle-class children were comfortable within the dominant regulatory discourses of the early childhood setting, especially if they resonated with the dominant discourses of their families. How children whose dominant family discourses are not congruent with those of their early childhood setting construct their experiences in these settings would be a useful focus for future research.

Despite the ease with which the children in this study appeared to take up these regulatory discourses, an unsettling question remains: are these the discourses with which we really want preschool children to engage? As Foucault (1980) reminds us, discourses speak us into existence; they 'shape our understanding of what is possible and desirable' (Dahlberg et al., 1999, p. 31). In taking up these discourses, certain understandings of themselves as participants in the preschool community are spoken into existence (Foucault, 1980). If these children understand that their teacher's role 'is to explain, order and control the world for children' (Cannella, 1997, p. 153), then these understandings will shape their subjectivities, or way they see themselves, as learners. Does the challenge for early childhood educators, therefore, become one of envisaging alternative discourses that children might take up, ones that might 'give a different shape to their experience' (Gee, 1996, p. 141) of early childhood settings?

The difficulty is that the discourses that we, too, have taken up as early childhood educators, researchers and policy-makers 'can hide from us other ways of thinking . . . They come to seem inevitable, natural, normal, practical, common sense' (Gee, 1996, p. 86). Consequently, our accustomed ways of thinking about our practices and assumptions become naturalized – and 'other ways become hidden – impossible and inconceivable' (Wright, 2000, p. 169). And yet, we need to become aware of 'what we are doing, in order to begin to address adequately how we might do things differently' (Gore, 1998, p. 248).

One strength of this study is that it has shown how children's perspectives can unsettle our accustomed ways of thinking. This process of unsettling can create spaces that invite 'critical and productive questions' (Dahlberg et al., 1999, p. 134) about how we want children to perceive their teachers and construct their early childhood settings. Such questions might include:

- What identities and roles do existing discourses enable children to construct and enact, both for themselves and for their early childhood educators?
- What identities and roles do these discourses preclude or marginalize?
- Do we want children to see us primarily as regulators?
- Are we regulating what we do not really need to regulate (Gore, 1998)?
- What alternatives might we have, given the climate of escalating regulatory requirements in which early childhood teachers themselves work?
- What might these alternatives look like in practice?
- How might we challenge children's constructions of their early child-hood teachers, or encourage them to explore possibilities for constructing teachers differently?
- What would be the point of doing so?
- How could we create spaces in which other possibilities and discourses might become possible?
- What changes to social and cultural practices might be required for children to construct and portray their experiences of early childhood settings differently?
- What visions do we have, as early childhood educators, researchers and policy-makers, of what might be possible?

Questions like these might assist us to gain a greater insight into our work with young children and their families.

Conclusion

This study has contributed to the small but growing literature about the ways in which children construct their teachers and early childhood settings. It began with the intention of investigating how children perceived and portrayed their male preschool teacher but quickly expanded beyond its initial focus on gender to highlight the pervasiveness of discourses of regulation in the children's responses regarding their portrayal of their teacher. The study reinforces the need to encourage the critical conversations that have recently begun to emerge about power in early childhood settings and suggests that there would be value in early childhood educators and children collectively engaging in critical and reflexive conversations about dominant discourses and taken-for-granted practices. Such conversations may create spaces in which we might begin to envision new possibilities, including new kinds of relationships between children and early childhood teachers. As Jones notes, by listening to children we might learn to 'think differently' (2002, p. 139) about what we may not previously have thought to question.

Acknowledgements

I wish to thank Bill and the children who participated in the study for making this investigation possible. The study was funded by a Macquarie University Research grant.

Notes

1   In the State of New South Wales, both service types provide education and care programmes. Unlike preschools, many child care centres operate for extended hours. Most cater for children aged from 2 to 5 years, while others also accept younger children.
2   Bill's views about how his gender and work as an early childhood teacher intersect are reported in more detail elsewhere (Sumsion, 2000b).

References

Armstrong, J. and Sugawara, A.I. (1989) Children's perceptions of their day care experiences, *Early Child Development and Care*, 49: 1–15.
Cameron, C. and Moss, P. (1998) Men as carers for young children: an introduction, in C. Owen, C. Cameron and P. Moss (eds) *Men as Workers in Services for Young*

Children: Issues of a Mixed Gender Workforce (pp. 11–28). London: Institute of Education, University of London.

Cannella, G.S. (1997) *Deconstructing Early Childhood Education*. New York: Peter Lang.

Dahlberg, G., Moss, P. and Pence, A. (1999) *Beyond Quality in Early Childhood Education and Care: Postmodern Perspectives*. London: Falmer Press.

Daniels, D.H., Kalkman, D.L. and McCombs, B.L. (2001) Young children's perspectives on learning and teacher practices in different classroom contexts: implications for motivation, *Early Education and Development*, 12(2): 253–73.

Davies, B. (1989) *Frogs and Snails and Feminist Tales: Preschool Children and Gender*. Sydney: Allen and Unwin.

Diamond, K.E. and Cooper, D.G. (2000) Children's perspectives on the roles of teachers and therapists in inclusive early childhood programs, *Early Education and Development*, 11(2): 203–16.

Evans, P. and Fuller, M. (1998) Children's perceptions of their nursery education, *International Journal of Early Years Education*, 6(1): 59–74.

Farrell, A., Tayler, C., Tennent, L. and Gahan, D. (2002) Listening to children: a study of child and family services, *Early Years*, 22(1): 27–38.

Foucault, M. (1977) *Discipline and Punish: The Birth of the Prison*. New York: Pantheon.

Foucault, M. (1980) 'Prison talk', in C. Gordon (ed.) *Power/Knowledge: Selected Interviews and Other Writings 1972–1977* (pp. 37–54). New York: Pantheon Books.

Gee, J.P. (1996) *Social Linguistics and Literacies: Ideology in Discourses* (2nd edn). London: RoutledgeFalmer.

Gore, J.M. (1995) Foucault's poststructuralism and observational educational research: a study of power relations, in R. Smith and R. Wexler (eds) *After Postmodernism: Education, Politics and Identity* (pp. 98–111). London: Falmer.

Gore, J.M. (1998) Disciplining bodies: on the continuity of power relations in pedagogy, in T.S. Popkewitz and M. Brennan (eds) *Foucault's Challenge: Discourse, Knowledge and Power in Education* (pp. 231–51). New York: Teachers College Press.

Holligan, C. (2000) Discipline and normalization in the nursery: the Foucaultian gaze, in H. Penn (ed.) *Early Childhood Services: Theory, Policy and Practice* (pp. 134–46). Buckingham: Open University Press.

Jones, L. (2002) Derrida goes to nursery school: deconstructing young children's stories, *Contemporary Issues in Early Childhood*, 3(1): 139–46.

Klein, E.L. (1998) How is a teacher different from a mother? Young children's perceptions of the social roles of significant adults, *Theory into Practice*, 27(1): 36–43.

Leavitt, R.L. (1994) *Power and Emotion in Infant-Toddler Day Care*. New York: State University of New York Press.

MacNaughton, G. (1998) Improving our gender equity 'tools': a case for discourse analysis, in N. Yelland (ed.) *Gender in Early Childhood* (pp. 149–74). London: Routledge.

MacNaughton, G. (2000) *Rethinking Gender in Early Childhood Education.* Sydney: Allen and Unwin.

MacNaughton, G. and Newman, B. (2001) Masculinities and men in early childhood: reconceptualising our theory and our practice, in E. Dau (ed.) *The Anti-Bias Approach in Early Childhood* (pp. 145–57). Sydney: Longman.

Mayall, B. (1999) Children and childhood, in S. Hood, B. Mayall and S. Oliver (eds) *Critical Issues in Social Research: Power and Prejudice* (pp. 10–24). Buckingham: Open University Press.

O'Kane, C. (2000) The development of participatory techniques: facilitating children's views about decisions which affect them, in P. Christensen and A. James (eds) *Research with Children: Perspectives and Practices* (pp. 136–59). London: Falmer Press.

Ryan, S., Ochsner, M. and Genishi, C. (2001) Miss Nelson is missing! Teacher sightings in research on teaching, in S. Grieshaber and G.S. Canella (eds) *Embracing Identities in Early Childhood Education: Diversity and Possibilities* (pp. 45–59). New York: Teachers College Press.

Sheridan, S. and Samuelsson, I. (2001) Children's conceptions of participation and influence in pre-school: a perspective on pedagogical quality, *Contemporary Issues in Early Childhood*, 2(2): 169–94.

Smith, A.B., Ballard, K.D. and Barham, L.J. (1989) Preschool children's perceptions of parent and teacher roles, *Early Childhood Research Quarterly*, 4: 523–32.

Summers, M., Stroud, J.C., Stroud, J.E. and Heaston, A. (1991) Preschoolers' perceptions of teacher role and importance, *Early Child Development and Care*, 68: 125–31.

Sumsion, J. (2000a) Oppositional discourses: deconstructing responses to investigations of male early childhood educators, *Contemporary Issues in Early Childhood*, 1(3): 259–75.

Sumsion, J. (2000b) Negotiating otherness: a male early childhood educator's gender positioning, *International Journal of Early Years Education*, 8(2): 129–40.

Wright, J. (2000) Disciplining the body: power, knowledge and subjectivity in a physical education lesson, in A. Lee and C. Poynton (eds) *Culture and Text: Discourse and Methodology in Social Research and Cultural Studies* (pp. 152–69). St Leonards, Sydney: Allen and Unwin.

Yelland, N. and Grieshaber, S. (1998) Blurring the edges, in N. Yelland (ed.) *Gender in Early Childhood* (pp. 1–14). London: Routledge.

6 Who can speak?

Silence, voice and pedagogy

Jonathan G. Silin

Over the past two decades I have been an advocate for building curriculum out of children's lived experiences – whether the small seemingly inconsequential events that take place in the playground or singular, incomprehensible moments such as occurred on September 11, 2001. My work has been concerned with identifying and supporting voices not found in most classrooms, for example, people with HIV/AIDS, Gay and Lesbian families and students, the homeless, and other disenfranchised groups.

While a concern for voice continues to be a central theme of my work, my observations in an economically depressed urban school district, where I am director of research for a major reform initiative, have caused me to question my assumptions about voice and silence (Silin and Lippman, 2003). Here the children continuously record, document, and share every experience. Journal writing is the required first activity in all K-6 classrooms and when the children go on a field trip, it is always written about before the day is over. In an era of intensified accountability feedback is individual, immediate, and carefully worded. It seems as if every moment must be pedagogically meaningful. In these, as in so many classrooms around the country, literacy appears to take precedence over life.

To be honest, my interest in the unspoken, knowing in and through the body, has also been prompted by caring for my elderly and extremely fragile parents. Where once I heard silence only as an indication of oppression and constraint in the classroom, I have now begun to hear other meanings as well – silence as a communicative act, an essential component of human development, a moment to be savored rather than papered over. But let me explain.

We live in a noisy world. The impatient sounds of fax and answering machines; the continuous clicking of laptop computers; cell phone beepers going off at the most inopportune moments punctuate our daily lives. There is little opportunity for silence to speak, and, when it does, we are often too busy to listen. In the summer that I rode the bus between my home on Eastern Long Island and the hospital in New York City where my father lay voiceless, the result of losing most of his larynx to cancer, I was especially aware of the intrusiveness of the new technologies. The cacophony of sounds on these weekly trips was a stark contrast to the silence that reigned in my father's room.

When my mother and I said goodbye to my father before his operation, somewhere deep in the bowels of that gigantic hospital, we did not know if his larynx would be salvaged. Seven hours later, seated in a sterile gray room, the youthful Dr Lee, still dressed in green operating suit, plastic shower cap, and tennis sneakers, patiently assured us that he had been able to save two-thirds of my father's right larynx. He will have a natural if somewhat sandpapery voice.

Seeing my father in the recovery room later that afternoon, still heavily sedated, lifeless and waxy yellow, the frustration of being temporarily without voice did not seem so pressing. He had weathered the operation well, and I knew that he would speak in two to three weeks when the shunt in his throat was removed. It was only the next morning, as I entered his room, that the full impact of my father's situation became evident. Angry, filled with rage, he kept trying to speak and yet no words emerged from his mouth. Then I noticed, on the bed, the first of a dozen yellow legal pads that were to be his primary mode of communication. Written in his clearest print, all capital letters, were these instructions – GET MY SON IMMEDIATELY – followed by my phone number.

Asking my father to nod when I suggested various reasons for his distress, it quickly became clear that the room to which he had been moved, containing three other patients and no partitions, was far too public a space for this very private, partially blind and voiceless octogenarian.

As I began to negotiate with the hospital personnel for a new room, the words my father had written in my absence resonated throughout my body. Although my mother was standing by his side during this time, a position she had taken up over 63 years ago, he knew that her own frailties would render her ineffectual. How few words it took for my father to communicate his panic and dependency. How unnecessary it was to speak about my responsibility.

In the weeks following the throat surgery, my father learned to communicate with gesture and pen. His needs and his discomforts began to form a regular pattern. After a short while, it was easy enough to second-guess his wishes. The legal pads allowed for more complex conversations. I came to accept the silence as the only way to wait out the recovery. There was little to be said.

Sitting with my father day after day, I became aware of the complicated, changing textures of our silences. There were moments when the silence seemed to create an unbridgeable gap that separated us into different worlds. There were others when it allowed us to be together peacefully, without straining to make small talk or to interpret our frequently misunderstood words.

Silence was a relief, a refuge in which we could be present without demanding or intruding. In the context of this father–son relationship, silence was certainly a new way to express care.

Ironically, I was not there three weeks later when the shunt was removed, and my father spoke his first words. My brother called from the hospital room and casually asked if I wanted to speak with my father. For the first time in my life, the sound of his voice brought tears to my eyes.

Caring for my parents, I have come to appreciate anew the surprising ways that professional and personal lives may intersect. For just as I use my early childhood skills in caring for my increasingly fragile parents – breaking down complex tasks into component parts, paying close attention to transitions and the introduction of new health aides – I am also prompted to rethink many assumptions about teaching and learning. What would happen, for example, if we gave equal attention to silences as well as words in our classrooms, to the students who don't speak as well as to those who find their voices so easily? Why must children write in journals each morning, describe the field trip in detailed sentences, summarize every book in carefully crafted paragraphs?

The quiet weeks after my father's first throat surgery and the years of further operations that led to his permanent loss of speech made me increasingly curious about silence. At the same time, I want to acknowledge that the seeds for this interest were probably planted long before. For like many other gay people I grew up with a heightened sensitivity to the strategic need for silence, for keeping my own counsel. As a child I experienced strong feelings of difference that were not specifically linked to longings for other boys or men, but they did contribute to a rich inner life. I first made this link in early adolescence when questions of voice became erotically charged. Then, I lived in a space defined by the tension between revealing enough to attract another and concealing enough so as not to be discovered by those who might do me harm. Silence functioned as a source of strength as well as constraint, a way to read the complexity of the social world and to write my desires into the hearts of others.

As an adolescent during the 1950s, I learned that our silences, like our words, await the interpretation of varied reading and listening audiences. I also learned that it is often better to remain silent than to use language belying our experience. The ponderous tomes which I covertly perused in libraries and bookstores, employed a pseudo-scientific vocabulary that seemed to have no relationship to the feelings and emotions that pulsed through my body.

Today, even though I can choose to refer to myself as homosexual, gay, or queer, I am still painfully aware of the constraints that labels place upon us and stymied by the gap between experience and articulation. These reservations about language do not constitute a rationale for silence. Rather, they underline an existential reality – much of human experience is unspeakable, unimaginable.

During the 1960s, as a young adult and early childhood teacher, I was used to busy classrooms filled with the sounds of young children at work. Neither silence nor stillness seemed 'developmentally appropriate'. Charged with the task of encouraging children to verbalize their thoughts and feelings, I did not consider that the acquisition of language is a mixed blessing. Along with the parents, I welcomed the children's use of words as an unalloyed indication of development and integration into the social world.

But language also imposes order and control, culture and constraint. We seldom think about what is lost (Phillips, 1999). Linguistic competency is achieved through distancing from the preverbal self, and often at the cost of the rich, if chaotic, emotional life of the pre-school child. Language inhibits the new and unrehearsed, the raw and embodied expressions of ideas. Words bring safety and containment. Failed attempts at communication remind us of what it is like not to talk. As a classroom teacher I only wanted to improve the children's verbal skills. Today, I think more about how to sustain fluency between the children's spoken and unspoken lives.

In a society that values rational discourse, there is little space for the unspoken. The goal of education in a democracy is to transform potential conflict into logical arguments that are posed and defended by independent, autonomous actors (Walkerdine, 1990). When schools emphasize the practice and achievement of reason, silence is viewed as absence or failure. More often than not, silence is assumed to reflect some kind of individual or social pathology.

But what if the uncensored celebration of voice is understood as a reflection of class and culture as well as an indication of individual growth? What if we considered the ability to remain still as a critical social skill and silence an essential aspect of our humanity?

In the postmodern world educators accentuate the social nature of identity formation, the ways that we come to see ourselves as members of distinct, at times overlapping, groups. We value explicit expressions of identity and schools in which differences are emphasized.

Early in life, however, we also develop identity by remaining silent (van Manen and Levering, 1996). When we begin to withhold information or feelings, we start to experience ourselves as separate from rather than merged with those around us. When interior dialogue develops, we are aware of self in a new way. It is here too that we form our sense of spiritual connection to the larger world. Just as adults nurture language, we also need to protect the interior spaces in which children come to know themselves.

I suspect that many teachers are more skilled at enabling those who do not speak to find a means of expression than at reading silences. Reviewing an early draft of this chapter, a close friend and colleague asked: What does it mean to teach the unspoken? How do children come to value silence?

The challenge, it seems to me, is to clear a space in the midst of the usual classroom chatter for silence to emerge. Three strategies may be helpful in making a place for silence. First, teachers can build an increased tolerance in themselves and their students for the discomfort that often comes when difficult questions are posed in the classroom (Britzman, 1998). The conversations I will report in what follows make clear that socially relevant curriculum addressing children's lived experiences can be discomforting. Silence isn't easy.

Second, teachers can offer diverse materials and experiences that challenge the hegemony of the written/spoken word. The arts provide essential tools for children to make sense of their experience and to imagine how others live (Gardner, 1983; Greene, 1995). Teachers can also structure times for guided silences – meditation, yoga, music, movement, and acting exercises – so that children can experience a heightened awareness of self as well as the relief that comes with a momentary loss of self.

Finally, teachers can attend to the 'pleasures of forgetting' described by Jardine and Rinehart (2003). For while writing may bring a certain mindfulness, at the same time it may also undercut a potential for renewal and regeneration. What about the value of letting go, of allowing experiences to come to an end without trying to capture and preserve them? This is to leave aside the endless accumulation of artifacts upon which teachers have come to rely as proof of student learning and our own pedagogy.

My fascination with silence comes after a quarter century of increased attention to issues of voice (Gilligan, 1982; Belenky et al., 1986). Feminists have used the metaphor of voice to describe the struggles of women to speak the truth of their lives and to establish more equitable social institutions in which their words can be heard. My history as a gay teacher attests to the way that I have benefited from the contemporary focus on voice and the identity politics in which it is embedded (Silin, 1999). Having achieved the right to speak in contexts once prohibited to me, I do not want to terminate the discussion of voice or to exclude other newer speakers from the public arena. However, I do want to draw attention to the complex ways that silence and voice may function in schools.

In my own work with teachers, I often ask them to set aside the desire to teach in order to become researchers. I want them to listen carefully to the voices of children. This means both practicing the art of remaining still, something hard for active teachers to do – if I am not talking how can I be teaching? – and tolerating the discomfort that may arise from the silences of the children.

My students are often surprised by what happens. The assignment is to invite the children to talk about their everyday lives, to describe their social worlds. A prompt in the form of a question is often in order. For example, what do you know about families? Has anyone ever seen a homeless person on the street? What would you like to know about HIV/AIDS? Then it's up to the good teacher, turned researcher, to remain silent, to teach nothing, and to listen to everything.

Hilary Lewis has a strong commitment to hearing the children out. As a white, middle-class teacher in a poor, African-American Head Start center, she knows how developmental norms often ignore cultural context, silence community values, and label children as failures. This experience leads her to redefine her primary role as 'community builder' rather than 'facilitator of individual development'.

She introduces the subject of homelessness to her 4- and 5-year-olds by telling them about her encounter with a homeless woman and her child on the subway ride to work. Hilary wonders aloud if the children have ever been asked for money. Receiving positive replies, she probes for why people might need money. The children answer that it might be for clothes, a house, food, 'a sofa, chairs, tables, a bed, covers and furniture', a clock, panties, paper for writing, toys for the baby, a dog to play with the baby, and 'a TV so she can see if it's hot or cold and because you might want to watch something on cartoons'.

In the midst of this conversation, the children begin to talk about their experiences of moving from one house to another, with belongings packed in boxes, feelings of fear, anger, sadness, and excitement cascading all over Hilary's carefully prepared lesson plan.

At the next meeting the children explore what it might be like to be hungry, the dangers of sleeping on the street and in other public places. Again, mid-way in the conversation, the children turn to moments of discomfort in their own lives, for example:

Shanequa: Sometimes my mom go to see my dad, but I was alone with my brother, my big brother, and my big brother play music, and I was sick on the music, that's why my mom not here.
Hilary: One time you were alone with your brother and you got sick?
Lynda: From the music?
Hilary: You didn't like the music?
Shanequa: (shakes her head, lower lip jutting out) And I was alone, and I sat on mommy's bed and I said, 'I want my mom.'

Hilary acknowledges how difficult it can be when caregivers leave us and another round of stories is unleashed.

Jessica: My mommy goes away and my big sister makes me sit down in the room.
Devon: My brother be hitting me.
Ariel: My sister hit me!
Jahkiem: My cousin don't let me play.
Dawn: Me and my sister watch TV. But it is scary cause my mother not there.

In the end, the children agree that the best remedy for these unpleasant moments is to report them to their parents.

A third meeting begins with a book about a family living in a shelter. Now some of the children share their own experiences of eating in soup kitchens and sleeping in shelters where Kim observes, 'They have beds and all the kids sleep with the big kids.' Naturally this leads to a discussion of sleeping arrangements in the children's own houses with stories about brothers and sisters who sleep together, moms and dads who do not; children who sleep with their parents, and others who seem quite confused about which beds they regularly occupy.

No matter how complicated the domestic arrangements may seem to be, all the children identify with the child in the storybook who is frequently separated from his mother. Again, there is a flood of stories about the difficult times of childhood with examples of parents who are unable to pick them up at school, older siblings who fail to take responsibility for them, school bus drivers who become angry, children being left unattended in neighborhood stores, and mothers who cry on being reunited with their children.

Hilary's conversations tell us that children know about homelessness through first-hand experience, from observations of others, and by making inferences from their own lives. They also tell us that children move easily between the subject of homelessness and moments of dislocation, abandonment, and separation in their own lives.

Like Hilary, I see this movement not as an egocentric concern with self but as an empathetic attempt to grasp the lives of others. More important than a set of facts about homelessness, Hilary is teaching her students that they can craft their own stories, that adults will listen to them, and that the classroom can become a community of caring learners.

Like Hilary too, I sometimes put on my researcher hat while teaching. The first night of the 2001 Fall semester fell on Tuesday, September 11th. Needless to say, my plans for that session, like so much else in so many people's lives, were consumed in the fires that engulfed the Trade Towers. Because of the idiosyncrasies of the academic calendar, we did not meet for another three weeks. When we finally convened, I asked the students to tell about where they had been that eventful September morning and how the young children in their care had responded.

My students reported a range of reactions. There were increased requests to visit the school nurse during the following days with all manner of bodily aches and pains, expressions of fear for loved ones, and an overwhelming desire to get back to the routines that make school a safe, predictable place.

Paradoxically, in this course entitled 'The Social Worlds of Childhood' there was barely a mention of September 11th in the following weeks. In their own way, the students were indicating that they too simply wanted to get back to 'normal', to the routines that make them feel safe. So I decided to honor their silence, just as I would have done with children, and reluctantly continued with the planned syllabus.

Working in a very different context, Patricia Lent, a teacher at P.S. 234 directly across the street from the Trade Towers, was faced with the same tension; the desire to take full account of extraordinary events and the need to move forward. Upon relocating to a temporary classroom several days after 9/11 she reflected:

> What about the curriculum? Shouldn't I take responsibility for getting my program back on track? Shouldn't I be concerned about third graders falling behind? Shouldn't I start insisting that they do their best work? Perhaps I should have, but I didn't. None of us had gotten back to normal. None of us could handle a lot of pressure. None of us remembered what our best work looked like . . . I did believe, while we were at school, that it was important for the children to be busy, it was important for them to work together, and it was important for all of us to accomplish something.
>
> (Lent, 2002, p. 4)

Lent reports that she and her students read, sang, played math games, practiced cursive writing and continued to talk about what had happened. In early February when P.S. 234 returned to its own building, the class began a serious social studies curriculum about Eastern Woodland Native Americans. While the children were clearly ready for this, Lent also left plenty of time for discussion, for the children to tell and retell their stories throughout the year.

Unlike Lent's students, most of my own had not been quite so close to ground zero or forthcoming with their stories. So near the end of the semester I decided to test the waters again, this time using a video filmed in a classroom of 5- and 6-year-olds just days before (Edstrom, 2003). In the video Matthew is busily at work stuffing small wooden figures into the open space created by the crosshatch design of his block building. The structure, like several others in this classroom, towers above the children. Sandra is carefully sending other people down a slide that extends out from the upper floors of the building and reaches to the ground. A patchwork of small carpet samples has been assembled to cushion their arrival. Near the shelves Kassim is methodically stacking smaller blocks in piles of six and pushing them across the floor, destination as yet unknown.

After a brief question and answer period about the video, I asked my students what was happening in their own schools in response to 9/11. They talked about a plethora of charity drives including walkathons, bake sales, and toy collections. A few noted that their own schools have become the recipients of charity. In one case this had resulted in a pen-pal project with children from the Mid-West. In another, the school simply distributed a huge quantity of cuddly animals it had received to all the first graders, without any explanation.

Charity helps to ameliorate the conditions of those in need and to calm our anxiety. I would argue that educators have a far more difficult task as well, that is, to help children make sense of their experience. As Mathew, Sandra, and Kassim demonstrated, children have abundant curiosity about their world and the structures in which they live and so many of their parents work. Nor are they lacking ideas about how to make them safer. Soon after the evacuation slide first appeared in the block area, their teacher brought in a newspaper article about newly proposed emergency strategies for high rise buildings, including rope slides. She moved quickly to support and extend the children's thinking.

As our conversation progressed that night more than two months after the Trade Center tragedy, Jena spoke about the apathy with which some of her 6-year-olds approach their daily journal writing. She expressed frustration that they were not able to use detail, develop full storylines, or even identify stories that they want to tell. I doubt, however, that it is the children who lack imagination. In our rush to get kids reading, we all too easily forget that young children still learn in and through the body. In addition to words, children need other tools such as blocks and sand, paint and clay, wood and construction supplies, that allow them to ask questions, re-present what they know, and solve problems. Unfortunately, these are slowly disappearing if not totally absent from the many classrooms in which I observe (Silin and Schwartz, 2003).

Against the odds, however, I persist in believing that it is the teacher's job to see the potential for learning in their students' representations of the world. How is a 7-acre site containing 100s of floors cleared and where does the rubble go? Why are fires burning weeks after the collapse? Why are subway stations still closed? How is the Hudson River held back anyway? Here are the makings of a rich curriculum filled with science and social studies, and math and literacy as well.

Needless to say, children also have the right *not* to talk about 9/11. Because something is unspoken, however, does not mean it is unthought, or that it will not be voiced in the future. My years of helping teachers talk about difficult social realities have taught me that the responses of young children may come long after the formal discussions led by adults have ended.

Well into December 2001, my former student, turned colleague, Ali Nash, described several conversations among her 5-year-olds. At the time, she taught science at PS 89 also directly across the street from the Trade Towers. Ali and her students had harrowing experiences on September 11 as they were forced to run for their lives.

It was late morning when Tim was drawing a full page 'world map', with lots of green and blue, and a few splotches of red.

Bruce: Why is it red?

Tim: That's Afghanistan. It's red because it blew up!

Bruce: It didn't blow up, because Osama Bin Ladin's still there. What about Tikestan, Pakistan, Initstan! (He excitedly recites a litany of other unrecognizable names ending in 'stan'.) They're pretty dangerous. Some people in Pakistan don't like America, so you should make it red.

Tim: It's all bad guys.

Bruce: Are you drawing Iran? (He touches Afghanistan.)

Tim: (insistent)   I'm NOT drawing Iran . . . I'm drawing China.

Bruce: What's the blue? Water?

Tim: China's not dangerous. China's helping us, I think.

Brian: How about America? How about you draw red, white and blue for America? (Brian hands Tim the appropriate crayons to realize his patriotic vision.)

While Tim, Brian, and Bruce are trying to make sense of shifting political realities, other children deal more directly with the emotional impact of September 11. Here Lena, a classroom teacher, questions 5-year-old Rebecca at the end of the day about her visit to Ali's science room:

Lena: What did you do today?

Rebecca: We had science. We learned about water.

Lena: What's your science teacher's name?

Rebecca: Her name is Ali. Jane is her mommy. [In fact Jane is another 5-year-old girl in the class.]

Lena: (after a moment's reflection) Um . . . Jane is Ali's mommy? What makes you say that?

Rebecca: Well, when we were running away from the World Trade Center, Ali was crying and Jane told her, 'It's going to be O.K.' And that's what mommies do.

To be clear: I do not want to minimize the human tragedies suffered by so many on 9/11. I believe, however, that it is the educator's responsibility to explore with her students how our society is responding to these difficult events, from managing the physical destruction at ground zero and imagining the site's reconstruction, to pursuing war in Afghanistan and Iraq. And, yes, this may mean encountering difficult emotions and unanswerable questions. But we will be so much the wiser for acknowledging our ignorance and for serving as models in our search for understanding.

An important caveat is in order here. For just as many of us were exhausted by the continual images of the collapsing Trade Towers on the news, so has the search for voice been sensationalized in the popular media. Radio talk shows, reality TV, self-help books, and the press thrive on personal confession. People recount their struggles with addictions to substances, destructive relationships, and the effects of childhood abuses in excruciating detail. Increasingly, individuals risk turning moments of real human suffering into public spectacles.

The experience of many children in schools also suggests that the achievement of voice alone does not necessarily secure social change. In the 1970s, for example, sociologists pointed out that open classrooms, in which children were encouraged to speak more freely and to engage with many kinds of materials, favor those who came from highly verbal middle-class homes (Sharp and Green, 1975; Bernstein, 1976). The behaviors and skills needed for success, that is independence, choice making, self-regulation were assumed and therefore not taught to children from the working class. The open classroom also created increased opportunities for professional surveillance. The more children display of their real emotional and social lives, the more ways they can be found wanting. As psychologists, learning specialists, reading teachers, and social workers hover over children, they bring with them new forms of testing, evaluation and repair.

In a similar vein, Foucault (1978) argued that the spoken and unspoken are not opposites but always reflect the same sociopolitical context, the same regime of truth. Thus, we speak about sex as something frought with danger, the source of deathly illness, unwanted pregnancies, and potential abuse. At the same time we are silent about sex as a site of pleasure, connection, and learning.

Words are notorious for the ways that they conceal and transform as well as tell the truth. More than celebrating the unfettered production of talk, teachers might better ask: Who can speak and who remains silent in my classroom? What can be said and what remains unspoken in our schools?

With respect to what can be said, consider the curious preparations for the war in Iraq by the New York independent schools in which my graduate students worked during the spring, 2003 semester:

> School One: Called an emergency meeting in February to inform staff that in case of a biological attack, the building would be sealed off from the outside world for two days. Sufficient food and water were stored. No drills for children who would be crowded into the basement were instituted, let alone discussions of the world situation.
>
> School Two: Told the faculty that it was prepared for a 6-hour lock down, planned a student drill, in this case interior hallways were considered safe, but again no curricular initiatives were undertaken.
>
> School Three: A week's supply of food was on hand but no preparations for a lock down were evident. Faculty were debating what to say to children but could not come to a consensus, so nothing was said at all.

School Four: Faculty attendance at a meeting about preparations for the war were optional and nothing was said to the children.

School Five: No talk or preparations had been made, and no conversations held with children.

School Six: Classroom discussions about war and war protests were preceding apace. Staff had offered a parent seminar on how to talk with children about war, but no physical preparations for a terrorist attack were discussed with staff.

These six stories represent a spectrum of responses. Almost all of the talk goes on among adults about specific procedures. With the exception of School Six, silence reigns in the classrooms.

With respect to who can speak, research continues to confirm that girls are still rewarded for remaining silent and well behaved in the classroom while boys are rewarded for speaking up and speaking out (Brown and Gilligan, 1993). Later as adults, women are often caught in a double bind when public displays of rational argument and private displays of emotionality are found to be equally suspect. The unspoken marks the possibility of the irrational, inexplicable, and uncontrollable. In our world, these possibilities are associated with the feminine and are kept at bay by the logic of the word.

Although silence is gendered feminine, it is women who are charged by society with facilitating the development of language in the home and in school. And it is women who are blamed when this passage into the world of reason is not successfully achieved (Grumet, 1988; Biklen, 1995). Researchers frequently find poor mothers at fault for speaking too little or in the wrong ways to their children. More generally, teachers, primarily women, are found to be the cause of failing schools.

To understand who can speak in our classrooms we also need to attend to the growing literature that examines the ways that language is used across cultures and social classes as well as genders (Tobin, 1995; Hammond, 2003). While many parents want schools to emphasize opportunities for children to talk and write about their personal experiences, many others want schools to focus on the skills and behaviors that will allow their children to join the economic and social mainstream. The former position is reflected in whole language and process writing programs, the latter position in the back to basics movement and its newest incarnation, Success For All.

In his 1982 memoir, *Hunger of Memory*, Richard Rodriguez offered the classic defense of a narrowly described skills-based education for minorities, the kind that he believed would go furthest in assuring their place in mainstream culture. In contrast, Lisa Delpit (1995) has advocated an education that enables minorities to negotiate a variety of instructional contexts and language communities. Rather than sacrifice a home culture for success in the public sphere, she is committed to helping teachers and families bridge the different worlds in which they may live. Delpit argues that some African-American parents are dissatisfied with progressive methods stressing self-expression and self-regulation. These approaches conflict both with their concern for maintaining clear distinctions between public and private spaces and their more directive modes of interaction at home. They are also suspicious of the potential for surveillance that progressive methods allow.

Few teachers or schools are purists. Children are not always silent in skills-based classrooms, nor do all children become talkers in whole language contexts. We have all known individual children who, either because of parental instruction or individual personality, are reserved, respectful, and silent in adult-controlled settings but who are capable of very different behaviors when among peers. Nevertheless, there are real differences in parental expectations that affect family–school interactions as well as our interpretation of a child's silence in the classroom.

Kate Delacorte, a director of the Downtown Little School, an early childhood center close to the World Trade Towers, writes about the different perspectives of the teachers and parents immediately following 9/11:

> The children had seen their world explode. Some had seen the planes hit, others had seen the fire and the smoke. They had seen people running for their lives and things falling from the sky. Some had witnessed people jumping from the towers. Others had been trapped inside their own smoke-filled buildings. Most had run or walked through chaos to find safety. They'd all seen, heard, experienced too much. They needed to understand in some small way what had happened.

The parents' needs were no less compelling. They needed to believe that their children hadn't really seen what they'd seen, that they hadn't understood the enormity of what had happened . . .

> The first day, a 4-year-old walked into the auditorium, talking as he crossed the threshold. 'A plane hit the World Trade Center and it fell just like this,' he said and let his sweater fall to the ground. He added, 'When it fell, it landed on a playground and killed all the children.' His mother told us, 'I don't think he really gets it.'

One focus of our school year was to help the parents accept what their children already knew so that they could help them understand it as much as it could be understood, and then to help them feel safe and protected. We wanted them to feel again as if they could keep their children safe and protected (Delacorte, 2003, p. 31). Kate Delacorte's story suggests that teachers must make the sometimes difficult distinction between denial and silence. They must promote discourse in the hope that it may eventually lead to silence or stillness more simply as a resting place.

My father's illness was not voluntary that summer six long years ago. It was the result of a critical illness and the intervention designed to save his life. It was an experience that I would not wish upon anyone. But it has intensified my awareness that in the classroom we can make critical choices about voice and silence. These choices are fundamental to our teaching. After all, when I speak, another doesn't. Silence opens space for others to announce themselves. When I speak, I may promote the belief that unsolvable personal and social problems can be fixed through the application of reasoned argument. Silence allows the ineffable to enter the classroom. When I speak, I augment my authority through the power of the word. Silence risks chaos and discomfort. When I speak, I may interrupt the inward dialogue through which we know ourselves best. Silence invites the spiritual to present itself in the classroom.

In an information-hungry society, where speed and change are valued over reflection and continuity, this curiosity about the power of silence is not calculated to make a teacher popular. It is, however, a position from which we can begin to appreciate that silence may be about presence as well as absence, care as well as neglect, thoughtfulness as well as mindlessness. In silence we take up a position alongside of our students rather than in front of them, and this may just be the biggest challenge of all.

References

Belenky, M., Clinchy, B., Goldberger, N. and Tarule, J. (1986) *Women's Ways of Knowing: The Development of Self, Voice, and Mind.* New York: Basic Books.

Bernstein, B. (1976) *Class, Codes and Control.* vol. 3. London: Routledge and Kegan Paul.

Biklen, S. (1995) *School Work: Gender and the Cultural Construction of Teaching.* New York: Teachers College Press.

Britzman, D. (1998) *Lost Subjects, Contested Objects: Toward a Psychoanalytic Inquiry of Learning.* Albany, NY: State University of New York Press.

Brown, L. and Gilligan, C. (1993) *Meeting at the Crossways: Women's Psychology and Girls' Development.* New York: Random House.

Delacorte, K. (2003) The children keep reminding us: one school's experience after 9/11, in A. McKersie and J. Silin (eds) *Teaching through a Crisis: September 11 and Beyond.* New York: Bank Street College of Education Occasional Paper #11.

Delpit, L. (1995) *Other People's Children: Cultural Conflict in the Classroom.* New York: New Press.

Edstrom, L. (2003) Building up: block play after September 11, in A. McKersie and J. Silin (eds) *Teaching through a Crisis: September 11 and Beyond.* New York: Bank Street College of Education Occasional Paper #11.

Foucault, M. (1978) *The History of Sexuality*. Vol. 1 Trans. R. Hurley, New York: Pantheon Books.

Gardner, H. (1983) *Frames of Mind: The Theory of Multiple Intelligences*. New York: Basic Books.

Gilligan, C. (1982) *In a Different Voice*. Cambridge, MA: Harvard University Press.

Greene, M. (1995) *Releasing the Imagination: Essays on Education, the Arts, and Social Change*. San Francisco: Jossey-Bass.

Grumet, M. (1988) *Bitter Milk*. Amherst, MA: University of Massachussets Press.

Hammond, M. (2003) On the bridge that we are building, in J. Silin and C. Lippman (eds) *Putting the Children First: The Changing Face of Newark's Public Schools* (pp. 126–40). New York: Teachers College Press.

Jardine, W. and Rinehart, P. (2003) Relentless writing and the death of memory in elementary education, in D. Jardine, P. Clifford and S. Friesen (eds) *Back to the Basics of Teaching and Learning* (pp. 73–84). Mahwah, NJ: Lawrence Erlbaum.

Lent, P. (2002) Teaching in the aftermath. Paper presented at the Annual Meetings of the National Association of the Education of Young Children, New York.

McLaughlin, D. and Tierney, W. (1993) *Naming Silenced Lives: Personal Narratives and the Process of Educational Change*. New York: Routledge.

Nager, N. and Shapiro, E. (2003) *Some Principles for the Education of Teachers*. Manuscript submitted for publication.

Phillips, A. (1999) *The Beast in the Nursery*. New York: Vintage Books.

Rodriguez, R. (1982) *Hunger of Memory*. Boston: Godine.

Sharp, R. and Green, A. (1975) *Education and Social Control: A Study in Progressive Primary Education*. London: Routledge and Kegan Paul.

Silin, J. (1999) Teaching as a gay man: pedagogical resistance or public spectacle? *GLQ*, 5(1): 95–106.

Silin, J. and Lippman, C. (2003) *Putting the Children First: The Changing Face of Newark's Public Schools*. New York: Teachers College Press.

Silin, J. and Schwartz, F. (2003) Staying close to the teacher, *Teachers College Record*, 105(8): 1586–605.

Tobin, J. (1995) The irony of self-expression, *American Journal of Education*, 103: 233–58.

van Manen, M. and Levering, B. (1996) *Childhood's Secrets: Intimacy, Privacy, and the Self Reconsidered*. New York: Teachers College Press.

Walkerdine, V. (1990) *Schoolgirl Fictions*. London: Verso.

PART 2
Rethinking Early Childhood Practices

7   Freedom to choose
Examining children's experiences in choice time

Sharon Ryan

Providing multiple opportunities for children to make choices is considered an essential element of high quality early childhood programs. By freeing the curriculum from teacher authority, early childhood educators believe that they are assisting all children to become independent problem solvers and skillful social negotiators. This chapter explores the liberatory assumptions underpinning children's choice making in the early childhood curriculum through the lens of poststructural social theory. Drawing on the findings of a qualitative case study of an urban kindergarten classroom, the stories of two children are examined for the ways they exercise, negotiate, and contest gendered power relations as they play with others in choice time. Presentation of these findings illustrates the different discourses that children enact through their play and how some of these discourses limit children's agency and identities as learners in the classroom. Implications for classroom practice and research are discussed.

Child-centered education based on developmental principles has long been advocated as the best and most equitable approach to teaching young children. This approach is evidenced for example, in the field's endorsement of the Guidelines for Developmentally Appropriate Practice (Bredekamp and Copple, 1997) as its consensus definition of high quality early education and in a variety of other early childhood curricula including High/Scope, and Reggio Emilia. In a child-centered education, the curriculum begins with the needs and interests of the child and responds to the unique characteristics of childhood. Teachers use their knowledge of how children develop to structure learning experiences that facilitate children's learning through play and discovery. Children, therefore, are viewed as active learners who require freedom from adult authority to explore ideas independently and make sense of their world (Sharp and Green, 1975; Burman, 1994). As a consequence of having some input and choice over their learning, it is believed that young children become independent and competent learners who are able to think and act in socially responsible ways (Sharp and Green, 1975; Walkerdine, 1984; Davies, 1993).

In contrast to the oppressive practices of transmission educational approaches, advocates for a child-centered education argue that the emphasis on personal choice and freedom from adult authority in a developmentally appropriate curriculum responds to individual differences and ensures educational success for all. Charlesworth (1998), for example, argues that developmentally appropriate classrooms promote equity in educational outcomes for children from varying cultural backgrounds because they ensure access and participation in activities, and provide opportunities for children to learn in their own unique ways. In this chapter, I draw on poststructural social theory to explore the equitable assumptions underpinning a child-centered pedagogy. Specifically, I want to argue that the conceptions of power and agency on which child-centered approaches are based do not adequately address the complex ways classroom social relations are embedded and interconnected to other social meanings and practices. Following a brief description of poststructuralism, I will tell the stories of two children's experiences of choice time to illustrate the kinds of gendered power relations young children enact and undergo when they are given opportunities to make choices and engage in play 'free' from adult authority. In the concluding section, I explore some of the implications of these stories of learning in choice time for rethinking what we mean by child-centered education and the place of 'student choice' in such a curriculum.

Employing a poststructural lens in early childhood education

In child-centered pedagogy, power is conceptualized as a negative force held by particular groups of persons, like teachers, and used to constrain the actions of individuals such as students (Usher and Edwards, 1994). Agency, therefore, is freedom from the authority of others to be able to make rational choices and act consciously in the world (Walkerdine, 1990). By sharing authority with students, child-centered educators free children to become determiners of their own actions. Child-centered educators share authority with children in the learning process so that children become self-regulating and self-determining individuals (ibid.).

Alternatively, poststructuralism particularly as seen through the work of Foucault, assumes that power is not necessarily something an individual possesses as a commodity nor is it always negative. Power still involves 'acting upon acting others' (Usher and Edwards, 1994, p. 99), but from a poststructuralist perspective, power is productive and expressed through discourse. Discourses are socially and historically constituted systems of ideas or fields of meaning that carry particular effects of power. The knowledges (ideas and meanings) constituting a particular discourse are sets of rules which differentiate true from false, determining what counts as knowledge, and what can be said and done by whom (Foucault, 1980). Thus, power in its connection to knowledge (power-knowledge) circulates in social relations by individuals taking up particular discourses; 'speaking and writing them into existence as if they were their own' (Davies, 1993, p. 13).

As human beings we do not reside in one stable discourse but instead we belong to different social groups (e.g. gender, race, class, culture, adult), each group circulating its own discourse and enacting practices that define what it means to be human (Davies, 1990). Individuals, therefore, can be constituted as powerful, or alternatively, they may be rendered powerless, depending on the discourse in which they are positioned. As an early childhood educator for instance, I can be and feel quite powerful in my daily work with young children because of the early childhood discourse which values the complexities of this work. Yet, when I interact with a group of scientists, the agency I feel as a teacher is quite often lost, because the scientific discourse does not always view the relational aspects of teaching young children as 'real work' compared to the empirical and rational work of science.

Thus, power relations are negotiated by individuals by either taking up the subject position offered by a particular discourse, or contesting their categorizations through competing discourses at sites of contradiction and conflict (Foucault, 1980). Agency from a poststructural perspective, therefore, is fluid, tied to discourses and the meanings given to subjectivity within a given discourse. When poststructuralism is used as a lens for considering children's interactions during self-initiated activity, the focus concerns not only the form and content of children's learning but the kinds of discourses and power relations that are shaping learning. It is to the study of children's talk and action as discursive productions that this chapter now turns.

Studying the dynamics of power in children's play

The setting for this study (Ryan, 1998) was an urban kindergarten classroom in the north-east of the United States that served a diverse population of students, most of whom were from low socio-economic backgrounds and predominantly of African-American or Latino descent. The experienced and highly skilled teacher of this classroom, Alison, enacted a dialogic curriculum (Dyson, 1993) in which children had many opportunities to shape the curriculum and social life of the classroom. One of the key ways this was achieved was through a daily choice time. This was the period of the school day when children were freest, being able to select from a wide range of activity choices and engage in play for approximately an hour with minimal teacher direction.

Using qualitative procedures of field notes, as well as audiotaped and videotaped recordings, I collected in-depth descriptive data of the children's talk and action during choice time over a five-month period, spending from 2–4 days a week in the classroom. To gain the research participants' insights into the kinds of power relations going on in choice time as well as to prevent the researcher's theoretical lens from being the only lens through which data were interpreted, the children were asked to give their own readings of what they saw in particular videotaped episodes of choice time events.

The compiled data record was subjected to a critical discourse analysis that involved searching for contradictions, conflicts, and resistances. What was said by participants at these sites of conflict was examined for the truth claims or knowledges used to produce particular power effects. From this analysis, it was possible to discern the discourses operating in and through children's play and the meanings being given to students' identities during choice time. Analyses of the experiences of Luz and Steven in choice time illustrate that even when there is freedom to choose, the potential to exercise autonomy over one's learning is also at the same time constrained by various discourses.

Creating new storylines: Luz's story

Choice time was an important part of Luz's day because, in her words, without choice time, 'we would never get to change areas'. Choice time meant Luz had more options and more of her favorite activities were likely to be 'open'. During choice time Luz tended to use a combination of power-knowledge strategies to negotiate her place as a valued friend and player in the social relations that took place in these areas, but the strategy she found most effective was creating new storylines.

Luz was an articulate and inventive teller of stories who could shift from one drama to another with great ease, using this knowledge to negotiate her subjectivity and that of others as valid players and worthwhile friends. When other children tried to change the story, requiring her to do something she did not agree with or there were conflicts in the drama, Luz would often say 'let's pretend' as an effort to either insert a new direction for the current drama or transform the script completely. Consider, for example, the following drama in which Luz is threatened with being killed off and, therefore, possibly excluded from future play.

Luz has been crawling around the house area playing a kitty when she takes a teacup from the sink where Sarah and Jocelyn are playing.

>   1. Sarah: Give me. (Luz moves away and pretends to drink from the cup.)

2. Sarah: (to J) Kitty's eating, she's drinking, um (whispers) poison.
3. Jocelyn: Oh! (Turning to look at Luz)
4. Sarah: (Pointing to Luz) You die because that was poison.
5. Luz: No that was, that's not poison!
6. Sarah: Yes, it was. Yes, it was.
7. Luz: It was kitty food.
8. Sarah: Nu-uh, it was poison.
9. Jocelyn: It was poison. It was poison. It was poison. (They are both standing over Luz.)
10. Luz: (Standing up) Pretend there was no poison in that cup.
11. Sarah: Well, it was and you died. You died already.
12. Luz: I got to get another cup. (Looks in nearby cupboard for a cup)
13. Sarah: No, you gotta die. You dead. (Standing next to cupboard using her body to make it more difficult for Luz to search for a cup)
14. Luz: Pretend you got a new kitty at the store.
15. Sarah: Mom, let's buy a cat.

Here 'let's pretend' is used by Luz to prevent exclusion in three different ways. The first attempt, a simple reversal of Sarah's and Jocelyn's claims that she was drinking poison proved ineffective (turn 5). Sarah's determination to keep with the story of poisoning is seen in the way she positions her body as a physical barrier to Luz's second attempt at protecting the role of the kitty (turn 13), that is, getting a new cup so that she does not have to drink poison and die (turn 12). Luz's third suggestion of a rewriting of the storyline is successful (turn 14); and with Sarah's acceptance that she needs to purchase a new kitty, Luz retains her life and role in the drama. By being able to continue in the play, Luz positions herself as a socially competent child and student.

Thus, through the use of 'let's pretend' Luz could become powerful with her peers and teacher. In these situations, her talk was not perceived as irritating by the children but an important knowledge source that enabled her to be socially acceptable, capable of playing co-operatively, and not always doing things her way.

However, when Luz tried to negotiate her gendered identity in the games of the boys, she found that 'let's pretend' alone was not always an effective power-knowledge strategy. Luz loved to enact domestic storylines and quite often chose to play in the house area, duplos, playdough and the blocks, creating quite intricate games with people enacting the routines of daily living. On this particular day, however, Luz had been trying to get involved with the boys in the house area who were creating weapons and engaged in different forms of superhero play. Prior to this incident she had already suggested getting tied up as a way to gain a place in the play but the boys had decided that they were the ones who wanted to be tied up. So what she did was to try a new storyline that involved a rather drastic measure.

Tom, Sebastian, Jesus, are creating lengths of snap cubes and inserting them up their sweater sleeves as concealed weapons. Luz, who has been feeding the dogs, starts to tidy up the house area around the boys.

1. Tom: Oh no, the bad guy. The bad guy's going to come. We got to get them. We got him.
2. Sebastian: Good. Just everyone get out. We're staying here by ourselves.
3. Luz: Can we come in with this, cause look guys. (She's holding some house effects)
4. Jesus: Her do it.
5. Luz: Pretend we're, pretend we're –
6. Sebastian: Because we're love jedders.
7. Luz: Pretend that all of the girls that are here were dead.
8. Tom: Okay . . . But we knew their names.
9. Sebastian: Yeah. Luz, you've been in heaven all day long.
10. Tom: Yeah, then we came for, met her.
11. Sebastian: Yeah.
12. Luz: Okay.
13. Tom: Oh, somebody tied her. Somebody tied her.
14. . . .
15. Sebastian: Hey, guys. Oh no, here they come. Hide guys, hide.
16. Tom: Hide! Hide!
17. . . .
18. Luz: We need to lock everything. So they won't come in.
19. Sebastian: Tell Tom not to get in. He can't hide. We're just going to lock it. (They scurry round covering each other up and pretending to hide when Tom changes the storyline suddenly.)
20. Tom: I'm Wolverine.
21. Luis: I unlash the, yah.
22. Luz: Stop it! You can't!
23. Sebastian: You're going to be the better of any.
24. Jesus: Yes, leader.
25. Luz: Wait guys! Wait, let's play judges and there are a lot of people who are judges.
26. Boys: (Keep talking about their weapons to each other)
27. Stacey: (Comes over to Luz) You ain't in here.
28. Luz: Fine! I'm not going to bother you. We're in the dining room. We're in the dining room. Look all these things for the dining room. (Pointing to cups and things strewn around the house area)

Although it took Jesus' acknowledgement to the boys that it was okay for Luz to play (turn 4), it was the extreme measure of pretending to kill off all the girls through which Luz managed to position herself as part of the boys' play (turn 7). But this role was as a love interest, someone needing rescuing from the 'love jedders' as Sebastian called himself and the other boys (turn 6). When Tom changes the plot by declaring himself Wolverine of the X-Men (turn 20), Luz appears to lose any place in the drama (turn 22). Despite attempts to renegotiate her position by creating a new story of judges in which they can all be equal (turn 25), the X-Men and superheroes win out. This leaves Luz with little choice but to retreat back into the familiar discourses of domesticity in the dining room (turn 28).

Interestingly, Luz continued to use this strategy of creating a storyline of segregation as a means to gain access and participation in the play of the boys.

The children have been studying fire engines and firehouses as part of the transport curriculum. Tom's dad, a firefighter, has visited the school this morning; and at choice time the boys return to their large firehouse in the block area that they had built the day before. Luz has a truck with people in it and drives it along the vacant length of block area until she comes to the wall of the firehouse and stops. It is almost impossible for her truck to turn around.

1. Luz: Sebastian! . . . Sebastian!
2. Sebastian: Yeah.
3. Luz: Who made this? (Pointing to the firehouse) Who made this?
4. Sebastian: Me.
5. Luz: Is this is a bridge?
6. Sebastian: This is . . . no!
7. Luz: Is this is a hospital? [another theme running throughout the children's play]
8. Sebastian: A firehouse.
9. Stacey: Well, how are we going to pass? (She has moved her truck behind that of Luz's.)
10. Katerina: Easy. Go like this. (And she demonstrates walking over the wall and into firehouse)
11. Sebastian: No! You can't get on our firehouse.
12. Tom: I know. We just make a, we just we just turn this. (He moves one of the large blocks so a wall of the firehouse is open.) They share.
13. Sebastian: No!
14. Luz: They have a fire in their house.
15. Sebastian: Stop it. Stop it. (He confers with Tom and Jonathon.)
16. Stacey: Then we can get through?
17. Luz: There's a fire in our house.
18. Tom: No, if we just . . . then they can pass.

19. Sebastian: I don't care.
20. Stacey: I *can't* pass!
21. Jonathon: See, they can pass. They can pass. Hello! Look it. (Jonathon goes and walks over to a point in the wall.)
22. Luz: Look, a door. (Points to a block)
23. Jonathon: They can pass. (Walks back over the wall that Luz is calling a door)
24. Stacey: How you know you get in there, Sebastian?
25. Sebastian: You can only come in through the door, okay? (He moves a block to open the wall.)
26. Luz: Okay. (She begins to move her truck, Stacey follows.)
27. (Sebastian sits by the door of the firehouse watching Luz and Stacey. Luz takes her truck and physically places it and herself in the firehouse.)
28. Stacey: (Still outside) Guys, we want to play with it.
29. Tom: No!
30. Sebastian: You can't play in here.
31. Luz: The girls can't come in, only the boys right? (She leans over and places her girl person/prop outside the door.)
32. Sebastian: Only the boys can play. Okay, come in. (He leans over and scrutinizes people, picking up a girl.) She can come in because she has a dog. Oh, that's a cat. (He brings her in.) These children can come in because I like them.

Although the firehouse was so huge that there was minimal space available for the girls to build, Sebastian argues that the girls cannot access his firehouse by claiming ownership; he built the fire house so only he and the boys can play in it (turns 11 and 15). While Tom and Jonathon suggest ways the girls can pass through with their trucks and people (turns 12, 18, and 21), without upsetting their firehouse, Sebastian remains steadfast (turn 19). Sitting on the outside of the wall, however, Luz begins to negotiate access by invoking a storyline in keeping with the firehouse theme – she attempts to get the boys involved in a game about fires (turns 14 and 17). As the boys reject this suggestion, Luz offers the idea of a door in the wall to resolve the issue of how people pass through, though not play, in the firehouse (turn 22). This door allows her to physically place her body in the firehouse. Having gained physical access, Luz then articulates the unspoken rule that has prevented her access – 'only the boys' can play. It is by invoking this rule, rather than by creating the storyline of the fire that permits Luz access and eventually the opportunity to play in the firehouse.

Poststructural readings of these stories illustrate that being able to create storylines with apparent fluidity and ease was both a source of power and constraint for Luz's social work in choice time. It was a technique that often allowed Luz to gain entrance to the play of others, sometimes to even lead the drama; but when it came to playing with the boys, Luz's value was directly tied to stereotypical categories associated with being a female. In these episodes, despite Luz's command of storylines, the gendered discourse prevented Luz from taking on the strong and action-oriented roles in the play because she was a girl, and girls were viewed as being weak and needing rescuing.

Bodily knowledge: Steven's story

Like many boys in studies of children's gendered play (e.g. Davies, 1989; MacNaughton, 1994; Jordan et al., 1995), Steven preferred physical strategies to verbal ones to exercise power in his world. In fact, Steven seemed to learn physically, as he was one of the most coordinated students in the classroom and someone who always used his body in inventive ways. Choice time was also a favorite part of Steven's school day and not surprisingly Steven tended to choose those learning areas that had the potential for lots of action, like the blocks, house area, duplos, and table games. To negotiate and maintain his prominent place in the social order, Steven drew on his bodily knowledge – both physical strategies, and topics of taboo – as tactics of power.

Physical strategies

Steven would use materials in new and very physical ways to gain access to a social group, as the following episode illustrates:

In the block area, Tom and Sebastian have been creating a building together which keeps on changing its function, at this point in time becoming a hospital. Throughout this play they use the toy people to enact their dramas associated with the building's function. Steven has been watching these boys while working on his own construction.

1. Sebastian: Hurry up. Hurry up. I'm back from the hospital. We got dead.
2. Tom: She's in jail and he – she's in jail and he's sick.
3. Steven: (Approaches them trying to put a car on top of their building)
4. Tom: Better not knock that thing down. No. No! Don't you dare. I'm telling the teacher.
5. Steven: (Laughs)
6. Tom: I'll knock the building down on your head.
7. Steven: I'm not. Watch this. (He drops a person from the top of building.)
8. Tom: Ooh!
9. Steven: Knock the people down.

10. Tom: (Drops a person down from the top of the building) Oh. Did you see that it bounced over there and in there?
11. Sebastian: Watch this Steven. *Watch this.*
12. Tom: *I'm surprised that* my brain got all of that.
13. Sebastian: Steven! Watch this. Say yoho. Yoho.
14. Steven: Yoho. Yoho.
15. Tom: Steven, you know what? I threw him down from here and it bounced off – off Sebastian's truck.
16. (They all begin to throw the people off the building, giggling a lot.)

In the initial phase of this episode, it does not look like Steven is going to gain entrance to the drama because Tom perceives his physical stance as dangerous to the building he and Sebastian have created. In this instance, Tom appears not to view Steven's physicality as a positive aspect of Steven's identity as a co-player, because he may break down his building. To deter Steven, Tom employs several claims to truth, first, a classroom rule that 'you shouldn't knock down other people's buildings', second, the threat of going to a higher authority (turn 4), and finally, when these do not have the desired effect (turn 5), a physical threat (turn 6). It is Steven's use of a physical strategy, however, that prevents him from being excluded. By throwing materials off the top of the building Steven sets off a completely new episode of play (turn 7) in which the other boys test out different acts to attain Steven's approval (turns 13, 15, and 17). Whereas Steven had been seen as an outsider, a threat, his use of physical strategies enabled him to become the leader of the play. This leadership was short-lived, however, as Steven accidentally touched Tom's building and some blocks tumbled to the floor, which led to Tom getting angry and seeking teacher help.

These physical strategies Steven employed were not limited to the inventive use of materials, but more frequently involved using his body as an instrument of power. Steven enjoyed employing this kind of power-knowledge strategy to exert power over boys as well as girls, particularly those who were perceived to be 'weaker' in the social order as in the following episode.

It is almost clean-up time, and Steven has come to the rug to put something away. Reading the song chart with the wand [the special pointer Lara uses to point out words to children as they read] are Tyrone and Ryshan. They try and turn the song chart over to the next one but experience some difficulty, so Steven comes over and assists them.

1. Steven: (Standing right in front of Ryshan, holding onto his arm and speaking close to her face) Do you know where I came from? I came from, came from . . .
2. Ryshan: (Smiling at Steven, she tries to push him away.)

3. Tyrone: (Holds magic pointer and whispers something into Steven's ear)
4. Steven: (Pointing his finger at Tyrone) And you don't need that [pointer].
5. Tyrone: I turn you into a prince. (Taps Steven on the head with magic pointer and his hand) Well, I turn you into a princess. (Taps Ryshan)
6. Ryshan: (Giggles.)
7. (Tyrone goes to tap Steven on the head again but Steven stops the wand in mid-air, holding onto it while Tyrone tries to push it towards his head.)
7. Tyrone: Stop!
8. Steven: (Lets go of pointer) Don't turn me into a princess. I be a girl.
9. Tyrone: I turn you into a prince. (Goes to touch him with pointer. Seeing the pointer heading his way, Steven dodges it) I turn you into a prince. I'm turning you into a prince! I turn you into a prince. (Steven looks at the song chart as Tyrone taps him on head.)
10. Tyrone: (To Ryshan, tapping her on head with pointer) I turn you into a princess, again.
12. All: (They sing 'Twinkle twinkle little star' as Tyrone points to the words with the pointer.)
13. (Steven starts to chase Ryshan around the song chart.)
14. (Ryshan tries to go the other way then positions herself next to Tyrone giggling nervously.)
15. Steven: (Grabs her with both arms) Got ya!
16. Ryshan: (Pushes him away and stands by Tyrone speaking to him) He do that to his other girlfriend down there (points to another area). That's his other girlfriend. What's down there?
17. Tyrone: (No response.)
18. (Steven is sitting waiting behind the song chart and leans underneath and grabs at Ryshan's legs.)
19. Ryshan: Ah! (She moves away where he can't reach her.)
(Clean-up is called so they leave the song chart to find a book.)

At first glance this might appear to be the innocent play of children. It's just a game of chase after all. However, Thorne (1995) argues that beneath the surface of such chases is a gendered terrain, accompanied by intense emotions and the blurring of boundaries between play and aggression. Moreover, Davies argues that the bipolar categories that define maleness and femaleness in our world require that children commit themselves to one gender or another. To produce themselves as masculine boys need to regularly enact the dominant discourse of what it means to be masculine 'through oppressive acts of domination and control of their environment' (1989, p. 89).

In this episode Steven can be seen to be defining and asserting his masculinity against Tyrone (turns 4, 7, and 8) and Ryshan (turns 1, 13, 15 and 18).

Tyrone was a child some defined as a 'gender-bender' in the class, openly expressing his love of mermaids and the color pink. When Tyrone approaches Steven with the magic wand, Steven is wary, using his body in powerful ways to prevent Tyrone from touching him (turns 7, 8, and 12) and by declaring his membership in the male gender category (turn 8). Tyrone then pronounces Steven a boy by naming him a prince and he repeats this several times as if to make it clear to Steven that he recognizes his masculinity and thus to protect himself from physical threat (turn 9). For her part, Ryshan helps set off the physical pursuit (turn 2) and then acts the powerless female to Steven's strong male as he attempts to catch her. To facilitate the chase, Ryshan employs physical strategies – she tries pushing Steven away, moving herself far enough, but not too far so that he can continue to pose a threat (if she wanted to get rid of him she could have left the rug, for example) and positioning herself next to another child (turn 14). Ryshan also acts the helpless one by supporting Steven's efforts to maintain his masculinity, and in doing so, ascribes less agency to her own identity.

Being aggressive and physical was not the only form of bodily and sexist knowledge that Steven employed as a technique of power in choice time. In some interactions, Steven used discursive strategies in which he spoke of bodily topics that he knew would gain him attention from other children.

Topics of taboo

Conversations about bodily functions and sexuality are funny and pleasurable to children because they are one way they can transgress official discourses of the classroom and the authority of adults (Dyson, 1997; Grace and Tobin, 1997). Expressing thoughts and feelings that were supposed to be 'off-limits' or rude in the classroom was used by Steven to impress others, to gain their admiration and their inclusion and choice time allowed him to engage in this kind of banter. In the following example at writing and drawing, Steven got everyone on his side because he spoke about sexual aspects of women's bodies.

Tyrone, Callie, Maqueda, and Katerina are drawing and writing while Steven hovers nearby. The news of Callie's and Steven's like for each other seems to have become public news today. Luz and Alicia have teased Callie about it and the children at the table are excited. Their talk has been about Steven.

1. Tyrone: He don't like girls.
2. Callie: Yes he does.
3. Steven: (Comes to the desk) I like big girls and women.
4. Kids: Ooh!
5. Steven: I like to touch them.
6. Kids: Ooh! (They giggle.)

7. Steven: I like to touch this. (Pats hand on his breast)
8. Kids: Ooh!
9. Tyrone: (Talking about his drawing) I make Steven big with hair.
10. Callie: (Laughs.)
11. Tyrone: I make the hair so good! Look at you Steven. (Shows him the drawing)
12. Steven: I'm telling. (He goes off and hides behind the pillar listening and watching.)
13. Tyrone: He not going to tell.
14. Katerina: He's going to tell.
15. Callie: No.
16. Katerina: Yes.
17. Callie: No.
18. Katerina: Yes.
19. Steven: (Re-enters drawing and writing and stands by Tyrone)
20. Tyrone: You got.
21. Steven: I'll tell you about naked girls.

By speaking the unspeakable, of talking about desire and touching women's sexual body parts Steven demonstrates his willingness to transgress adult authority (turns 3, 5, and 7). The 'oohs' from the children indicate that Steven has impressed them with his knowledge and daring (turns 4, 6, and 8). Also indicative of his inclusion is Tyrone creating a drawing about the partnership of Steven and Callie (turn 9 and 11). At the same time, however, there is a dark side to Steven's pleasure in speaking about women's bodies in this sexual way. Steven is speaking a sexist and dominant masculine discourse that positions women and girls as 'other' in society (Walkerdine, 1990). Talking about such taboo topics like sexuality may be a way Steven crosses borders of authority in the classroom and reasserts his masculinity and popularity in the child discourse, but at the same time, the humor of the situation evoked by the child discourse (i.e. taboo topics help children to transgress their marginal positionings in adult–child discourse) precludes the girls from resisting Steven's positioning of women as objects of men's desire, and by implication, themselves.

In summary, then, choice time allowed Steven and Luz opportunities to be agents in their social worlds. On the other hand, choice time and the kinds of play these children engaged in were also a discursive practice that perpetuated stereotypical gender differences that provided quite different opportunities for Luz and Steven to exercise authority in their world. Luz and Steven were both being competent learners in choice time as defined by the developmental discourse – they were able to choose activities, follow through on those choices and engage in productive play – but despite being able to make choices and take authority for their learning, they were not always equally powerful.

In choice time Steven was able to assert his physical authority and engage in practices that reaffirmed his masculinity. Alternatively, Luz, an assertive, intelligent, and articulate girl who sought to move beyond the power accorded females in the domestic sphere, was sometimes limited by the dominant discourse that positions females as less powerful in relation to males. In order to maintain a place in the boys' dramas Luz often had to renegotiate her desire to be strong and a leader of the play with the boys' positioning of her as a supportive female to their positions of fireman and superheroes. Thus, the discourse of child-centered pedagogy with its emphasis on free play validated boys practicing sexism by exercising overt physical and verbal power over girls (Walkerdine, 1990).

Rethinking student choice in the curriculum

Children's play is not a neutral space but rather is a political and negotiated terrain. A poststructural lens on children's play suggests that if we are going to continue our commitment to equitable experiences for children in our programs, then we may need to rethink our definitions of being child-centered. Student choice is important, but instead of choice being conceptualized as freedom from adult authority, our interactions need to focus on helping children to understand the choices offered by different classroom discourses (Davies, 1990) and the power effects of such choices. Together with children we need to examine play and learning from multiple perspectives, construct multiple readings of the texts of classroom play in order to examine and question the authority on which they are enacted into being. This may require active participation in children's play and the use of other spaces like the circle (Ryan and Ochsner, 1999) to explore with children the discourses that constitute our taken-for-granted meanings of what it means to be a boy or a girl, for example, and illustrate the kinds of contradictory and multiple identities individuals can take up in resistance to typical binary categorizations like male/female, teacher/student, adult/child, etc. Such interventions can take many forms but at their core is the need for early childhood educators to shift the ways we observe, interpret, and intervene in children's learning.

Rethinking child-centered education so that we might achieve our goals of educational equity poses new challenges and possibilities for those of us in early childhood education. Poststructuralism with its emphasis on power as a fluid and central aspect of social lives offers one pathway for this important work. It allows us to see how young children and teachers can be at the same time both powerful and powerless, agents and recipients of change in their worlds. By examining learning and teaching as discursive performances that shift and change, that have multiple meanings and multiple possibilities, we open up a space to create new and more inclusive ways of teaching young children.

References

Bredekamp, S. and Copple, C. (1997) *Developmentally Appropriate Practice in Early Childhood Programs Serving Children from Birth Through Age 8* (rev. edn). Washington, DC: National Association for the Education of Young Children.

Burman, E. (1994) *Deconstructing Developmental Psychology*. London: Routledge.

Charlesworth, R. (1998) Developmentally appropriate practice is for everyone, *Childhood Education*, 74: 274–82.

Davies, B. (1989) *Frogs and Snails and Feminist Tales: Preschool Children and Gender*. St Leonards, NSW: Allen and Unwin.

Davies, B. (1990) Agency as a form of discursive practice, a classroom scene observed, *British Journal of Sociology of Education*, 11: 341–61.

Davies, B. (1993) *Shards of Glass: Children Reading and Writing Beyond Gendered Identities*. St Leonards, NSW: Allen and Unwin.

Dyson, A.H. (1993) *The Social Worlds of Children: Learning to Write in an Urban Primary School*. New York: Teachers College Press.

Dyson, A.H. (1997) *Writing Superheroes: Contemporary Childhood, Popular Culture, and Classroom Literacy*. New York: Teachers College Press.

Foucault, M. (1980) *Power/Knowledge: Selected Interviews and Other Writings 1972–1977*. New York: Pantheon Press.

Gallas, K. (1998) *Sometimes I Can Be Anything: Power, Gender and Identity in a Primary Classroom*. New York: Teachers College Press.

Grace, D.J. and Tobin, J. (1997) Carnival in the classroom: elementary students making videos, in J. Tobin (ed.) *Making a Place for Pleasure in Early Childhood Education* (pp. 159–87). New Haven, CT: Yale University Press.

Jordan, E., Cowan, A. and Roberts, J. (1995) Knowing the rules: discursive strategies in young children's power struggles, *Early Childhood Research Quarterly*, 10: 339–58.

MacNaughton, G. (1994) 'You can be dad': gender and power in domestic discourses and fantasy play within early childhood, *Journal for Australian Research in Early Childhood Education*, 1: 93–101.

MacNaughton, G. (1997) Feminist praxis and the gaze in the early childhood curriculum, *Gender and Education*, 9: 317–26.

Ryan, S. (1998) Freedom to choose: a poststructural study of child-centered pedagogy in a kindergarten classroom. Unpublished doctoral dissertation, Teachers College, Columbia University, New York.

Ryan, S. and Ochsner, M. (1999) Traditional practices, new possibilities: transforming dominant images of early childhood teachers, *Australian Journal of Early Childhood*, 24: 14–20.

Sharp, R. and Green, A. (1975) *Education and Social Control: A Study in Progressive Primary Education*. London: Routledge and Kegan Paul.

Silin, J.S. (1987) The early childhood educator's knowledge base: a reconsideration, in L. Katz (ed.) *Current Topics in Early Childhood Education*. Vol. 7 (pp. 17–31). Norwood, NJ: Ablex.

Thorne, B. (1995) *Gender Play: Girls and Boys in School*. New Brunswick, NJ: Rutgers University Press.

Usher, R. and Edwards, R. (1994) *Postmodernism and Education*. London: Routledge.

Walkerdine, V. (1984) Developmental psychology and the child-centered pedagogy, in J. Henriques, W. Holloway, C. Urwin, C. Venn and V. Walkerdine (eds) *Changing the Subject: Psychology, Social Regulation and Subjectivity* (pp. 153–202). London: Methuen.

Walkerdine, V. (1990) *Schoolgirl Fictions*. London: Verso.

8 Learning to be a child
Cultural diversity and early years ideology

Liz Brooker

The outer door opened and Amadur and Mohiuddin were shepherded in by their mothers. As it closed behind them, all four stood stiffly just inside the room, staring ahead. Mrs Goode approached them with a welcoming smile: 'Hi there, come on in, lovely to see you! Mums, you can go, these two will be fine. Come on boys.' She took the hands of the 4 year-olds and led them cheerfully towards the sandbox, leaving their mothers to exchange glances and then exit, backwards through the door. Amadur and Mohiuddin stood beside the sandbox looking blank and bewildered. Mrs Goode collected shovels, gave one to each of them, and dug industriously herself. After a few moments both boys dutifully squatted on the floor and began to dig, in imitation. They continued this way for some time, and Mrs Goode, after praising their efforts, moved off to another activity. The two boys, who were cousins, slowed their shovelling, stopped, and stared at each other.

(Field notes, All Saints' School, 7th September)

Introduction

Like Amadur and Mohiuddin, I was new to Mrs Goode's classroom that September (although, like them, I had visited in the previous term, before the summer break). Unlike them, however, I at once felt completely at home in the room, a glorious oasis of informal, child-centred, play-based learning in the midst of a rather squalid inner-urban neighbourhood. And like Mrs Goode, I was confident that the environment would soon become equally comfortable and natural for these boys, who had never experienced anything like it before.

It took me a year of observation and participation in Mrs Goode's room, and a long period of reflection afterwards, to think through these assumptions and weigh up the benefits for young children from diverse class and cultural backgrounds of the early years provision they are offered. 'Thinking through' involves moving beyond the particular experiences of particular children in particular settings, to discovering the underlying meanings of such encounters. This chapter attempts to present this process, showing how a range of theoretical understandings can help us to make sense of our work with young children and their families, in the same way that they try to make sense of our provision. In order to do so, it argues, we need to examine both our beliefs about Early Childhood Education, and our beliefs about the nature of childhood itself.

The All Saints' study

The All Saints' study (Brooker, 2002) was an attempt to answer certain persist-ent questions arising from my own experiences of teaching young children. The questions were about the differential group outcomes for children from different social and cultural backgrounds – differentials which persisted des-pite all our efforts, as educators, to offer an inclusive and appropriate curric-ulum for all children. For, while every *individual* child comes to school with a unique combination of knowledge and skills, gifts and talents, and may make unpredictable progress in school learning, the idea that whole *groups* of chil-dren should have lower achievement than other groups is clearly unaccept-able. In particular, I was interested in discovering what might be the lasting effects on children's learning of the actual transition from home to school, the process in which a 'child' is transformed into a 'pupil', with all that that entails.

The design of the study also grew out of my own professional experi-ences. As an Early Years teacher, I believed that children's learning could be understood by observing the children carefully, in every aspect of their behaviour, and by uncovering the perspectives of their families and the prac-tices of their homes and communities. Having worked in multicultural com-munities, I was particularly interested in the ways that culturally different home experiences might shape children's school careers. In order to focus the inquiry, my year of participant observation in the setting concentrated on the experiences of a sample of 16 children, constructed so as to reflect the factors research has shown to influence children's early achievement: ethnicity, sex, social class and age. My hope was that the ways these 16 individuals behaved and learned in their shared classroom environment might reveal something about the ways that different children experience the transition from home to school. Observation of the children was supplemented with a series of structured data collection activities, including home visits and interviews with the families of the children, assessments at the beginning and end of the year, structured observations in the classroom, interviews with the children, audits of classroom provision, and interviews with the classroom practitioners.

The setting – the 'Reception class' at All Saints' Primary School – was selected because it seemed to offer an exemplary and very inclusive Early Years environment. It was an informal and explicitly child-centred classroom in a small and welcoming multicultural school in a poor neighbourhood. The class teacher in her turn exemplified many of the characteristics we look for in an effective early childhood teacher: she was a lively and articulate, as well as reflective, practitioner, open and friendly in her manner, and open to innovation, and to researchers. Since she knew many of the families of the incoming children, she helped with the construction of the sample, and provided important background information throughout the year.

After meeting all the families before the summer holiday, I was ready to observe and record from the moment the classroom door opened in September, and ushered the 4 year-olds into their new role as school pupils. As the months went by, and data accumulated, it became clear that many of my own assumptions were being challenged. The ideology of Early Childhood Education, an essential part of my own professional identity, was one of the first assumptions to be questioned.

Early childhood education: the child and the 'nursery inheritance'

Historians of childhood, whose work is increasingly widely read in the context of the new sociology of childhood (Mayall, 2002), have shown that constructions of childhood vary not only with the social and cultural setting in which they are situated, but also with the particular historical moments which shape those settings. In Britain, for instance, we know that medieval and Victorian childhoods were different from those of today; and that the childhood of poor children was never viewed in the same way as that of the rich (Hendrick, 1997). Other cultures have parallel histories. In every society, that is to say, the 'child' and 'childhood' are socially constructed concepts as well as lived realities – socially constructed by the powerful ideas and interests of the society, in response to its current economic and political needs, and religious and moral beliefs (James and Prout, 1997).

Institutions, however, create their own constructs, and it is widely recognized that the western, minority-world 'institution' of Early Childhood Education (Dahlberg et al., 1999) has evolved its own persistent, and passionate, view of childhood. The origin of these beliefs – in the philosophy of the Enlightenment and the project of modernity, and in the thinking of a pantheon of nineteenth- and twentieth-century 'pioneers' (Pestalozzi, Froebel, Owen, McMillan, Montessori, Isaacs) – is familiar, and frequently recounted (Anning, 1991). The relationship of some aspects of this ideological tradition (Pollard et al., 1994) to the regimes of truth of developmental psychology, was proposed by Walkerdine (1984) and Burman (1994), and has been scrutinized more recently by those, like Dahlberg and her colleagues, who have been committed researchers in the early childhood field.

The concept of childhood contained in this ideological tradition or 'nursery inheritance' (Bennett et al., 1997) has undergone surprisingly little change over the past three centuries, a period in which national views of childhood have undergone frequent reversals (Hendrick, 1997): the natural and basically innocent child of Locke and Rousseau was present in Pestalozzi's school and Froebel's kindergarten, and subsequently in the nurseries of Owen and McMillan, Steiner and Isaacs. The concept had its heyday in the 1960s, when English nursery and infant schools were viewed internationally as a beacon of liberal and progressive practice. And it has held on, sustained by the idealism of practitioners and professionals, through periods of conservative backlash, to emerge in the 1980s and 1990s in the guise of Developmentally Appropriate Practice (Bredekamp and Copple, 1997). Ironically it is the latter manifestation which has triggered some of the sharpest critiques of the concept (see, for instance, Lubeck, 1996; Soto, 2002).

The ideology of Early Childhood Education, then, has constructed an enclosed and self-sufficient world within which such concepts are taken-for-granted, 'natural', self-evident and 'true'. It is a tradition which both defines and defends its own realities, when necessary, creating barriers to protect itself and its children from harmful outside influences, usually those of governments intent on formalizing early learning.

An idealized picture of the 'Early Childhood' child might depict one who is:

- full of potential, naturally curious, and eager to learn;
- active, outgoing and communicative;
- independent, autonomous, and able to show initiative;
- capable of selecting and sustaining self-chosen games and activities;
- able to learn through play and exploration.

Such a child is assumed to develop through universal stages, common to all children.

The 'ideal environment' envisioned by the Early Childhood tradition for this 'ideal child' reflects these characteristics. It is a place which offers the time, space, opportunities and resources for active exploratory play, through which children can construct their own learning, at their own pace and in their own way. The 'play ethos' (as discussed by Smith, 1994, and Bennett et al., 1997) has therefore been seen as the key feature of such an environment.

The child as a learner at All Saints'

Mrs Goode's classroom at All Saints' School exemplifies such an environment, providing a space within which learning can be accomplished through *play* and *fun*. The school takes in children from a variety of ethnic backgrounds, with a common low socio-economic status. The staff, though aware of cultural differences, are confident that their chosen pedagogy is appropriate for children from different backgrounds, since all children, despite the idiosyncrasies of their early experience, are essentially similar, with similar needs. Mrs Goode argues that 'the range of experiences that they've had, before school, is so huge – you have to give them the *best* environment', and when interviewed she clearly articulates the features of such an environment:

> It has to first of all allow them to have independence, so they can actually direct their own time . . . They've got to be able to choose, they've got to make choices, and they've got to be able to maintain things independently, things that interest *them*, the sort of things that *they* will then learn from; and you have to have enough opportunity for them to develop their social skills, because that's one of the most important things; and they have to have a *wide* range of activities that they've actually experienced and explored, different experiences, different sensory things . . . they also *must* have space, and they must have freedom to move about within it . . . and they must also have fun, things must be of interest to them. There must be that kind of informality of learning.

'Learning', in this classroom, comes about as a result of children's self-directed, self-motivated explorations, rather than as a result of 'teaching'. Granting children independence is an important aspect of the ethos, and Mrs Goode refers frequently to 'letting the children just be, and letting them explore': 'you look for independence, how independent they can be, and again it goes back to maintaining their own activity'. Underlying this 'independence' of course is a strong belief in *individualism*, in the child's uniqueness as a psychological entity: a core belief in developmental psychology, and in what Elkind (1997) calls the concept of 'child nature', but not nearly such a strong conviction among families from non-Western cultures.

The role of the adults in this environment is to make provision that is truly child-centred, 'developmentally appropriate' for children who are aged 4 and 5. The principal requirements then are *space*, for children to be active; *time*, for children to learn at their own pace; *freedom* to choose activities and sustain them; and interesting and imaginative resources for *play*. The child's role, as we have seen, is to move about independently and select among the concrete sensory experiences on offer, showing the motivation to sustain involvement in activities of his or her own choosing; and to have *fun*. Since it is 'natural' for children to play, they are able to learn through play, without even knowing it. As the nursery nurse explained to me, 'It's actually, the major aspect of learning for this age group is actually play, it is actually how they learn.'

However, this central tenet of the 'nursery inheritance', familiar to all early educators, is not taken for granted by all the children's families.

All Saints' families: concepts of childhood

The beliefs of the children's families were less explicit than those of their teachers, but eventually clarified themselves from the layers of data – informal conversations and observed behaviours, at home and in the classroom, as well as taped interviews. Among the families of UK origin, (whom the study refers to as 'Anglo' families), a somewhat weaker version of the teachers' beliefs prevailed. From their perspective, children were viewed as rather specialized beings, at a distinct stage of development, whose early childhood in particular was a sacrosanct phase, characterized by a complete lack of responsibilities, and complete freedom to play. All the mothers could narrate their own children's early development in detail, and remembered what they had played with at different stages; each child was viewed as an individual whose unique development and personality could be compared both with familiar developmental milestones, and with siblings and the children of friends and neighbours. All of them indicated that their parental responsibilities included noticing and attending to the child's own preferences. In differing degrees, they reported that they had been 'down on the floor playing with them' in their children's early years at home. Certainly they knew all about their children's toys and imaginative games, and had attempted to cater for these, at the same time as hoping, somewhat against their convictions, that their children were *learning* something useful from their play.

Just as the world of early childhood was accorded a special status, requiring constant adult attention and care, the world of adults was viewed as equally separate by most of these families. From around seven in the evening, childish things were banished, and children were safely tucked up in their own rooms (which were decorated with childish images – Thomas the Tank Engine, fluffy bunnies – and equipped with nursery rhyme tapes and children's videos). The adult world had a private life of its own, a respite from all the child-centred work of the day. This at least was the model, which all the 'Anglo' parents aspired to. Those who failed to meet some of the implicit criteria – who had no time to play or no money for toys, whose children refused to go to bed, or watched adult videos – apologized for these lapses. These parents were also identified as deficient by other parents, and sometimes by the staff, who measured various aspects of their parenting against their view of a 'normal' childhood.

The lives and beliefs of the Bangladeshi families provided a complete contrast to this 'Anglo' perspective. Their small children, rather than occupying a sphere of their own, were integrated into the mixed-age community of the extended family. Several co-slept with their mothers and siblings of all ages, and none had a room of their own. Their early care was undertaken by the extended family – by older siblings, and adults who went to their restaurant jobs in the evening – and they often passed their time at home observing and helping in the routines of these older family members. Mothers, when asked about their 4-year-olds' favourite toys and pastimes, looked blank. They were surprised that I should expect them to describe what their children did during the day, while older siblings were at school, since these under-fives were either accompanying their parents in household routines, or occupying themselves quietly out of sight of their mothers. Children's play was certainly of no account to their mothers: they were concerned for their children's safety and happiness, but this concern did not involve taking a 'childlike' perspective. Their descriptions of their children were of a 'good girl, always helping', or a boy who 'likes to put his hand with mummy's hand'. They did not identify such activities as children's responsibilities, or as 'work', but simply assumed that their children would make such a contribution. The Anglo families, by contrast, more often characterized their children as 'obsessed with Teletubbies' or 'good at drawing' or 'a tom-boy, always prefers to be out on her bike and get muddy'.

The Anglo parents, one might say, cherished their children's very 'childishness': their children had a time, a space and a life-style of their own, and were expected to behave in child-specific ways. (Both Dunn (1987) and Tizard and Hughes (1984) have highlighted the assumption, derived from this perspective and reinforced by picture-books and children's décor, that children aged 4 are concerned with 'special, childish interests, mainly to do with mothers, babies, dolls, teddies and animals', whereas research suggests they are also intensely interested in the world of adults.) The Bangladeshi families, by contrast, valued their children's adaptation to, and participation in, the family: their children shared the time, space and activities of household members of all ages. Like the Punjabi families whose views were explored in earlier studies (Dosanjh and Ghuman, 1998), they were not intent on cultivating independence or individualism in their children, but interdependence.

The All Saints' families: beliefs about learning and learners

The differing cultural expectations each group held for their children were further revealed in their views about learning, and in the ways that they tried to prepare them for school. The Anglo families' awareness of the appropriateness of play encouraged them to hope that their children were *learning* while playing, even if they found this hard to believe. When their children started school, in a free-play classroom, they approved but also admitted that they were looking forward to some more concrete evidence of their children's learning:

> Yeah, the school's fine. Even if they play now, you know they're going to learn in the end . . . (Kelly's mother)

> I think the school's OK, they have to learn to play before they learn to work. (Joshua's mother)

Many admitted too that their own child would be 'suspicious' of any attempts by their parents to 'teach' them, so that any efforts they made in this direction had to be disguised, or made to seem casual. Kelly's mother reported, 'She won't look at books if I'm in the room, she knows I'll be watching her!', while Cameron's mother described the lengths she went to in inventing alphabet-learning games, 'otherwise he thinks I'm trying to teach him something'. Among these families, as among parents in an earlier study, 'The prevailing belief . . . is that the success of educational efforts lies in how well they are disguised as play' (Lightfoot and Valsiner, 1992, p. 407). When children enter the reception class, parents feel easier: their children may *appear* to be playing all day, but they are in the care of experts who can be trusted to ensure that they are learning at the same time.

For the Bangladeshi families, the reverse is true: in most households, once their older children return from school, an hour or two is set aside for concentrated home tuition which includes all but the youngest children. These sessions (like the children's mosque school classes) offer a clear demonstration of the ways that parents believe that learning is brought about. Children aged 4 to 18 are found seated round the dining-table, doing their school homework or being taught by their parents. Even the 4 year-olds may be copying lines of writing, memorizing alphabets (sometimes two or three different alphabets) or reciting numbers or names of common objects from workbooks sent by relatives in Bangladesh. Most parents emphasized to me that their children needed to 'study hard', at home and at school, in order to do well. The vision of sand and water, blocks and toys, which greeted them in the Reception classroom, was a severe test of their faith and trust in their children's teachers. One father spoke for all, and articulated the views that the Anglo parents may also have held, when he asserted, in a slightly challenging tone, that 'Anything you are teaching her, she is learning': like other Bangladeshi parents, he could not conceive of children as 'learning' without being taught.

Two aspects of the information collected from parents gave additional clues to their beliefs, and to the specific effects these beliefs may have had on their child-rearing practices. One was an item in a questionnaire administered to all the parents in the class, asking what they thought parents should teach, and children should learn, before they started school. The skills listed included dressing and toileting, sharing and turn-taking, and the ability to speak and communicate. Most of these skills received similar levels of support from all parents; but the one which attracted *most* support from the Anglo parents, and very low support from Bangladeshi parents, was the last of these. While English-speaking parents knew that communication is important in school, Bangladeshi parents seemed to feel that learning to listen, rather than learning to talk, was the most important skill.

The other item was a rather difficult question put to all the parents in a follow-up interview: *How can you tell if a child is going to do well and get on at school? What is such a child like?* The question was not an easy one to answer, but most parents were able to describe some of the attributes which would identify a 'good learner', and again the cultural divide outweighed the individual differences between respondents. English-speaking parents collectively evoked a child who is 'always busy . . . always doing something . . . and coming up to you, telling you about it . . . showing you what they're doing . . . you can tell by the way they come up to you, what they say'. The Bangladeshi families (like Abu Bokkar's mother, quoted below) described children who learn through listening intently, rather than through speaking up. Inevitably, they were giving their children quite different expectations about life in the classroom.

Life in the classroom: learning through play?

When Amadur and Mohiuddin walked through the classroom door, the scene that met them was unlikely to have been the one they had expected. Their parents, like the other Bangladeshi parents, had made clear to them what school was all about ('sit quietly and listen to the teacher', 'stay in your seat and study hard', 'don't speak, just do as the teacher tells you', were the phrases that recurred in interviews). The qualities the community inculcated in children, and expected in pupils (as their Quranic classes confirmed) were those of stillness, obedience and respect; of submission to the teacher who was imparting the knowledge without which the children would, as another father put it, 'be nobody' when they grew up.

All of the Bangladeshi families had tried to make their child into the kind of child who could learn from a pedagogy of direct transmission of knowledge, from teacher to learner. As one mother proudly asked,

> When Abu Bokkar knows 10 words, why are there children who will not know one word? Because when teacher is teaching them, they are

> listening in this ear and taking it out of the other ear: Bokkar doesn't
> do that, he is listening properly and putting it in his head!

Unfortunately for her, and parents like her, this was not the way that learning came about in Mrs Goode's classroom. On the contrary, learning was planned to occur as a result, not of 'sitting still and listening quietly', but of using the time and space, freedom and resources to make energetic and often boisterous choices, to challenge, explore and discover.

In the first term, observations of the 16 children showed their very uneven and varied responses to the learning opportunities they were offered. Amadur and Mohiuddin, for instance, did not take long to discover, at one level, what was expected of them. After a few days of looking over their shoulders at Mrs Goode, and checking on the behaviour of other children, they got stuck into energetic playing: shovelling sand, or pouring water, for up to an hour at a time; tipping out jigsaws or dominoes; sitting at the computer moving the mouse in circles. Most of the time they were silent, but when they took a break from this industrious activity they would stand and chat with other Bangladeshi boys, or wander the room with them, arm in arm, or disappear to the toilets and washrooms. Outwardly, by learning 'how to play', they were adapting to the pedagogy of the classroom. But (like some others in the room) they may not have been 'learning *through* play'. Recent research on pedagogy (Siraj-Blatchford et al., 2002) has supported the claims of Vygotsky (1978) and Bruner (1986) about the importance of the social contexts of learning. It reminds us that there is much more to 'learning' than endless repetitive shovelling of sand or shuffling of jigsaws: that moving children's learning forward requires the intervention of 'more experienced others', adults and children who can support children in extending their existing knowledge into new domains. Without such interaction, children's play activities may keep them busy and occupied but fail to engage their thoughts – the kind of activity described (Wood and Attfield, 1996), as 'hands-on' but not 'brain-on'.

While an Early Childhood training and pedagogy gives us hope that, if children are playing, they are also learning (something), these observations of the children confirmed that play *in itself* was insufficient. In order to benefit from the pedagogy – to learn through play – a child needed to display the appropriate learning dispositions and enjoy appropriate social relationships, both with adults and with 'more experienced' peers. The personal and social characteristics required for this – the characteristics of the 'right kind of child' for this classroom, were described in the entry assessments for Personal, Social and Emotional Development, assessments which were made of all the children during their first few weeks at school.

Assessing children's 'readiness' to learn

Statutory entry assessments of each child, obligatory in the UK from 1998 to 2002, measured both the core areas of academic learning – Speaking and Listening, Reading, Writing, Mathematics – and also specific aspects of children's social development. Not surprisingly, the knowledge and skills of the Bangladeshi children – assessed largely through the medium of English – compared poorly with those of the English-speaking children in their class. More disturbing were their scores on the Personal, Social and Emotional scales, which purported to describe, not the child's learning, but the child herself or himself. The five-point scales were well matched to the qualities identified by Mrs Goode in her accounts of how children learn in their settings: they were headed, respectively, Initiative; Relationships; Co-operation; Involvement; Independence; and Behaviour. The practitioner, after observing the children in their first few weeks of school, had to decide where on each of the six scales each child should be placed. 'Initiative', for instance, had descriptors ranging from 1: 'timid' to 5: 'curious problem-solver'; 'Involvement' from 1: 'flits' to 5: 'concentrates'; and 'Independence' from 1: 'dependent' to 5: 'independent'.

For all six aspects, the Bangladeshi children were awarded much lower scores than their Anglo counterparts. Amadur and Mohiuddin, for instance, scored only 1 for 'Initiative', and 2 or 3 for 'Relationships', 'Co-operation', 'Involvement' and 'Independence'. As viewed by the adults who made the assessments, they were, self-evidently, lacking in the qualities needed for successful adaptation to the classroom environment, and so were perhaps not 'ready' for school learning. In comparison with their Anglo class-mates, it seemed, they were less able to take turns, share, co-operate, form relationships, make choices, show initiative, persevere, and communicate. These developmental 'deficits' meant that it was difficult for them to access the curriculum offered in the classroom, where the particular style of learning that was offered required all these forms of social behaviour. By behaving, more or less, in the ways their parents had instructed, the Bangladeshi children were constructing themselves, in the eyes of the school, as poor learners, with limited access to the goods on offer in this rich and inviting classroom.

Becoming a pupil: a chancy business

As the year went on, some of the Bangladeshi children took their cue from English class-mates and began to involve themselves in the kinds of play conducive to the planned learning outcomes. By half-way through the year, it was possible to see which of them were beginning to access the benefits of the active experiential learning on offer: those with older siblings in the school (several informed me, when I asked how they knew what to do at school, 'My sister tell me, so I know'); those whose parents had the confidence and expertise to come in and speak to teachers; those with a relative with an English education; and those who acquired a special friend who was English and could induct them into activities.

Girls, on the whole, fared better than boys in this respect. Some showed considerable skill in making and sustaining relationships, and most developed one or two companions who helped them to acquire the classroom rules for social behaviour *and* learning behaviour. The boys in the group took much longer to discover these rules, and in consequence remained far more detached from the classroom culture which developed as the months passed. The few children, including Amadur, Mohiuddin and a solitary girl (Tuhura) who never appeared to acquire the types of behaviour that were valued, dropped steadily further and further behind, until they barely participated in the life of the classroom. In the summer months, when more intensive instructional activities were gradually introduced to the class, these three were almost always left to choose in the free-play areas, where observations showed them apparently day-dreaming and desultory. The attractively presented activities, and the cheerful kindly adults, had failed to engage them at the right time, and they now seemed to have retreated to their own solitary worlds.

By the end of the year, each of the 16 children had a distinct pupil identity, inscribed in their school profiles and reports, which would go with them into the years of formal learning. Their early days in the classroom appeared to have set each on a path towards success or failure, a path from which it would be difficult to deviate in future. Some aspects of their progress could be traced to individual differences of home experience and parenting, but underlying these were the broader, cultural, differences which were making it much harder for the Bangladeshi children to achieve. The direct clash of beliefs and practices between their parents and their teachers meant that they had double the work to do on starting school: not just 'becoming a pupil', a task all children must accomplish (Willes, 1983; Pollard, 1996; Boyle and Woods, 1998), but becoming a different kind of child from the one their family and community had created. For those who succeeded, it was a remarkable triumph of energy and determination.

Learning the lessons of the All Saints' children

Any attempt to derive lessons for practice from these findings is fraught with risks. First, it would clearly be wrong to abandon our hard-won play pedagogy in favour of formal instructional methods. Equally wrong, I would argue, would be an attempt to colonize our ethnic minority or working-class families through intensive parent education, to bring them into conformity with white middle-class perspectives: cultural imperialism of this kind, spreading the western message into non-western communities at home and abroad, is not appropriate. Nor should we place our hopes in the more gradual colonization which comes about through the slow erosion of minority cultural practices, the incremental assimilation of children and families into the mainstream, generation by generation.

Instead, we might first use the example of the All Saints' children to interrogate our own beliefs about children and their needs (Woodhead, 1997), acknowledging that the variety of children's cultural backgrounds calls, not for a one-size-fits-all learning style, but for a range of learning styles. Re-thinking the characteristics we value in children would require us to re-think the entrenched cultural bias often shown in our provision for their learning; and it would require us too to re-think the ways that we assess the knowledge, skills and dispositions they bring to school. These are not new challenges: thoughtful educators (such as Ladson-Billings, 1992) have been making this argument for a dozen years now – indeed, some persistent advocates of DAP now claim that this is what the guidelines originally intended (Hart, 2002; Hyson, 2002).

Second, we might interrogate our frequently uncritical advocacy of the effectiveness of play – any play, all play – and ask whether our children are necessarily benefiting from the activities provided in early childhood settings. Again, this is not a new challenge. Well-designed research studies (Sylva et al., 1980) have always discriminated between the activities, and the environments, which can be shown to extend young children's thinking, and those which merely keep them busy, and help them to pass the time pleasantly. But the early childhood lobby, fearful of a return to formal instruction, has held to its mantra of 'play at any cost'. This work/play dichotomy, we must now recognize, has long outlived its usefulness: many of the young children, around the world, who undertake economic work to support their families or pay for their own education, are also learning from, and gaining pleasure from, their tasks (Woodhead, 1999). Less controversially, we can consider the example of the Reggio preschools, where children, rather than being exhorted to play, are invited to work at their own projects, and do so with a seriousness and persistence not always seen in nursery settings (Rinaldi, 1993). For play to 'work', we might acknowledge, there is almost always a need for social interaction and the shared construction of knowledge.

Third, we ourselves must work hard to develop dialogues with parents about our beliefs and our goals for young children. Minority and working-class parents have frequently been viewed as 'hard to reach' if not actually 'uninterested' in their children's learning, although research (Huss-Keeler, 1997; Siraj-Blatchford and Brooker, 1998) has shown otherwise, and the All Saints' families certainly did not fall into this category. But such parents may also be viewed as simply ignorant or wrong in their beliefs about learning – as were the Bangladeshi families of All Saints' End. The work/play dichotomy, again, can be responsible for constructing barriers between parents and teachers, as well as between children and their learning: such barriers can only be overcome by serious and respectful *listening*, and not by a home–school dialogue which assumes the school is always right. If we start with the assumption that all parents, as well as all teachers, wish children to succeed in their learning, we can go on to discuss our beliefs about what we want children to learn – socially as well as academically – and how we think this learning is best achieved. In the course of such dialogues, terms like 'work' and 'play' are best avoided, since they conjure up unwelcome meanings and associations for both parents and practitioners. We can focus instead on our shared concerns for children's 'learning', and perhaps also on the 'instruction' which (as Vygotsky claimed) occurs whenever a child is shown or told something by a more experienced learner, including during play activities.

Finally, the most important reminder from Reggio for other early childhood settings may be the emphasis on *relationships* as the foundation for children's development and learning. Too much of western pre-school education has been based upon 'solitary explorer' models derived from developmental psychology (Sylva et al., 1976). Vygotsky's account of the social context of learning, a context in which knowledge is constructed *between* individuals, rather than simply *within* the individual child, has generated an alternative research tradition, which emphasizes the development of intersubjectivity and the instructional role of a shared focus and shared culture (Bruner, 1986; Schaffer, 1992; Siraj-Blatchford et al., 2002). Such research supports the view of the Reggio child as 'most of all, connected to adults and other children' (Malaguzzi, 1993: 10).

None of us will under-estimate the difficulties facing teachers with large groups, too little help, and too many children speaking an unknown language. The only fruitful way forward in such situations, we might conclude, is to put all our efforts into supporting children's personal and social development, engaging with children in ways which include them in the classroom culture, and modelling the behaviours and skills they need to work together to support each other. These are far more significant skills than, for instance, learning the curriculum of colours and numbers, letters and names, which many early childhood settings still prioritize, and which children will teach each other once they have acquired the social skills for peer tutoring and collaboration. The interdependence and collective spirit traditionally taught by Asian families, for instance, may support this undertaking better than the individualism that we in the West have tended to cherish.

References

Anning, A. (1991) *The First Years at School*. Milton Keynes: Open University Press.

Bennett, N., Wood, E. and Rogers, S. (1997) *Teaching Through Play*. Buckingham: Open University Press.

Boyle, M. and Woods, P. (1998) Becoming a proper pupil: bilingual children's experience of starting school, *Studies in Educational Ethnography*, 1: 93–113.

Bredekamp, S. and Copple, C. (eds) (1997) *Developmentally Appropriate Practice in Early Childhood Programs* (rev. edn). Washington, DC: NAEYC.

Brooker, L. (2002) *Starting School: Young Children Learning Cultures*. Buckingham: Open University Press.

Bruner, J. (1986) *Actual Minds, Possible Worlds*. Cambridge MA: Harvard University Press.

Burman, E. (1994) *Deconstructing Developmental Psychology*. London: Routledge.

Dahlberg, G., Moss, P. and Pence, A. (1999) *Beyond Quality in Early Childhood Education and Care: Postmodern Perspectives on the Problem with Quality*. London: Falmer Press.

Dosanjh, J. and Ghuman, P. (1998) Child-rearing practices of two generations of Punjabis: development of personality and independence, *Children and Society*, 12: 25–37.

Dunn, J. (1987) Understanding feelings, in J. Bruner and H. Haste (eds) *Making Sense: The Child's Construction of the World*. London: Methuen.

Elkind, D. (1997) The death of child nature: education in the postmodern world, *Young Children*, 11: 241–5.

Hart, C. (2002) Contribution to colloquium, 'Developmentally Appropiate Practice: continuing the dialogue', *Contemporary Issues in Early Childhood*, 3(3): 447–9.

Hendrick, H. (1997) Constructions and reconstructions of British childhood: an interpretative survey, in A. James and A. Prout (eds) *Constructing and Re-constructing Childhood* (2nd edn). London: Falmer.

Huss-Keeler, R. (1997) Teacher perception of ethnic and linguistic minority parent involvement and its relationship to children's language and literacy learning: a case study, *Teaching and Teacher Education*, 13(2): 171–82.

Hyson, M. (2002) Discussion, 'Developmentally appropriate practice: continuing the dialogue', *Contemporary Issues in Early Childhood*, 3(3): 454–7.

James, A. and Prout, A. (1997) A new paradigm for the sociology of childhood? in A. James and A. Prout (eds) *Constructing and Re-constructing Childhood* (2nd edn). London: Falmer.

Ladson-Billings, G. (1992) Culturally relevant teaching: the key to making multicultural education work, in C. Grant (ed.) *Research and Multicultural Education*. London: Falmer.

Lightfoot, C. and Valsiner, J. (1992) Parental belief systems under the influence, in

I. Sigel et al. (eds) *Parental Belief Systems: The Psychological Consequences for Children*, (pp. 393–414). Hillsdale, NJ: Lawrence Erlbaum.

Lubeck, S. (1996) Deconstructing 'child development knowledge' and 'teacher preparation', *Early Childhood Research Quarterly*, 11: 147–67.

Malaguzzi, L. (1993) For an education based on relationships, *Young Children*, Nov. 93: 9–13.

Mayall, B. (2002) *Towards a Sociology for Childhood: Thinking from Children's Lives.* Buckingham: Open University Press.

Pollard, A. with Filer, A. (1996) *The Social World of Children's Learning*. London: Cassell.

Pollard, A., Broadfoot, P., Croll, P., Osborn, M. and Abbott, D. (1994) *Changing English Primary Schools?* London: Cassell.

Rinaldi, C. (1993) in C. Edwards, L. Gandini and G. Foreman (eds) *The Hundred Languages of Children: The Regio Emilia Approach to Early Childhood Education. Norwood. NJ: Ablex.*

Schaffer, R. (1992) Joint involvement episodes as contexts for cognitive development, in H. McGurk (ed.) *Childhood and Social Development*. Hove: Lawrence Erlbaum.

Siraj-Blatchford, I. and Brooker, L. (1998) *Parent Involvement in One LEA: Final Report*. London: Institute of Education.

Siraj-Blatchford, I., Sylva, K., Muttock, S., Gilden, R. and Bell, D. (2002) *Researching Effective Pedagogy in the Early Years*. DfES Research report, London: HMSO.

Smith, P. (1994) Play and the uses of play, in J. Moyles (ed.) *The Excellence of Play.* Buckingham: Open University Press.

Soto, L.D. (2002) contribution to colloquium 'Developmentally Appropriate Practice: continuing the dialogue', *Contemporary Issues in Early Childhood*, 3(3): 449–51.

Sylva, K., Bruner, J. and Genova, P. (eds) (1976) *Play*. Harmondsworth: Penguin.

Sylva, K., Roy, C. and Painter, M. (1980) *Childwatching at Playgroup and Nursery School*. London: Grant McIntyre.

Tizard, B. and Hughes, M. (1984) *Young Children Learning*. London: Collins.

Vygotsky, L. (1978) *Mind in Society: The Development of Higher Psychological Processes.* Cambridge, MA: Harvard University Press.

Walkerdine, V. (1984) Developmental psychology and the child-centred pedagogy: the insertion of Piaget into early education, in J. Henriques et al. *Changing the Subject: Psychology, Social Regulation and Subjectivity*. London: Methuen.

Willes, M. (1983) *Children into Pupils*. London: Routledge and Kegan Paul.

Woodhead, M. (1997) Psychology and the cultural construction of children's needs, in A. James and A. Prout (eds) *Constructing and Re-constructing Childhood* (2nd edn). London: Falmer.

Woodhead, M. (1999) Combatting child labour: listen to what the children say, *Childhood*, 7(1): 27–49.

Wood, E. and Attfield, J. (1996) *Play, Learning and the Early Childhood Curriculum.* London: Paul Chapman.

9 Questioning diversity

Jeanette Rhedding-Jones

This chapter interrogates the concept of *diversity*, an important aspect of the postmodern condition. It argues that diversity, as a concept, should matter in contemporary society and the education systems that are embedded in them, and it should not be treated superficially, or in a tokenistic manner. Diversity is understood in various ways within early childhood education. We need to carefully consider how early childhood educators perceive diversity since it can have far-reaching implications for the ways in which we enact our professional lives. In this chapter the concept of diversity is made problematic. Various observations and recordings made in day care centers in North America and Europe are critically questioned in relation to the current issues. These contexts were observed when visiting children aged 2 to 5 years of age in care settings. The examples are chosen to create focal points for interrogation and to illustrate the ways in which diversity is enacted. The field notes and the references that are analyzed within this chapter have been arranged so that diversity is considered from a variety of perspectives within management discourses, to see how diversity may be encountered in early childhood education contexts. The chapter considers the ramifications of this and asks if the term *diversity* is still a term that is relevant in contemporary times. At the end of the chapter the implications for professionals in early childhood education are drawn together. The aims of the chapter are to do the following:

- to show that diversity is a critical issue and, as such, the term needs to be carefully considered;
- to assist readers to consider the ways they might deal with 'diversity' in early childhood education practice;
- to question the practical and discursive positioning of early childhood education in relation to the wider discourses of diversity.

A political agenda for change is built into the chapter. For example, one critical issue is related to the integration of ethnic and linguistic 'minorities' in early childhood contexts. This becomes problematic when it operates in practice as assimilation, rather than as transformation of the monoculture and the mono-lingual through a critical and anti-racist multiculturalism (May, 1999), and through strategies of anti-bias in early childhood education and care (Creaser and Dau, 1996; Derman-Sparkes, 1991; Makin et al., 1995). In focusing on diversity, the chapter deals with this issue as something that is able to be seen and heard; and also as a set of discursive constructions.

The *seeing* and the *hearing* that happens in the following scenarios can be through words, silences, actions and non-actions of the adults and the chil-dren. The first scenario is presented here for your critical interrogation. Here, I as the narrator, have juxtaposed my notes from everyday events from early childhood education and care settings. In New York, I was behind glass to 'observe' young children in a center. In Oslo, I spent two days with a group of visiting international people also observing early childhood education and care practices. We were invited into the Norwegian day care centers and the explanations were given in English. The scenarios I present in this chapter are framed by my note-taking at these centers. This was informed by my critical questioning, including issues such as: What is happening and not happening here in terms of diversity and language(s)? Who are the adults here? What are they saying and writing and why? As the narrator of the scenarios I was mindful not to be exempt from the critique.

Scenario One

> It is 11.30 a.m. and we're in the language room in the barnehagen [a day care centre in Norway, for children aged 3 to 5 years]. It has 'språk rom' (language room) written on the door. There are lots of testing and teaching objects visible, cards with pictures on them for example, and small toys. The barnehagelærer (day care teacher-carer) calls what happens in here 'mapping'. They map what each child can do with language.

> Teacher-carer: I use this book from Sweden and I can see how many words they know. I use [the book and the objects] to find out what they know [in Norwegian language]. To the parents, I tell them 'Speak your mother tongue'.
> Woman in observation group: At home. [not expressed as a question]
> Teacher-carer: At home. [expressed as an answer]
> Second woman observer: What about the father's language? [The teacher doesn't understand. She is, after all, trained in special pedagogy not in critical theory.]

From my reading, the issues here appear to be that:

1   This day care center does provide for children speaking another language at home, but it does so by locating the explicit teaching and testing of the national language behind a closed door, specifically for those children not from the nationally dominant ethnicity. By doing so the children's home languages are perhaps not seen as 'language' at all.

2   The English words here may not 'mean' what speakers of English at home might think. Similarly, the Norwegian language used by the children learning to speak it as a second or third language in this pre-school may not 'mean' what the Norwegians think it does.

3   The professionals in this scenario assume that they are able to 'map' what the children can do with language and that language is able to be rated and evaluated by people listening to it. By trusting the writers of the 'Swedish book', as experts from another country, the Norwegian teacher-carers are not trusting their own professional experience and knowledge.

4   The so-called 'mother tongue' is not valued in the day care center because that is where the normalized and colonizing language of Norwegian rules. If the children hear and speak their home languages only at home they soon learn that home is not the place that matters, at least that will be how they think Norwegians see non-Norwegians.

5   'Special' pedagogy has a lot to do with setting up pedagogical events like the one in this scenario. If 'critical' pedagogues decided what happened, then the events might be otherwise.

6   The questions asked by the two women observing in this scenario show that they are being critical: of gender matters (the 'mother tongue' and the 'father tongue') and of the split between the private home and the public pre-school (the implication that children must not speak their home language when not at home).

These narratives might benefit from postmodern readings, where readers resolve the split between narrative and exposition, and where there are many unfixed possibilities and implications for practice. The aim is to show that the creation of a critical diversity is crucial for early childhood education for a number of reasons. These include:

*   being able to better understand objections or resistance to the concept of 'diversity' particularly in its present use in early childhood education;
*   a desire to focus on the political justice aspects of equity rather than simply on the rhetoric of superficial aspects;
*   a consideration of resisting 'diversity' strategies favoring individuals, groups and cultures that are already well supported.

It is anticipated that people will have multiple interpretations of the con-
cept(s) of diversity, and these may actually be what help us to create contexts
for discussions which will have important implications for practices. What
this chapter cautions against are situations in which a term or word is adopted
without awareness of its discursive histories and effects. Meanings have to be
considered in context and related to practice. A problem with normalized
understandings of diversity is that they appear to require an 'add-on multiculturalism that "celebrates" exotic otherness' (Laubscher and Powell, 2003,
p. 221). Further, it might be contended that diversity might be more illusory
than real, as much of today's so-called cultural diversity is nationally constructed because of an underlying 'consumerist commonality' (Lo Bianco,
2000, p. 94). Early childhood education should aim to go beyond an 'add-on
multiculturalism' simply celebrating the exotic. What we are doing about the
national constructions of 'diversity' is not so clear.

Definitions and discourses

This section deals with diversity definitions in operation, that is, how usage of
the term diversity shows what people think diversity is, and then how this
might translate into practice. Discourses are about sets of practices that are not
always understood. They include describing and knowing what people do, and
what they say, and realizing the impact of values, life histories and socio-
cultural contexts on behaviors. Because diversity exemplifies what happens
with discourses and power, the term itself serves to show what discourses exist
and how they operate.

In early childhood education the term 'diversity' has been used in connection to support identity, difference and complexity (e.g. Grieshaber and
Cannella, 2001; Siraj-Blatchford and Clarke, 1998). These issues need to be
further explored in critical ways related to everyday practices in learning
environments with young children. In the scenario that follows, there is a
description of what was happening in practice, at a particular place and time.
It is relevant to consider what ideologies here are supporting identity, complexity and difference. What is managing diversity in the face of difference? Is
it pedagogy that normalizes the management of space, time and children?
Further, what definitions and discourses of diversity have allowed me as a
privileged White woman to here become a passive observer and critic?

Scenario Two

*Through the New York observation glass I view a young man sounding
sounds, a young woman psychology student that I was introduced to earlier,*

a mother and an assistant to the teacher-carers. The children are all in a circle. [cut] Now the children are lining up for the adults and going out the door. Don't know where to. The empty room has the usual pale wood midget furniture. Tokenly compartmentalized for child action of assorted kinds. The PhD student of psychology is now planning her dinner on the mobile phone . . . Outside the playroom the Parent Bulletin Board is up high above the lockers. Says 'For sale: car seat, baby swing, electronic'. The next notice is in Spanish. The third says 'Admission into session for prospective parents at . . . school'. On the far wall are 'Our Family Books'. These are published by four men I've not heard of: Don, Bill Jnr., Jo and Pete. In the corridor is information about bilingualism. A poster says something in an Asian script that I cannot understand.

The issues embedded here are many and include:

- Diversity is obvious in the parent notice board but not in what these 5-year-olds are actually doing, which is a normalized circle activity based around English-language phonics, followed by all lining up and going together to another room at the same time.
- Here the psychology student's phone calling appears to demonstrate a disengagement from early childhood practice and its critical issues.
- The men-as-experts who have published the books for the parents to read have very White and American names. Despite the Hispanic and 'Asian' languages of the families of these children, there appear to be no 'experts' from them. Further, there are no women 'experts' writing the books, despite the large numbers of women professionals in early childhood education, and the fact that the 'parents' I am seeing today are all mothers.
- By placing observers behind one-way glass the notion of childhood is perhaps quite close to animal-hood. If the children are not free to spy on adults, and to move among adults as they might wish, then what is in this scenario as a discourse of adult control and surveillance of the young? Because this is a day care center with most children speaking languages other than English at home, they are subjected to the observation glass in ways that 'majority' children are not, because visitors like me come to look at them.
- Although this institution is recognized as 'multicultural', the multi-culturalism is not made critical, as the catering for diverse language and cultures appears to be tokenistic. Effects of the diversity discourses and definitions here are that the languages other than English are visible or audible only on the parents' notice board, where Euro-American men appear as experts and 'Asian' and Hispanic parents communicate with each other.

- Managing diversity appears to be happening through the normalizations of psychology, the teaching of Anglo-American phonics, and the children all doing the same thing at the same time. By being with the children and the man who is their teacher-carer, the mother and the assistant and the psychology student are validating a non-critical pedagogy regarding diversity. Management via pedagogy thus eliminates bilingualism, despite the notice board's proclamation of it.

What follows links these diversity issues to general usage and then to management discourses more explicitly. In general usage, people in the Western world are likely to understand diversity as being about difference or variety. Because there is a variety of political developments associated with the language of diversity, we need to carefully scrutinize the political agendas with which diversity is associated. For example, in Australia a 1998 public service document says:

> Diversity relates to gender, age, language, ethnicity, cultural background, sexual orientation, religious belief and family responsibilities. Diversity also refers to the ways we are different in other respects such as educational level, work experience, socio-economic background, personality profile, geographic location, marital status and whether or not one has a carer.
>
> (Bacchi, 2000, pp. 75–6)

Here new diversities, such as family responsibilities, have crept in, but race and disability are left out. So our critical questions of this management discourse of diversity must be: Who wrote this and what was their agenda? How might this kind of distortion of diversity materialize within the institutions for pre- and early schooling? What are the effects for the people already in power? Coming from the adjective 'diverse', the term 'diversity' has only recently become part of everyday vocabularies. How it got there and whether it should stay are the underlying questions of this chapter. As ways into studying a problematized term or word then, what the chapter does next is consider diversity as it is used in differing discourses. For early childhood education professionals, what are the implications of the political positionings that follow as discourses?

Management discourses

Business management discourses are supposedly outside education as a discipline and as a university faculty. But education also has a management rationality, and so do the institutions funding day care centers, schools and research projects. Hence what administration is, what leadership is and what a political decision is, are closely tied to how diversity is constructed and viewed. Early childhood education links closely to all of these, though it has its own systems of leadership, administration and decision-making. Although it may seem unusual to consider what happens in the world of business, the reason for doing so is to caution against powerful and seductive discourses, definitions and practices that shift location into other arenas such as early childhood education.

In pointing out some effects of management discourses, the chapter works towards constructing a critical diversity. In management discourses, diversity is taken up as a desirable quality, but it is sometimes manipulated so that it suits the agendas of the managers rather than the interests of the clients. For early childhood education the critical issue is to decide what is acceptable from a particular discourse, and to know where and how to resist what happens. In management the current idea is that teams working together reflect the attributes of various groups, but in practice some of these management solutions need critical questioning. This questioning should also regard the links between management discourses and early childhood education management. Managing diversity can then be seen as sometimes problematic.

Managing diversity

Bacchi, writing in a critical way about managing diversity, says 'the language of workplace diversity is supplanting equal employment opportunity' (2000: p. 64). Further, a management discourse is positioning 'managing diversity as the way "forward" '. Here 'the words "reasonable" and "practicable" will . . . become the hallmarks of workplace initiatives in relationship to equity in the future' (ibid., p. 67). Bacchi (ibid., p. 68) describes 'the post-1996 emergence of "workplace diversity programs" in both state and federal public service documents' in Australia and demonstrates the kinds of critique that might be useful to engage in within early childhood education, rather than the acceptance or transfer of the discourse from the management arena.

We will now consider how *mainstream diversity* can have a homogenizing effect on people and how *productive diversity* views diversity in less rigid ways, and is potentially more useful for early childhood education.

Mainstream diversity

With mainstream diversity the focus is on the 'other': on individuals seen as 'different'. Here, as with all management discourses of diversity, the social justice of diversity may be only rhetoric, and not actual. Bacchi says that the effect of a mainstream approach is to totalize and individualize. This means that 'qualitative differences among employees are equalized or averaged and translated into workplace norms governing behavior and performance' (2000, p. 71). The problem with mainstream diversity is that it simplistically ignores the groups and the cultures, in its focus on ways that individuals are different from each other, and its attempts to make them the same. With this approach the focus is on who is 'different' or 'other' from yourself. Here difference and otherness are *not* seen as a normal part of everyday life, but as something to be got rid of, reduced or glossed over. Mainstream diversity, as a homogenizing approach, aims to make everyone appear as similar as possible. So what is done in the workplace, the play-places and the classrooms is the same everywhere, regardless of who the children and their families are. Following this, how children and staff are judged is in relation to some expected 'average' which is constructed after the dominant culture's values. Here 'competence' and 'quality' are critical issues. What tends to dominate is conformity.

We can see mainstream diversity happening in the higher education institutions of early childhood, with spin-off effects in schools and preschools. Scenario two is an example of it happening with children, whose behavior and performance are governed by normalizations. In scenario three the children as individuals are taught and tested in a special room, as 'others' to normalized Norwegians. Without this practice though, would the 'others' still learn the Norwegian language before going to school? What would happen here if the teacher-carer professionals who are ethnic Norwegians were themselves constructed as 'others', and lacking in the particular skills acquired by migration and multilingualism? What are the national responsibilities of immigrants to become assimilated? Why are there no 'ethnic minority' professionals in this pre-school? Here is a third scenario which might provide some answers.

Scenario Three

>   While she works with the children, the Pakistani Norwegian who is an assistant tells me without my asking, and in our only common language, which is Norwegian, that she only has grunnskole. [Primary schooling, which might have been until she was 16, but she could have been as young as 12. She has had no formal, institutionalized education since then.] So she can't go further, she says. She means she can't do a course, because she doesn't have the schooling prerequisites to get in.
>
>   She has the children in a circle, and is singing Norwegian songs to them. Not one of these children is of Norwegian background. All are here as children whose parents have recently migrated. They need to know the songs for when they go to school next year. The woman assistant wears the salwar kamij [traditional Pakistani women's clothes: matching loose long and

all-covering tunic, loose long trousers and long scarf]. I have my salwar kamij *at home, from when I worked in Bangladesh. I wear the* salwar kamij *to the formal dinner that night.*

In considering this scene it is useful to raise some questions. For example:

- How is the assistant positioned as 'other'?
- How do she and I decide to position ourselves?
- Was my subsequent wearing of the *salwar kamij* a token gesture to make me feel better about my education and wealth?
- Was it to differentiate myself from the others at the dinner?
- Why are these children not learning Pakistani songs?
- What are the effects of the assistant singing in Norwegian while embodying the non-Norwegian?
- How are we to understand the desire for difference and the desire for non-difference happening at the same time?

Some of the problems associated with mainstream diversity are that 'this insistence upon "individual differences" can mean simply bypassing groups' (Bacchi, 2000, p. 71). So my scenario-writing risks an emphasis on the assistant and myself as individuals, without acknowledging the groups and cultures we represent. These include not only ethnicity, race and language but age, socio-economic class, gender, sexuality, religion and ability. Here what appeared as a scenario showing something of 'multiculturalism' becomes by the agency of this pre-school assistant, a focus on her socio-economic positioning in relation to mine. This shows at the level of personal contact, which is where early childhood education always is, and must be, that we *cannot* get rid of our own subjective positioning in relation to 'others'. The subjective is always there, and it is often preferable to the pretence of being objective. This, however, is not about 'individual differences' as some kind of modernist essentialism, but about the complex and changing positionings of the self in postmodernity. A mainstream approach to diversity is not addressing these complexities.

Productive diversity

In contrast to the approach of 'managing diversity' and 'mainstream diversity', a newer 'productive diversity . . . emphasizes the need for . . . members of organizations to change, to learn new languages, for example, and to learn to assess the value of different ways of doing things, instead of insisting that there is only one way' (Bacchi, 2000, p. 68). Here a productive diversity in institutions will be *against* 'shared vision and corporate culture, teams, win–win conflict situations, benchmarking, setting standards, quality management'. Its underlying discourses, says Bacchi, are social justice, understanding and individual differences. Productive diversity then (Cope and Kalantzis, 1997) might move an institution beyond assimilation and the prevailing practice of organizational monoculturalism. For early childhood education this seems preferable to managing diversity.

Cope and Kalantzis' model of 'productive diversity' is based on the concept of culture as cohesion through diversity and focuses on 'the dynamic relationship of differences in the establishment of common ground' (1997, p. 16). Diversity, they say, is a critical issue to be negotiated, with qualitative differences in value systems, ways of thinking and ways of communicating (ibid., p. 144). Further, it 'is not just a matter of hiring a few people of "minority" background . . . Productive Diversity changes everything we do in organizations because it changes the fundamentals of organizational life' (ibid., p. 209).

As with the other scenarios, I put forward the following for various analyses, critiques and deconstructions. Some questions to ask of it and indeed of all the scenarios, are:

- What appears to be happening with diversity as it is differently constructed by differing discourses and the approaches within them?
- What aspects of each scenario may be seen as *managing diversity, mainstream diversity, productive diversity,* and *token diversity*?
- Further, what other discourses of diversity might exist?

Scenario Four

> *It's very very hot. The children are all inside the* barnehage, *in Norway. There is no water play. Outside there is fenced land around the (day care) building but no-one has mown the lawn so it's just long weeds. This is cultural difference. Here there seems to be no pedagogical use of the earth. There could be a gently running hose, shady trees for outdoor play, growing vegetables for children to eat, flowers not from a florist shop. What could these mothers from African countries, Turkey and Pakistan (or any mothers from anywhere else) do with this day care centre's land? Are they unlearning their relationship to seasonal growth? Or just trying to be as Norwegian as possible after their migration? Inside the water-less* barnehage *one of the children is trying on my sunhat. As I don't stop him the hat turns into everybody's dress-up prop, with sideways glances from the mirror to see what I will do. Here they don't wear hats.*

As a *productive diversity*, the scenario might demonstrate a cohesion through diversity because the children and the mothers appear to be acting as one group. Yet this is not a *productive diversity* because what is being produced is more of the same Norwegian monoculture. So diversity, at least at that moment, in my writing of it, has not been negotiated as a critical issue, with changes to practice-as-usual. Here the practices regard the exceptionally hot weather and the uses of the land and the play areas, and the non-use of water. As an Australian living in Norway I find the Norwegian-ness of the curriculum choices foreign. For the children and the mothers from African countries, Turkey and Pakistan, this may be their only experience of a pre-school. So how could they, or others without experience of doing things differently, imagine it otherwise? How could we, without experience of the home nations of the mothers imagine what their 'diversities' might request, desire or construct?

Critical discourses

What has become increasingly evident is that diversity is a political term and may be used in a variety of contexts in order to appease and placate. For example, Chandra Mohanty (1990) wrote of the challenges for education, regarding race and voice. She spoke against 'the analytic categories and political positionings ... that position Third World women as a homogeneous, undifferentiated group leading truncated lives' (p. 180). Calling for reconceptualization she says:

> The challenge of race resides in a fundamental reconceptualization of our categories of analysis so that differences can be historically specified and understood as part of larger political processes and systems. The central issue, then, is not one of merely *acknowledging* difference; rather, the more difficult question concerns the kind of difference that is acknowledged and engaged. Difference seen as a benign variation, for instance, rather than as conflict, struggle, or the threat of disruption, bypasses power as well as history to suggest a harmonious and empty pluralism.
>
> (p. 181)

In addition, Mohanty warns of 'a discourse of "harmony in diversity" '. To make this clear she analyzes 'the workshops on "diversity" for upper level (largely white) administrators' regarding 'the operation and management of discourses of race and difference' (p. 184). She also analyzes 'the women's studies classroom' and says 'the links between these two educational sites lie in the (often active) *creation* of discourses of "difference" '. Speaking of universities, Mohanty says (p. 191), 'the liberal nature of the institution as a whole, is the sort of attitudinal engagement with diversity that encourages an empty cultural pluralism and domesticates the historical agency of Third

World peoples.' Given that Third World peoples would now be called 'from The South' or 'from Developing Countries', the critical question is: Could this also be said about early childhood institutions?

Like Bacchi (2000), Mohanty (1990) also highlights the problems associated with a discourse of individualism, where each person is supposed to be representative of their own cultural group just by being there; and where we say everyone is valuable. Following Mohanty, we need to go beyond the token gestures of setting up special 'units' to support diversity and staffing them with workers from the monoculture. We need to engage in discussion and then to act on the critical issues, so that all voices and bodies are heard, seen and valued. Such action will mean some of us have to move out so that others may move in.

Here LeCompte et al. (2003) suggest that 'difference may more properly be seen as ordinary – or even extraordinarily valuable'. In saying this, they point to political relationships between diversity, divergence and difference, and emphasize the dangers of current normalizations. As with the Australian public service definitions of diversity (Bacchi, 2000), the relativity of privilege makes problematic some of what happens in the name of equity and social justice. Le Compte et al. make such matters critical by linking them to essentialism and stigma.

Early childhood education discourses

This section very briefly presents some key writings within early childhood education. First, we look at text by Viruru (2002) whose research focused on fieldwork with young children in her homeland of India. She says: 'the concept of Relation is that it is opposed to the idea of "essence" . . . To exist in Relation, is to be part of an ever-changing and diversifying process, whereas to be reduced to an essence is to be fixed with permanent attributes' (ibid., p. 37). Here then are no expected categories, no unchangeable values, no core personalities and no predictability. Viruru's diversifying is a process: a verb and not a noun. An 'ever-changing and diversifying process' exists because of our relations with other people, other discourses, other positionings. Here is not a diversity with people as its objects. Rather this is about the subjective and fluid processes of not being the same, and of changing according to who you are with, or where you are at a particular point in time (e.g. Rhedding-Jones, 2001, 2002a, 2002b, 2003a, 2003b). It might be contended from postmodern readings that Viruru aligns herself with critical theorists such as Bhabha (e.g. 1994, 1996) and Mohanty (1990), by resisting the noun 'diversity'.

From professional literature for early childhood practitioners the practical advice about what should be done about *linguistic diversity* is: make sure that families are key participants and learn from them; maintain and develop the languages the children bring from home; make the programs culturally and linguistically relevant; have all children explore other languages; cater for bilingual children and see bilingualism's advantages (after Makin et al., 1995, pp. 69–104). Related strategies for working with *anti-bias* are: plan for change; change policy and procedures; develop the staffs' professionalisms; have more information and communication between families and staff; record keep about children's sense of identity, languages and self esteem (adapted from Khoshkhesal, 1998). Also closely related are *anti-discriminatory* approaches that: shape policies and practices by reviewing and revising organizations; acknowledge discriminations; understand and accept anti-discriminatory principles; change procedures of recruitment, selection and promotion of staff; examine and learn to understand oppression; implement culturally appropriate curricula not monocultural curricula; intervene in children's processes of learning if this is discriminatory. In the UK these approaches specifically target inequality and 'diversity' regarding black children, refugees, children as girls and boys, traveller children (Gypsies), children with disabilities, and children from homosexual families (Brown, 1998, pp. 45–6).

As what-to-do advice for teachers and carers this is focusing on the children and staff themselves, rather than on the management matters of how to manage, how to make diversity productive, how to appear to be catering for it. However, given economic rationalism, such curricula and institutional strategies are constantly at risk. Further, unless we develop critical perspectives around diversity and take up matters of social justice, the term 'diversity' (with its management connotations) could actually displace the anti-bias, anti-discriminatory approaches, the equity work and the critical multicultural work currently being developed and conducted. I am therefore asking people to be conscious of any shift towards a 'new term', and its political implications and possible negative consequences. This is not just about fashion and the comings and goings of 'hot words'. It is about the dangers of being politically manipulated into something you did not know about. In this case, if we follow some of the management approaches, the 'something' could be the future of ethnic and racial minorities in early childhood education.

Conclusion

Throughout this chapter I have posed questions and interrogated practical manifestations of diversity. We now have to ask whether diversity, with all the problems here interrogated, is still a term we want. If we say we are working for a critical diversity, then this would differentiate the reconceptualizing of diversity from that which is non-critical, such as those in the management approaches, and perhaps some of the early childhood education approaches also. The chapter has presented various scenarios and critiqued and problematized the notions of diversity to show that, from critical perspectives, diversity is not a word to be adopted and used without thought. Seen as a critical issue, diversity is 'loaded' with complexities, innuendoes and omissions. Thus, I have tried to offer, via the scenarios from practice with children, critical insights on the problematization of difference and inclusion: of integration, assimilation and transformation of cultures, institutions and people. What is evident is that we need to make problematic our definitions of difference in relation to diversity. This means looking critically at what is happening as practice in the name of 'diversity', so that difference becomes usual, and what becomes problematic is normalization. Further, we need to ask critical questions about socio-economic diversity, and the structural inequities that cause it. For example, we might:

- make diversity plural, as *diversities*;
- see that culture is not fixed;
- not categorize people into homogenous groupings;
- focus on equity and social justice in our everyday actions and words;
- prepare both children and adults to become change agents via challenging stereotypes and norms of behavior;
- raise our own awareness of what middle-class *whiteness* entails;
- be wary of management discourses and programs and their applicability to early childhood education;
- critique and transform the relations of power in early childhood settings.

Through these actions we might then facilitate and construct *critical diversities*.

References

Bacchi, C. (2000) The seesaw effect: down goes affirmative action, up comes workplace diversity, *Journal of Interdisciplinary Gender Studies*, 5(2): 64–83.

Bhabha, H. (1994) *The Location of Culture*. London and New York: Routledge.

Bhabha, H. (1996) Culture's in-between, in S. Hall and P. Du Gay (eds) *Questions of Cultural Identities*. London: Sage.

Brown, B. (1998) *Unlearning Discrimination in the Early Years*. London: Trentham Books.

Cope, B. and Kalantzis, M. (1997) *Productive Diversity: A New, Australian Model for Work and Management*. Annandale, NSW: Pluto Press.

Creaser, B. and Dau, E. (1996) *The Anti-Bias Approach in Early Childhood*. Woden: Australian Early Childhood Association, Harper Education, Australia.

Derman-Sparkes, L. and the ABC Task Force (1991) *The Anti-Bias Curriculum: Tools for Empowering Young Children*. Washington DC: National Association for Early Years Curriculum.

Grieshaber, S. and Cannella, G.S. (eds) (2001) *Embracing Identities in Early Childhood Education: Diversity and Possibilities*. New York: Teachers College Press.

Khoshkhesal, V. (1998) *Realising the Potential: Cultural and Linguistic Diversity in Family Day Care*. Sydney: Lady Gowrie Child Centre.

Laubscher, L. and Powell, S. (2003) Skinning the drum: teaching about diversity as 'other', *Harvard Educational Review*, 73(2): 203–24.

LeCompte, M., Klingner, J. and Campbell, S. (2003) Editorial call for papers on theme issues, *Review of Educational Research*, 73(4): iii–iv.

Lo Bianco, J. (2000) Multiliteracies and multilingualism, in B. Cope and M. Kalantzis (eds) *Multiliteracies: Literacy Learning and the Design of Social Futures*. London and New York: Routledge.

Makin, L., Campbell, J. and Jones Diaz, C. (1995) *One Childhood, Many Languages: Guidelines for Early Childhood Education in Australia*, Pymble, NSW: Harper Educational.

May, S. (ed.) (1999) *Critical Multiculturalism: Rethinking Multicultural and Anti-Racist Education*. London: Falmer Press.

Mohanty, C.T. (1990) On race and voice: challenges for liberal education in the 1990s, *Cultural Critique*, Winter 1989–1990: 179–208.

Rhedding-Jones, J. (2001) Shifting ethnicities: 'native informants' and other theories from/for early childhood education, *Contemporary Issues in Early Childhood*, 2(2): 135–56.

Rhedding-Jones, J. (2002a) An undoing of documents and other texts: towards a critical multicultural early childhood education, *Contemporary Issues in Early Childhood*, 3(1): 90–116.

Rhedding-Jones, J. (2002b) Doing diversity: dealing with complexity, difference and multiplicity in practice, theory and research methodology. Invited plenary presented at the International Education Symposium, 'Quality, Culture and Diversity in Education', Oslo University College, Norway, 7 May.

Rhedding-Jones, J. (2003a) Feminist methodologies and research for early childhood literacies, in N. Hall, J. Larson and J. Marsh (eds) *Handbook of Early Childhood Literacy* (pp. 399–410). London: Sage.

Rhedding-Jones, J. (2003b) Questioning play and work, early childhood and pedagogy, in D. Lytle, *Play and Educational Theory and Practice* (pp. 243–54). Westport, CT: Praeger.

Siraj-Blatchford, I. and Clarke, P. (1998) *Supporting Identity, Diversity and Language in the Early Years*. Philadelphia, PA: Open University Press.

Viruru, R. (2002) Colonized through language: the case of early childhood education, *Contemporary Issues in Early Childhood*, 2(1): 31–47.

10 Secret children's business

Resisting and redefining access to learning in the early childhood classroom

Sheralyn Campbell

The political ideals of socially-just early childhood teaching

Socially-just teaching in Australia emerged from historical ideals of reforming disadvantaged children and transforming them into model citizens (Brennan, 1998). Like the progressive education movement in the United States, early childhood education in Australia was committed to reconstructing and improving society. Over more than a century early Australian reformist teaching has blended with liberal feminist ideals, anti-discriminatory practices and multicultural government policies.

MacNaughton and Williams (1998, pp. 220–1) have illustrated that in Australia today most early childhood teaching approaches may be identified within one of five typologies. Each approach makes claims to similar ideals of social equity and cultural inclusion. However, these five approaches differ as they move from simple or tokenistic representations of diversity and difference, to political engagement with the social, cultural and political milieu of the early childhood classroom. The latter can be characterized as an anti-discriminatory approach to teaching.

An anti-discriminatory approach to early childhood teaching attempts to confront and change the politics of human relationships, and the institutionally supported inequities in early childhood knowledge and practices. It is committed to an ethos which ensures that every child has access to learning and relationships. These approaches are not new (see Derman-Sparks and The ABC Taskforce, 1989; Hopson, 1990; Stonehouse, 1991; Dau, 2001). However, after more than a decade of equity activism it would seem that a child's 'access' to learning and relationships remains a site of political struggle in many early childhood classrooms.

For example, in 1998 I recorded this conversation in an early childhood classroom as a group of boys began using construction materials:

1. Henry (3) and Richard (3.5) to Mick (5): You can't play with the Mobilo!!
2. Anne (teacher): Why can't Mick play?
3. Richard: Cos he doesn't know how to do it.
4. Anne: Well, you could show him how.

(98FN: 12.5)

These words show how a child's access to play with their peers and to particular types of learning is often the subject of negotiation and struggle. In moments like these children use claims of 'differences' to privilege some understandings of what is 'normal', 'necessary' or 'desirable', and not others. In effect, children are saying 's/he is not like me' and therefore should not be here. These claims underpin and authorize a range of techniques that children then use to include and exclude others in learning and relationships. They are the subject of this discussion about what anti-discriminatory approaches to teaching should be targeting, and how these approaches can move beyond simplistic responses to inequities. They impel teachers like me to ask 'What makes it possible for children like Mick to be included in play with others?'

Many anti-discriminatory approaches to situations like these in early childhood classrooms (e.g. Derman-Sparks, 1989) are permeated by developmental constructions of the child. These constructions at times act to unintentionally relegate politics between children and between teachers and children to the remoteness of a child's immaturity or cognitive and social skills (see Campbell, 1999, 2001). They act to explain Richard's and Henry's exclusion of Mick as natural or normal for any child who is not yet able to play co-operatively. Using these approaches the easy answer to Mick's inclusion lies with responses like the one given here by Anne. Teachers can change exclusion by helping children like Richard and Henry to scaffold learning for Mick. These two boys could use their expert knowledge to show Mick how to build. The issues that teachers address in responses like these are differences in children's cognitive, physical, social and cultural knowledge, skills and abilities. When teachers respond to developmental differences, they do not necessary engage with the sexist, racist, and classist political effects invoked in and by children's words and actions.

However, when the complexities of 'race', class and gender are layered over Mick's attempt to use Mobilo, there are another set of questions that come into focus. These questions attend to the productive effects and differences of how power is exercised between and for people in such moments.

Layering politics over play

Mick was a child who, as a Pacific Islander and migrant to Australia, spoke English as a second language. Mick's parents were both working and studying and struggled to make ends meet. Richard's and Henry's first language and cultural histories were located in middle-class White Australia. These additional layers of detail provoked me to ask 'What were the politics of how Mick could access learning with Richard and Henry?' Specifically,

- What did it mean for Mick, Richard, or Henry and for Anne when a Western form of commodity knowledge (i.e. using Mobilo) was valued and prioritized as the means by which Mick could be included in learning and relationships? Who was included or excluded by this prioritizing, and how?
- What did it mean when Richard and Henry were elevated to the positions of 'teachers' of Mick, and designated as the gatekeepers of when and how he could be included as a boy using the construction materials? Who was privileged and marginalized by this positioning, and how?

These questions displace the developmental naturalness and normalcy of exclusions by entangling the children, their learning and their teacher in a web of political effects. These effects are produced and contested in and by what people think, feel, say and do in an early childhood classroom.

The contested terrain

Michel Foucault identified the contested terrain of human life as the site where change is possible because it is where competing forces of power and knowledge are at work in the struggles between people. He took a unique view of power as a productive rather than oppressive force that could not be possessed or owned by any individual. Rather, he saw relations of power-knowledge exercised in and through a web of effects that are produced discursively between people (Foucault, 1994). In his genealogies of mental illness, prisons and sexuality, he showed how people are constituted as subjects of competing historical discourses that have institutional and personal support. As subjects of discourses, people are also entangled in and by the production and exercise of relations of power-knowledge with many different effects. The exercise of these relations of power and knowledge govern how it is possible to be a person in the social world, making some ways more desirable and pleasurable than others. This was shown in the moment between Anne, Richard, Henry and Mick when a middle-class White Australian way of being a boy was privileged over other possibilities.

Foucault believed that wherever power is discursively exercised, there are also possibilities for resistance to the authorizing knowledges. These are the places where change is possible. For example, in the Mobilo scenario, Anne's words were an attempt to contest and resist how some boys used Mick's lack of skills and knowledge to justify excluding him from play. However, resistance in itself does not guarantee that changes will alter the effects of how relations of power-knowledge circulate. As Usher and Edwards have cautioned: 'Changing practices do not . . . do away with power but displace and reconfigure it in different ways. These reconfigurations and displacements cannot simply be assumed to be more humane or democratic' (1994, p. 91). Their caution invokes the question:

> Would Anne have changed the 'racist' politics of Mick's exclusion simply by ensuring that the three boys all used the construction materials, or would 'racist' politics have continued in another form?

This question stands as a testament to the necessity of ongoing scepticism in anti-discriminatory teaching. It suggests that the work of anti-discriminatory teaching in the early childhood classroom will never be 'done'. Teachers must always be vigilant for the effects of how relations of power-knowledge are produced, exercised and resisted between people.

In the next section of this chapter I want to show how one group of children 'resisted' the attempts of their teachers to ensure that every child had equal access to learning. I will also show how seeking out these moments of 'resistance' and overlaying them with the politics of gender enabled these teachers to glimpse the oppositional secret business in which children were engaged. This secret business involved children in actively displacing and reconfiguring the teacher's discourse of 'equal access to learning' with a discourse of gendered separations.

The pointers to how these relations of power-knowledge were produced, exercised and resisted lay in the daily discursive struggles between teachers and children, and between children.

Teaching for equity

> Bella (3 years) to [Anne] her teacher: . . . *If people say I can't play with them, . . . I'll just say to them it's for everybody*. (Campbell, 2001, p. 123)

This fragment of conversation was recorded in 1998 when I worked in Spider Room (the 3–5 years room) of an inner urban early childhood classroom with three early childhood teachers, Anne, Leyla and Meg.

We had been working together to reflect on what it meant to understand and use an anti-discriminatory approach to teaching. We called our approach *socially-just* teaching. For us, socially-just teaching was often concerned with ensuring that every child had access to learning. This meant teaching with children in ways that guaranteed any child could choose and use the spaces, the learning experiences and the relationships in the classroom.

When we heard Bella's words we initially felt that we had succeeded in creating equal access to learning for the children in Spider Room. Bella's words confirmed for us that what we said and did as teachers had enabled her to exercise her power to choose to play anywhere, and also to challenge anyone who said that she couldn't. In our classroom, we believed that everyone had access to learning regardless of gender, 'race' or class.

Teaching practices

Anne, Meg and Leyla used three key understandings and practices to support equal access to learning for all children. These were:

- equal rights to a fair share;
- signposting a fair share;
- empowering children to claim a fair share.

Equal rights to a fair share

In Spider Room, the teachers believed that everyone was entitled to a fair share of resources, experiences and learning opportunities. However, for the teachers a fair share did not always mean an 'equal' share. Like many of the government policies that underpin how public funds are distributed, the teachers had instituted a system of distributing each child's share of resources using a needs-based model of sharing and turn-taking.

Their formal 'turn-taking' system enabled each child to be allocated a turn in the sequence of their request, but a child's share (sometimes equated with how long they played at an experience) was a more fluid affair.

The teachers gave some children more time at an experience, or more materials, than others. This was because the teachers viewed children as individuals who could and should be placed at different points of a developmental continuum. The differences between children meant that some needed, and were given, a longer turn because they started behind others in individual skill level, experience or development. Likewise some children were given more materials because of the complexity of their thinking, skills and creative representations. The effect of how teachers worked to support each child's access to learning was to distribute children across the share and turn-taking system based on differences in their knowledge, skills, interests and abilities.

Signposting a fair share

The classroom spaces also held signposts to guide children in interpreting the system of sharing and turn-taking. These signposts indicated to children how resources should be shared using a one-to-one correspondence between people and items. For example, four chairs at the drawing table meant that four people could work together; two strings at the bead threading cushions meant that two people could work together; a symbol of three people on the wall meant that three people could work in the home corner and so on. Most children indicated that they read and used these signposts independently of the need for teachers to intervene. The signposts were designed to enable children to be self-governing within the system of sharing and turn-taking. Chris (4) showed what this looked like with Illana (4) and Rowena (3):

1. Chris: (looked around the room) We need a three people game that we can all fit!
2. Illana and Rowena: Yeah!

They moved to the dramatic play area with a symbol of four people on the wall (Campbell, 2001, p. 118).

(98FN: 21.5)

Empowering children to claim a fair share

Although the environment held clear signposts to children about how to share or take a turn, the teachers were also proactive in supporting a child's rights to choose to play anywhere. In particular, they worked hard to empower each child with the knowledge, skills and abilities that would enable her or him to use the system of turns and claim access to her or his choice of play.

The teachers each observed, listened to and intervened in children's learning to ensure that everyone could choose to access learning experiences. Their interventions took a range of forms that included:

- restating a formal written or informal memorized list of turns;
- helping a child to understand or invoke the system of turns;
- challenging a child who was being unfair to others within the system of turns.

For example, when Illana (4) wouldn't share the dolls and dolls house with Kaarin (4), Meg intervened. She gave Kaarin some words to use with Illana so that she could negotiate her share of the resources within the system of turns:

241. Meg: OK. Well, you need to ask her again and ask her to listen to you. And if she's not ready and not quite finished playing the game,

> you need to ask her if it is your turn when she finishes . . . you need to make sure she's listening this time. (Campbell, 2001, p. 120)

In this way Meg believed that she had mediated an entry point to the system of turns for Kaarin. She felt that Kaarin could use this entry point in order to assert her choice of and rights to learning with Illana.

Power relations and resistance at work

As we looked for the productive effects of relations of power-knowledge in the system of sharing and turn-taking, we found that the children used a range of techniques of resistance to our discourse of social justice. They actively engaged in the 'secret business' of inscribing gendered differences across the system of sharing and turn-taking.

The children used three techniques for resisting the system of sharing and turn-taking. These were:

- inserting private commodity ownership;
- colonizing and regulating spaces;
- enlisting a teacher's political activism.

Inserting private commodity ownership

The classroom domain was a realm of publicly owned resources in which boys or girls had equal claim to a turn or share. However, on many occasions children showed how private commodity ownership could be used as a technique of resistance to the teachers' intent of gender equity.

Leyla recalled one such moment:

65. Leyla: Penny and Olga had nail polish and said Andrew couldn't have any because he was a boy. When I talked about the fact that boys could wear nail polish, suddenly there wasn't enough nail polish [to share], so he couldn't have [a turn] anyway (Campbell, 2001, p. 124).
(98AT15: 65)

While Leyla had intended that her challenge of the two girls would make gender invisible and thus include Andrew, the two girls had successfully negotiated and reconfigured Leyla's discursive shift. Without citing gender, they continued to exclude Andrew from the nail polish by invoking the untouchable domain of private commodity ownership. However, the effects of their exclusion remained gendered. Boys were unable to use nail polish with girls.

Colonizing and regulating spaces

While the signposts in the room were designed to enable boys and girls to choose to have a turn anywhere, children were able to insert a gendered social order by colonizing and regulating the spaces. For example, on one occasion at the dough table the teachers' signposts had indicated that two people could play. There were two chairs with two sets of cutters. Alison (3) stood watching Eric (3) and Henry (3). The two boys read Alison's silent observation as a possible entrance to their play.

> 2. Eric (looking at Alison): There's no room!
> 3. Henry looked up and smiled at Eric. Their eyes met.
> 4. Henry (still smiling broadly looked at Alison): Nooo.
> 5. Eric (smiled widely and said sarcastically): Soooorrry!
> Alison moved away silently and without protest (Campbell, 2001, p. 178).
>
> (98AT29: 2)

On many occasions, these colonizations of the spaces designed for everyone enabled children not only to enact gendered exclusions but also to regulate the sorts of play that was undertaken within these gendered spaces. For example, Kaarin and Fiona used a two-person space to ensure that only they had access to Fiona's Barbie doll. However, Fiona showed how remaining a girl in that space depended on practicing gender in a particular way:

> 29. Kaarin tipped Barbie upside down so her dress covered her face and her undies were revealed, then split her legs wide. Talking in a girlie high-pitched voice: *Hello Mister* (she giggled).
> 30. Fiona: Don't do that! We're not allowed to do that, Kaarin. Don't do that upside down 'cos it will hurt her . . .
> 31. Fiona took back her Barbie.
> However, later Fiona returned a Barbie to Kaarin and instructed her in how they could create Barbie's sexuality (Campbell, 2001, p. 131).
>
> (98AT1: 29)

While Kaarin's gender enabled her to access the space of Barbie play, Fiona regulated how she played as a girl to ensure that she got it 'right'.

Enlisting a teacher's political activism

On many occasions the children's resistance to social justice in the classroom depended on enlisting a teacher's proactive responses to unfairness. For example, Sally and Bella had made the block space into hairdressing salon for two people. They had been there for some time when Don and Henry began bumping the divider, growling and generally making implicit threats that indicated they were about to invade the space colonized by the girls.

> 60. Bella: We want to be on our own, don't we, Sally?
> 61. Don and Henry's growls became louder and the dividing partition began to shake as they bumped it.
> 62. Bella's voice raised with anxiety: *No coming in boys.*
> 63. Meg heard her and redirected the boys elsewhere, noting that the construction was 'just for two people'. The boys moved off.
> 64. Henry: Stupid girls.
> 65. Don: I know. (Campbell, 2001, p. 125)

> (98AT27+28: 60)

On this occasion, Meg had intended that her redirection would help the boys to understand and use the system of sharing and turn-taking fairly. However, instead her voice was enlisted by the girls and continued the separations between boys and girls. Meg's words and actions supported Bella's and Sally's continued practices of having a 'no boy' space. Meg's words and actions likewise confirmed for Don and Henry that the world is a gendered place.

The secret business of children

As we looked through the gendered lens of how children resisted our discourse of equal access to learning, it became clear that there were a set of rules that children used to govern play and relationships. For girls, this meant:

- not playing with boys;
- having and using knowledge of popular Western culture;
- owning and regulating the use of desirable commodities;
- investing in and sharing imaginings about heterosexual desires and pleasures;
- colonizing and regulating spaces.

Similarly, for boys, this meant:

- not playing with girls;
- having knowledge about building with Western construction commodities;
- knowing how to use bodies to invade spaces and dislocate girls;
- recognizing girls as undesirable;
- sharing imaginings about the desires and pleasures of physical power.

> (Campbell, 2001, p. 150)

When we sought out children's resistances to our teaching we found a contested terrain where children were engaged in the 'secret business' of reinstating their own gendered social order with sexist, heterosexist, classist and 'racist' effects. We saw how our efforts did not guarantee change to the politics of the classroom. Rather we watched as our discourse of social justice was displaced and reconfigured by how children practiced their gender. On one occasion Anne described this:

> Anne: [We had a meeting with the children to discuss boys and girls excluding each other from play experiences] . . . when we finished the meeting we disbursed them . . . They all actually went straight back to the same groups that we'd been talking about . . . excluding the boys from play . . . the boys went off into little groups [too].
> (Campbell, 2001, p. 166)

Attending to relations of power-knowledge in the classroom involves the teacher in necessarily asking questions about the productive and competing effects of discourses in the classroom. Specifically, it involves layering dimensions of gender, 'race' and class across the surface of interactions between people in order to ask questions about 'what else is going on here?' This offers the teacher another set of possibilities or 'stories' about how socially-just teaching is working, and how it is being displaced and reconfigured in and through resistances. For example, if I ask questions about 'what else might be happening' when Meg intervened on behalf of the girls who were playing in the block-hairdressing salon, there are a range of other stories to be told. These stories draw on the other discourses that may have displaced and reconfigured Meg's teaching for social justice. For example, Meg's words and actions may have supported:

- differences in the ways in which boys and girls believed and imagined blocks could and should be used, and with whom. Are there parallels here with documented differences in how boys and girls approach maths and science?
- discussions about how women and girls could form alliances that disrupt violent practices and intimidation perpetrated by men. This leads to the question: are there parallels here with feminist principles and practices?

These possibilities show the productive effects of relations of power-knowledge. In particular, they show how some configurations like the alliance between women and girls against masculine hegemony are politically desirable. Other configurations like the limitations in what it is possible for boys and girls to imagine in block play are less desirable.

Possibilities?

I have shown here how children can displace and reconfigure an anti-discriminatory discourse in order to engage in their own secret and political business. In the process, I have also shown that we as teachers were co-opted into supporting how children re-established their gendered social order. However, I do not wish to infer that this means there is no possibility for change. Instead, I hope it provokes questions about where we go from here in our anti-discriminatory teaching.

In my current work as a teacher with young children I am finding many opportunities for taking up this challenge. I am teaching in a small rural child care centre in Australia. Our town of 3,300 people faces many issues that include high unemployment, poverty, the impact of environmental sustainability on key industries like logging and fishing, drought, diverse family configurations and reconciliation with our indigenous community.

I have worked in this context for 12 months. The teachers, families and children that I work with have become central to how I engage in the complex business of changing what it means for me to teach for social justice. This has meant seeking the 'secret' and political stories that are produced in and by my own teaching within the early childhood classroom. I began this process in four ways. First, I sought out the strategies and tactics that children used to include and exclude each other from play. Second, I began to overlay these inclusions and exclusions with the different and political stories that they produced for me. Third, I reflected with my co-teachers about how we saw these strategies, tactics and stories in our own lives and in our teaching. Finally, I returned to the children with questions about the stories that my overlays and shared reflections had produced.

Seeking inclusion and exclusion

When children and teachers are understood as subjects of discourse, it is possible to see that we are each at various times different and contradictory people. As we position and are positioned within and through different discourses, we also are engaged in invoking a set of 'rules' or boundaries for what it is possible to think, feel, say and do as a subject. The struggles between children, in particular, the struggles which draw on or which attempt to disrupt these 'rules' or boundaries, have become personal pointers for me about how relations of power-knowledge are at work.

When I began to seek inclusion and exclusion between and for children I used categories that Gore (1998) had appropriated from Foucault's work in which the 'rules' or boundaries of discourses were invoked to effect or disrupt subjectivity. These were:

> *Surveillance*: expecting to be (or being) closely observed and supervised.
> *Normalisation*: comparing, invoking, requiring, or conforming to a standard.
> *Exclusion*: tracing the limits of what is understood to be undesirable differences.
> *Classification*: differentiating between groups or individuals.
> *Distribution*: arranging, isolating, separating, and ranking individuals.
> *Individualisation*: assigning individual specificity.
> *Totalisation*: assigning collective characters.
> *Regulation*: controlling by or invoking rules, restrictions, sanctions, rewards, punishments.
>
> (Gore, 1998, pp. 234–44)

Additionally, de Certeau's (1988) work provides some interesting paths for further exploration of these ideas. However, these categories have helped me to locate discursive struggles between children, and between teachers and children. At times these struggles involved moments that seemed insignificant at the time, but in later reflections showed a different set of possibilities or stories. For example, Tina and Luke were playing together at the bubble blowing. For some time I had been hoping that Tina would step outside of her good girl persona and take a 'ride on the wild side' with other children. I had been structuring some opportunities for Tina to 'break out' with boys like Luke. Luke was at times able to cross traditional gender boundaries and so offered interesting possibilities for how Tina explored other girlhoods.

It was late afternoon. Luke and Tina were giggling loudly as the bubbles overflowed their containers and threatened to drip onto the floor. Suddenly they were surrounded by a small group of children who variously watched and gave advice:

> George: Sheralyn, the bubbles are spilling on the floor! *[Surveillance, Regulation]*
> Annie (scornfully): Tina, that's not how you do it. You have to keep them in. *[Normalization]*
> Sabina: You've got paint on your dress now [Tina]! *[Regulation, Exclusion]*
> Pauli: Lukie, you made a big one. Its the biggest one I ever seen. Its bigger than the whole world. [laughing] Its gunna go right over the edge. [Tina] You can't do big ones like Lukie. Yours are just on the table. *[Classification, Distribution]*

Finally, I intervened. I was busy helping children who had rested to tie up shoe laces but I glanced up in response to George's words of warning to me about the bubbles going onto the floor. I reminded Tina to keep the bubbles on the table in the interests of safety. I let her know that if they went on the floor they would make it slippery *[Surveillance, Regulation]*.

As I used Gore's categories later to reflect on what had happened I met a story of power at work. George's words of warning to me had made me first watch and then tell Tina she needed to do 'it' differently. Annie and Sabina had used words that told Tina she was getting 'it' wrong and instructed her in how to get 'it' right. Paul ensured that Tina and Luke knew there were important contrasts in how they were doing 'it'. So what was the 'it' that they were doing. Was 'it' bubble blowing, or something else?

Overlaying stories of gender, 'race' and class

I found myself overlaying my story of how children should use bubbles safely, with other stories. I asked how had gender, race and class been invoked in and by the categories that children had used with Luke and Tina? For example:

- Were there stories that could be told of *classism* when Annie said to Tina 'That's not how you do it. You have to keep them in'. Annie prided herself on her knowledge of many Western commodities that Tina's family could not afford.
- Were there stories of *sexism* in Pauli's claims that Luke could blow bigger and better bubbles than Tina? Pauli rarely played with girls but often attempted to join play with other boys by demonstrating his physical prowess.
- Were there stories of *gender* and *race* in Sabina's concerns about how Tina was getting paint on her dress? Sabina often noticed and commented on the dress of girls who had different cultural histories to her own.

Reflecting on these strategies and stories

I returned to this moment in a discussion with my co-teachers. Specifically, I asked why I had cautioned Tina and not Luke about getting the bubble mix onto the floor. How could my concerns about 'safety' be displaced and reconfigured with a competing and gendered discourse that circulated in our classroom. Specifically, a discourse in which girls were feminized in ways that meant:

- they needed to play gently and be good;
- they needed to perform their femininity in some ways and not others;
- they were less skilful in the traditional domains of masculine play;
- their relationships with boys were based on gendered differences.

Together the teachers and I reflected on examples from our lives and from our teaching of a social order that depended on gendered differences like these. Some of the examples that we found included:

> Christine: (teacher) I grew up on a farm. I remember when I was screen cementing and a customer mistook me for a man. He was horrified with my father when he realized I was a woman. It wasn't women's work.
>
> Allan (4): [Boys] can play with Power Rangers and shooting games on the computer. Boys can play with girls. You play nicely when you play with girls.
>
> Anna (4, white Australian) to a Koori girl: If you don't get off the seesaw, I'll get my brothers to bash you up when they come in.
>
> (Seckold and Campbell, 2003, p. 15)

Returning to the children

These reflections helped my co-teachers to return with me to the children and ask questions about the issues provoked by our overlay of stories. These are two examples of how we have done this:

> Example 1
> I read the story of the *Paper Bag Princess* to the children. In the story princess Elizabeth has her castle destroyed and her prince abducted by a dragon. She outwits the dragon and rescues her prince dressed only in a paper bag. However, she chooses not to marry the prince when, despite her bravery, cleverness and resourcefulness he rejects her because she no longer looks like a real princess.
>
> When the children discussed the story, they confirmed that Elizabeth was wrong when she chose not to dress like a princess. They drew on classist and sexist 'rules' about relationships between men and women and supported the prince's rejection of Elizabeth. They assured me that how you dress matters in the world of being included in play.
>
> Example 2
> I used my Persona doll called Suzannah to recreate the story of exclusion that happened between the two girls on the seesaw. I asked questions about what Anna had said and how a person would feel if they were treated like that. I asked questions about how Suzannah, her friends and her teachers could respond to situations like this in the future.
>
> The children told me the things that they knew were part of my

discourse. They said Suzannah could say she didn't like what had been said. They told me that Suzannah could ask a teacher for help. They told me that everyone could just be friends.

In their responses the children showed me that they know there are different ways for men and women, boys and girls to work together in the social world. However, the reality of how discursive politics operate in their daily lives together mean that I am sceptical about their responses. I have seen how they resist, displace and reconfigure my discourse of social justice and how I am unconsciously also a conspirator in maintaining gendered, 'racialized' and classist separations. These separations mean that for children like Luke and Tina, or Mick, Henry and Don, access to learning remains contested and tenuous.

Continuing to teach for social justice

Teaching for social justice is an ongoing battle. Each teacher will necessarily find their own way of continuing the discursive struggle to change how children are able to access learning. For me the ongoing process involves:

- tracing how relations of power-knowledge are exercised and resisted at the site of the individual;
- troubling these relations of power-knowledge by overlaying them with the politics of gender, 'race' and class in ways that produce different stories about what is happening in my classroom;
- reconstructing these relations of power-knowledge with others by continuing to imagine, invoke and resist competing discourses of how we can practise our lives together.

To these ends, I have a set of questions that I find helpful in continuing to work for social justice. These are directed at the contested terrains in my classroom. Specifically, I ask:

- What is said, done and struggled over between people?
- How can these words and actions be read through the categories that point to relations of power-knowledge at work?
- How do others understand what is said, done and struggled over?
- What are the stories of gender, 'race' and class that can be told in and through these discursive struggles?
- In whose interests does each story work?
- How can I disrupt and change what is happening at both personal and institutional sites so that my classroom is more socially just?

In summary, this chapter has presented some examples of how power is discursively produced and exercised in early childhood classrooms. The examples show the ways in which children and teachers are entangled in, and by, the 'secret business' of constituting, displacing and reconfiguring the 'rules' and boundaries for access to learning. The examples map how competing understandings of access to learning include some children in play, and exclude others. In addition, this chapter offers teachers some strategies for engaging with (and in) moments of resistance to these 'rules and boundaries'. The strategies that are discussed lay siege to the politics of access to learning. They offer ways to target and contest the discourses that govern what each person can imagine, desire, say and do to be included in learning and relationships in the early childhood classroom.

Further reading

The following titles offer ideas for re-constructing socially just teaching in early childhood.

Brown, B. (2001) *Combating Discrimination: Persona Dolls in Action*. Stoke on Trent, Staffordshire: Trentham Books Ltd.

Campbell, S. and Smith, K. (2001) Equity observation and images of fairness in childhood, in S. Grieshaber and G.S. Cannella (eds) *Embracing Identities in Early Childhood Education: Diversity and Possibilities* (pp. 89–102). New York: Teachers College Press.

Centre for Equity and Innovation in Early Childhood (CEIEC) (2002) *Equity Adventures in Early Childhood* (CD-ROM). Melbourne: The University of Melbourne, CEIEC.

MacNaughton, G. (2003) Eclipsing voice in research with young children. *Australian Journal of Early Childhood*, 28(1): 36–42.

References

Brennan, D. (1998) *The Politics of Australian Child Care: Philanthropy to Feminism and Beyond*. Cambridge: Cambridge University Press.

Campbell, S. (1999) Making the political pedagogical in early childhood education, *Australian Journal of Early Childhood*, 24(4): 21–6.

Campbell, S. (2001) The definition and description of a social justice disposition in young children. Unpublished PhD thesis, the University of Melbourne.

Dau, E. (2001) *The Anti-Bias Approach in Early Childhood*. 2nd edn. French's Forest, NSW: Longman.

De Certeau, M. (1988) *The Practice of Everyday Life*. Berkeley and Los Angeles, CA: University of California Press.

Derman-Sparks, L. and The ABC Taskforce (1989) *Anti-Bias Curriculum: Tools for Empowering Young Children.* Washington, DC: National Association for Education of Young Children.

Foucault, M. (1994) Truth and power, in J. D. Faubion (ed.) *Power: Essential Works of Foucault 1954–1984* (pp. 111–33). London: Penguin.

Gore, J. (1998) Disciplining bodies: on the continuity of power relations in pedagogy, in T.S. Popkewitz and M. Brennan (eds) *Foucault's Challenge: Discourse, Knowledge and Power in Education* (pp. 231–54). New York: Teachers College Press.

Hopson, E. (1990) *Valuing Diversity: Implementing a Cross Cultural, Anti-Bias Approach in Early Childhood Programs.* Sydney: Lady Gowrie Child Centre.

MacNaughton, G. and Williams, G. (1998) *Techniques for Teaching Young Children: Choices in Theory and Practice.* South Melbourne: Addison-Wesley Longman.

Munsch, R.N. and Martchenko, M. (1980) *The Paper Bag Princess.* Toronto: Annick Press Ltd.

Seckold, C. and Campbell, S. (2003) Everybody helps on the farm: gender issues in rural early childhood settings, *Everychild*, 9(3): 14–16.

Stonehouse, A. (1991) Opening the Doors: Child Care in a Multicultural Society. Watson, ACT: AECA.

Usher, R. and Edwards, R. (1994) *Postmodernism and Education.* London: Routledge.

11 'Civilization of replicas'[1]
Disrupting multicultural pretend play props

Richard Johnson

Disneyland satisfies ... several of the deepest needs in contemporary culture that are otherwise not satisfied: the need for order, for mastery, for safety, and for adventure. What is it like to be in Disneyland? We walk down ordered paths and streets, carefully landscaped and scaled to give us a sense of variety and discovery. Architectural focal points capture our gaze as we move, pulling us from place to place. We travel passively through landscapes, on water, on rails, on wheels, surveying the whole of the contained spaces with a sense of mastery, a sense of the overall coherence of the total world.

(Orvell, 1995)

Introduction

In her visual cultural work Marianne Hirsch (1994) suggests that family pictures 'produce and reproduce dominant ideologies' and typically we enter that viewing of the family picture, like that diverse family in Figure 11.1, expecting to 'perceive what we are prepared to perceive' (ibid., p. 109). Hirsch's theoretical considerations reverberate strongly with my own particular personal and professional concerns as I consider the view (Grimshaw, 2001), what I see of the early childhood 'family picture' as one in which we also quite readily and without assumption 'perceive what we are prepared to perceive' – fixed, stable and happy, static and monolithic ideas we best know and have come to believe and be comfortable with in their various representation(s). In sharp contrast to this stance Hirsch (1994) then suggests that, instead,

> we consider how the camera and the image might, in the words of Jo Spence, be useful for its 'unfixing' rather than its 'fixing' qualities ... Here we must begin to question photographs, asking not what we think they show us ... but what they don't (can't) show us.
>
> (p. 110)

Figure 11.1   A family of puppets.

This *unfixing*, this *questioning* and searching for what they (i.e. images) don't/ can't show us is a 'return to the etymological roots of theoria – defined as an act of viewing, contemplation, consideration, insight' (Hirsch, 1994, p. 110), theory defined in relation to visuality. This type of theorizing is fundamentally active. For me, it is an attempt to move outside of the normative familial practices in the early education field, those familial practices upon which I've been 'raised' and raised myself as a child development undergraduate, and an early childhood education advanced graduate student. In this active, participatory movement I've been attempting to more dynamically call things into question (Johnson, 2001, 2003a) – things that once seemed stable, appeared to be fixed, looked as if they were normal and typical – but upon further viewing/ theorizing were seen to be strangely unfixed and unfamiliar. Returning to Hirsch's discussion of family pictures then, she offers, 'What I see when I look at my family pictures is not what you see when you look at them: only my look is affiliative, only my look enters and extends the network of looks and gazes that have constructed the image in the first place' (1994, p. 116).

In the movement, the shift away from the familial, the comfortable and the static, our looking, our interactive stance with and between an image 'suggests and evokes a story, a narrative continuity, an illusion of depth . . . they teach us how we look at images and how we invest them with story and with meaning' (ibid., p. 124). In this more critical perspective, in this opening up – our looking/our theorizing 'refuse[s] to participate in the narrative frameworks with which we are comfortable and instead insist on existing in the space of their production' (ibid., p. 124). Here we actively refuse to be 'sutured into the image' (ibid., p. 119) of tradition, suturing which typically demands that we comfortably and neatly fit, in a fixed and static manner. bell hooks refers to this refusal, to this positioning as 'oppositional looks' or 'a process in which the gaze functions as a site of resistance' (Bloom, 1999, p. 3). Other critical theoretical investigations, like Bakhtin's historical work on the 'cult of unified and exclusive reason', is beneficial here as he discussed the trap of limiting events into *a* particular, single consciousness. In this way if the event is only understood and critiqued within this single consciousness, then we run the risk of 'impoverishment and domination rather than mutual enrichment' (1990, p. 87).

The following discussion will illustrate how a critical theoretical stance can guide us to participate in a way of seeing, a way of theorizing, in 'which the process of investigation is part of the object of knowledge' (Bloom, 1999, p. 3). This work incorporates Kaomea's recent work that speaks to the 'anti-oppressive and decolonizing research methodologies that look beyond familiar, dominant narratives' (2003, p. 15), methods and notions that each share a Baudrillardian commonality of 'stimulating kinds of "break-in" into innovative areas of cultural investigation beyond the parameters and purview of more cautious discourse' (Zurbrugg, 1997, p. 5). Disruption and revision (Beckett and Cherry, 1994) are central to this movement and to this particular critique of normative representation in early childhood education as I, like others (Tobin, 1997; Jones, 1998; Canella and Viruru, 2004) possibly seek rupture as a 'means of escape' (Shaafsma, 1997, p. 256).

Reading normativity

The picture of the Forward Command Post in Figure 11.2 appeared around the time that the second Gulf War began. In my initial viewing of it I was first amazed to think that it might be a real toy for children to play with, especially

Figure 11.2   Forward Command Post.

in this anti-war-toy era we find ourselves embedded in (Carlsson-Paige and Levin, 1989). While part of me wanted to believe it actually was a real toy to be purchased and used, much like the many *Posts* we Americans continue to actively occupy and use in Iraq even as I craft this narrative, another part of me saw the ever-present irony and the critical parody in this 'Command Post'. Upon further critique and increased perusal of the image, it became easier and easier to engage with and imagine the usefulness of this pretend play toy, especially given that we were all being *bombarded* daily with similar war images from CNN, FOX, and our local affiliate TV stations. Upon continued viewing what made the Command Post continually easier to consider as a possible real toy was comparing it to other similar real toys and play props for sale in various early childhood curriculum catalogues. For instance, when I studied the two separate images in Figures 11.3 and 11.4 of the 'pretend play' police officer uniform and the doll's house, the man in uniform who carries a gun and upholds the law and a two-story home, I soon began to blur these two images, comparatively seeing them less and less as two distinct pictures – it was then that I more clearly visualized the Forward Command Post as a very authentic 'pretend play toy' or prop for children to engage with during their constructive play sessions.

Certain specific normative practices in early education today continue to support the idea that the simple addition (i.e., Orvell's earlier stressed need for 'order', 'mastery' and 'safety') of various types of curricular materials can

'They'll be ready to enforce the law with this authentic looking zippered jacket and cap.'
Figure 11.3 Police officer's uniform.

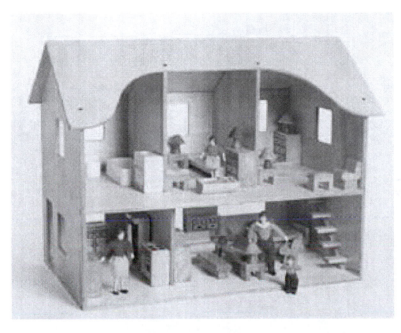

Figure 11.4   Doll's house.

bolster one's attempt to be a culturally sensitive practitioner, including the purchase and implementation of typical *diversity* materials like *Josephina* in Figure 11.5 and the selection of other typical multicultural props that follow in Figures 11.6 to 11.10.

Thinking back to the static multicultural processes I was first introduced to as an education student and further educated about and continued to witness over the years, and by interrogating current practices in Colleges of Education, I witness first-hand the 'what do I do on Monday morning?' attitude proliferating in education. These toys illustrate that. When I engage some of recent research on visual culture and representation (Jenks, 1995; Cortés, 2001; Fischman, 2001), I see the inherent danger of imposing simplistic additive structures (i.e., more racially 'correct' dolls and gender equitable materials equals attendance and adherence to multicultural education) into everyday pedagogical practices and professional development models. Common images such as those particular wooden figures above should appear as all-too-recognizable as they currently inundate the ranks of curriculum catalogues that cross all of our collective desks and coincide with the immense attempt to make ourselves into a more anti-biased, user-friendly group of practitioners. What intrigues me more than their recognizability is this notion of blurring of boundaries I briefly spoke to earlier. When I critically study these images again and again, just as I did earlier with the Forward Command Post, the blurred

Figure 11.5 Josephina.

Figure 11.6 House, furniture and black family.

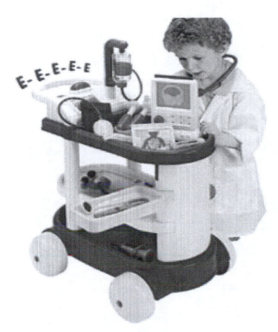

Figure 11.7 Medical cart.

sense or reading 'oppositionally' (Bloom, 1999) helps me effectively move theoretically against the normative aspects of these pictures, just as much of my recent work moves against different aspects of the field of early childhood education (Johnson, 2001, 2003b). My interests here are the lengths we go to resist, to contain, as we seek to protect normalized notions of children and childhood. The blurring productively helps me critique early education theory and practices that are distinctly interested in order, mastery, safety, clarity and making ALL apparent.

(Re)reading landscapes

Through the blurring, the oppositional looking, I better visualize how these specific figures and images hark to Umberto Eco's 'civilization of replicas' (Orvell, 1995, p. 148) that has resulted from an 'unhappy awareness of a present without depth' (Eco, 1986, p. 53). In his work, 'Understanding Disneyland: American Mass Culture and the European Gaze', Orvell notes that these replicas have 'arisen as part of a nation's effort to close distances by constructing ubiquitous replicas of itself' (1995, p. 148). As I interpret it, this work is similar to Baudrillard's accounts of *America*, whereby he posits we (i.e., Americans) actively attempt to construct 'a past and a history which were not their [our]

Figure 11.8   Pretend play Asian family.

Figure 11.9   Multicultural children puzzle.

own and which they have largely destroyed or spirited away . . . [things which are reconstructed as] something more real' (1988, p. 41). In fact, the appearance and usage of these replicant 'multicultural' dolls and toys are reminiscent of Baudrillard's simulacrum (Wilkerson, 2003).

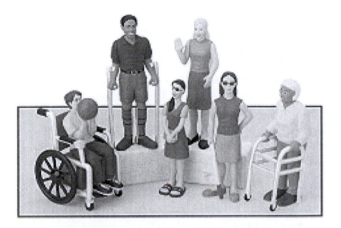

Figure 11.10 Friends with diverse abilities.

Viewing and being viewed by the data

In his work on the image, Bal (2001) discussed how meanings are produced in the visual experience(s). When we enter into a narrative production, whether it is the reading of a well-crafted poem or paragraph, the viewing of an abstract painting or an MTV video, each of these respective texts or narratives is 'an occasion for, not the cause of, meaning . . . [so] the reader articulates an ordering and reworking of the collection of possible meanings offered by the text and of additional possibilities brought in by herself' (2001, p. 76). Again, this works against the grain of the fixed, static, stable and happy, normative practices to which we've become accustomed to. This is not unlike the related proactive research position Lather advocates for, 'a multiplicity of readings by demonstrating how we cannot exhaust the meaning of the text, how a text can participate in multiple meanings without being reduced to any one, and how our different positionalities affect our reading of it' (1998, p. 125).

Unheimlich, the *unhomed* or that which is not 'at home' (Rogoff, 2000), runs counter to the 'homed', or that, maybe, which is fixed, stable and happy, static and monolithic (Hirsch, 1994), possibly that which is even more familial (i.e., known and familiar) in nature. From a research perspective, the '*awkward*' and '*strangeness*' as I critically engage this type of cross-disciplinary theorizing, is what entices me most about the relationship of visual culture to early education, especially when one attempts to critically engage notions of multicultural curricular tools and activities.

The few images I've shared here are increasingly popular images and curriculum materials and artifacts of primary education and other consumer industries today (i.e., tourism), perpetual images that surround you and I, our children and our collective psyche and mailboxes each week. These collective images, these dolls and action figures work to, 'create a world in which there is no reference to the past, and therefore no history ... [and by this] process, whereby everything bad that has happened in the past is erased or elided, everything that could be "historical" is instead rendered timeless' (Schaffer, 1996, p. 30). The more children and teachers and parents timelessly and unproblematically consume these products, these images, the more they/we risk participating in the remaking of the normative Western, colonial narrative(s).

Visual culture can be perceived in 'terms of particular and historically specific combinations of meanings and subjects – "scopic regimes" whose histories remain to be written' (Evans and Hall, 2000, p. 6). The consumer of 'images today "flips" through endless magazines, "channel surfs" on waves of TV shows [and the internet]' (Burgin, 2000, pp. 22–3) encountering a film through posters, toys, and other advertising images and books and comic strips before s/he first encounters it live. As active consumers we encounter visual images all the time and through 'collecting such metonymic fragments in memory' (ibid. p. 23), we come to be familiar with a visual image (film, video, toy, environment) we have not actually seen. In his work *In/different Spaces*, Victor Burgin shares that, 'visual culture – the combined product of "the media" and a variety of other spheres of image production – can no longer be seen as simply "reflecting" or "communicating" the world in which we live: it contributes to the making of this world' (ibid., pp. 21–2). Our understandings of children and their world(s), their knowledges, and their abilities are deeply influenced by the field of visual images and our multiple understandings and interpretations of them, or lack thereof.

In a critique of indigenous research, Stuart Hall noted that this type of critical cultural work has a 'profound, uneven and complex relation to the past which cannot be contained within fashionable nostalgia or simple reconstruction' (Beckett and Cherry, 1994, p. 54). Hall's commentary is vital as part of the critique of the visual image which represents the Constructive Playthings (2003) 'multicultural' prop or toy presented in Figure 11.11 – *Native American Village*. For instance, upon the critical viewing and further reading of the advertising under the Native American Village, Hall's sentiments (e.g., 'profound', 'uneven' and 'complex') leap off the page right at the viewer/reader. The catalogue's descriptive phrases (e.g., 'Get authentic' and 'encourages kids to re-enact the rich culture of Native American life', and 'There's even a "Medicine Man" as an extra bonus') speak quite clearly to this shallow notion of 'fashionable nostalgia or simple reconstruction'. Eco's earlier discussed work 'civilization of replicas' is witnessed here as possibly well-intentioned *multicultural* toys and props are in fact more recognizable as 'part of a nation's effort to close distances by constructing ubiquitous replicas of itself' (Orvell, 1995, p. 148). 'Authenticity', 're-enactment', the promise of 'there's even an added

'Get authentic savings on this busy playset that encourages kids to re-enact the rich culture of Native American life. Includes a 9 1/2"H vinyl teepee with plastic base, a totem pole, cooking utensils, tripod with kettle, horse, a family (Brave, Mother, Papoose, Child), 2 dancers, and other accessories. There's even a "Medicine Man", as an extra bonus. Ages 4 years +.'

Figure 11.11   Native American village.

extra bonus' – words of desire, exoticism, and consumption. These words, along with the images, continue to try to lure us, to tease us into really believing simplistic multicultural work as advertised can matter, can make a difference in the lives of children and future generations. This misleading work ultimately moves us backwards while we pretend to advance in our quest for social justice and education.

'Worlding the world'

In their work, Beckett and Cherry (1994) critique the close-knit relationship between theory and practice and how politics and texts have helped to shape each other. Their deliberations make strong connections to Gayatri Spivak's notion that 'the production of theory is in fact a very important practice that is worlding the world in a certain way' (1990, p. 7). Here Spivak is making reference to the fact that 'every socio-political, psycho-sexual phenomenon is organized by, woven by many, many strands that are discontinuous, that come from a way off, that carry their histories with them, and that are not within our control. We are inserted in them' (Harasym, 1990, p. 1).

   With this in mind, our (re)*imag*ined, rewritten multicultural curricula (the images, texts, materials, props, etc.) can begin to 'rewrite its own history as it should have been – indebted to those who had history before, and will continue to have a history well after' (Schaffer, 1996, p. 34). Images and the use of visual cultural practices (Metz, 1982) and theory can be an active part of this rewriting/reconceptualizing process, but it will take some work, for as Devereaux notes in her book, *Fields of Vision*:

real contemplation of images in traditional disciplines such as anthropology, history, and sociology has occurred . . . but the use of image, especially in video and film, as a means of serious intellectual discourse, has, outside the arts, remained exceedingly rare.

(2000, p. 4)

We have theoretical work to do!

As new connoisseurs of visual culture work, we're now more likely to be aware of how our interactivity, whether it is passive or active, has much stronger implications regarding the multitude of images we, and the students and children we work with, engage, than we have ever considered before. I acknowledge Bal's understanding that when I engage the visual, 'The work no longer stands alone: the viewer must now acknowledge that she makes it work; the surface is no longer still but tells a story of its and her making' (2001, p. 77). And in this 'making' I share Baudrillard's philosophical and pragmatic, 'willingness to be surprised; a willingness to undergo, undertake and to engage with the turbulence of contradiction, reversal, self-doubt, self-questioning, and the anguish and elation of re-definition, re-consideration, re-vision; a kind of existential experimentation' (Zurbrugg, 1997, p. 3).

Among current and future interests in the work of visual culture, my practices approximate what the field might consider. I'm seeking to find creative methods of attending to the complex number of ways that visual culture impacts our practices and our multiple disciplinary interests. My interests are similar to Banks' in that I too want to engage in 'an exploration by the visual, through the visual, of human sociality, a field of social action which is enacted in planes of time and space through objects and bodies, landscapes and emotions, as well as thought' (1980, p. 19). As educators, we have work to do, to actively anticipate and recognize different bodies, as the 'body is endlessly reconstructed and reinvented' (James et al., 1998, p. 150). The critical use of these curriculum catalogues and tourist images allows for a critique of a form of collective colonial memory and helps me to study how imperialism, 'involved not only territorial acquisition, political ambition and economic interests but also cultural formations, attitudes, beliefs and practices' (Ryan, 1997, p. 12). In our collective interdisciplinary (re)construction of these particular narrative structures we have to reassemble the past and the future by 'gathering and reusing [which] entail the bringing together of fragments, shards and snippets of disparate texts, objects, memories, writings and snatches of conversations . . . In gathering and reusing, fragments change context and meaning' (Beckett and Cherry, 1994, p. 52).

Like Britzman's critical work, looking itself is 'a practice much like speaking, writing, or signing. Looking involves learning to interpret and, like other practices, looking involves relationships of power. To willfully look or not is to exercise choice and influence' (2000, p. 10). I can choose to simply not look or to look uncritically, perhaps like so many tourists to Hawai'i – people who come to expect blue water, beaches, coconuts, suns, surf, luau, hotels, paradise – expectations built on how Hawai'i is packaged and sold before and after that sacred visit to paradise. This is not unlike these multicultural toys and props which intentionally 'seek to commodify real, living people, complex cultures, and environments into "sellable" products' (Au, 2001, p. 77). 'Sellable products' not unlike all the 'cute and quaint' play props and toys and dolls I revealed here and not unlike so much of the packaged early childhood curriculum products available on the 'market' today.

Note

1   Eco's 'civilization of replicas'.

References

Au, W.W.K. (2001) What the tour guide didn't tell me: tourism, colonialism, and resistance in Hawai'i. *Rethinking our Classrooms*, 2: 76–7.

Bakhtin, M. (1990) *Art and Answerability: Early Philosophical Essays*. M. Holquist and V. Liapunov (eds), trans. V. Liapunov. Austin, TX: University of Texas Press.

Bal, M. (2001) *Looking In: The Art of Viewing*. New York: Routledge.

Banks, M. (1980) Visual anthropology: image, object and interpretation, in W.J.T. Mitchell (ed.) *The Language of Images*. Chicago: University of Chicago Press.

Baudrillard, J. (1988) *America*. Trans. C. Turner. New York: Verso.

Beckett, J. and Cherry, D. (1994) Clues to events, in M. Bal and I.E. Boer (eds) *The Point of Theory: Practices of Cultural Analysis* (pp. 48–55). New York: Continuum.

Bloom, L. (1999) Introducing With Other Eyes: looking at race and gender in visual culture, in L. Bloom (ed.) *With Other Eyes: Looking at Race and Gender in Visual Culture*. Minneapolis: University of Minnesota Press.

Britzman, D. (2000) 'The question of belief': writing poststructural ethnography, in E.A. St. Pierre and W.S. Pillow (eds) *Working the Ruins: Feminist Poststructural Theory and Methods in Education*. New York: Routledge.

Burgin, V. (2000) *In/different Spaces: Place and Memory in Visual Culture*. Berkeley, CA: University of California Press.

Canella, G. and Viruru, R. (2004) *Childhood and Postcolonization*. New York: Taylor and Francis.

Carlsson-Paige, N. and Levin, D. (1990) *Who's Calling the Shots? How to Respond Effectively to Children's Fascination with War Play and War Toys*. New York: New Society Publishers.

Constructive Playthings (2003) *Catalogue*. https://www.constplay.com/family/default.htm (accessed 15 June).

Cortés, C.E. (2001) Knowledge construction and popular culture: the media as multicultural educator, in J.A. Banks (ed.) *Handbook of Research on Multicultural Education* (pp. 169–83). San Francisco: Jossey-Bass.

Devereaux, L. (2000) An introductory essay, in L. Devereaux and R. Hillman (eds) *Fields of Vision: Essays in Film Studies, Visual Anthropology, and Photography.* Berkeley, CA: University of California Press.

Eco, U. (1986) *Travels in Hyperreality.* Trans. W. Weaver. New York: Harcourt Brace.

Evans, J. and Hall, S. (2000) What is visual culture? In J. Evans and S. Hall (eds), *Visual Culture: The Reader.* Thousand Oaks, CA: Sage.

Fischman, G.F. (2001) Reflections about images, visual culture and educational research, *Educational Researcher*, 30(8): 28–33.

Grimshaw, A. (2001) *The Ethnographer's Eye: Ways of Seeing in Modern Anthropology.* New York: Cambridge University Press.

Harasym, S. (1990) Editor's note, in G. Spivak and S. Harasym, *The Post-Colonial Critic: Interviews, Strategies, Dialogues.* New York: Routledge.

Hirsch, M. (1994) Masking the subject: practicing theory, in M. Bal and I.E. Boer (eds) *The Point of Theory: Practices of Cultural Analysis* (pp. 109–24). New York: Continuum.

James, A., Jenks, C. and Prout, A. (1998) *Theorizing Childhood.* New York: Teachers College Press.

Jenks, C. (1995) *Visual Culture.* London: Routledge.

Johnson, R. (2001) Epilogue: reconceptualization as interruption, interrogative punctuation, and opening, in J. Jipson and R. Johnson (eds) *Resistance and Representation: Rethinking Childhood Education* (pp. 305–9). New York: Peter Lang.

Johnson, R. (2003a) The amorphous pretend play curriculum: theorizing embodied synthetic multicultural props. Paper presented at the annual Reconceptualizing Early Childhood Education Conference, Phoenix, AZ, January.

Johnson, R. (2003b) (Mis)Representations of identity in pretend play props: critiquing pretend play from a visual cultural perspective. Paper presented at the Annual Meeting of the American Educational Research Association, San Diego, CA, April.

Jones, A. (1998) Critical pedagogy. Unpublished manuscript.

Kaomea, J. (2003) Reading erasures and making the familiar strange: defamiliarizing methods for research in formerly colonized and historically oppressed communities, *Educational Researcher*, 32(2): 14–25.

Lather, P. (1998) Staying dumb? Feminist research and pedagogy within the postmodern, in H. Simons and M. Billig (eds) *After Postmodernism: Reconstructing Ideology Critique.* Thousand Oaks, CA: Sage.

Metz, C. (1982) *Psychoanalysis and Cinema: The Imaginary Signifier.* London: Macmillan.

Orvell, M. (1995) *After the Machine: Visual Arts and the Erasing of Cultural Boundaries.* Mississippi: University Press of Mississippi.

Rogoff, I. (2000) *Terra Infirma: Geography's Visual Culture*. New York: Routledge.

Ryan, J. R. (1997) *Picturing Empire: Photography and the Visualization of the British Empire*. Chicago: The University of Chicago Press.

Schaffer, S. (1996) Disney and the imagineering of histories, *Postmodern Culture*, 6(3): 1–36.

Shaafsma, D. (1997) Performing the self: constructing written and curricular fictions, in T. Popkewitz and M. Brennan (eds) *Foucault's Challenge: Discourse, Knowledge, and Power in Education*. New York: Teachers College Press.

Spivak, G. (1990) Editor's note, in G. Spivak and S. Harasym, *The Post-Colonial Critic: Interviews, Strategies, Dialogues*. New York: Routledge.

Tobin, J. (ed.) (1997) *Making a Place for Pleasure in Early Childhood Education*. New Haven, CT: Yale University Press.

Wilkerson, R.C. (2003) Dream replicants and the emergence of simulacra. http://dreamgate.com/pomo/replicants.htm (accessed 16 July).

Zurbrugg, N. (1997) Introduction: Just what is it that makes Baudrillard's ideas so different, so appealing? In N. Zurbrugg (ed.) *Jean Baudrillard: Art and Artefact* (pp. 1–6). Thousand Oaks, CA: Sage.

PART 3
The Emergence of New Technologies and Multiliteracies

12 Digikids
Young children, popular culture and media

Jackie Marsh

These are interesting times for early childhood literacy research. To begin with, there is little agreement in the field about what the nature of 'literacy' is. Take, for example, the argument about whether literacy is singular or plural in nature. Do children engage in multiple literacies (Cope and Kalantzis, 2000) or should the range of practices in which they engage be viewed as communicative practices, of which literacy – as a focus on lettered representation – is just one strand (Kress, 2003)? Second, the nature of the written word itself is changing profoundly as a result of advances in technology and the move from the primary textual site of the page to the screen. These 'digitextual practices' (Everett, 2003, p. 5) need to be embedded in an understanding of young children's early literacy development. This chapter explores these issues and draws on a number of research studies in which the communicative practices[1] of children aged between 2 years, 6 months and 4 years have been examined. The implications of this work for future research and practice in the field are also addressed.

New Times?

Some may question the need to argue for a careful analysis of young children's media practices, given that the new media age appears to be well and truly established. Unfortunately, popular discourse dictates that a case still needs to be made. Note, for example, the following news bulletin:

> There have been concerns that children, who have spent too long watching television and too little time talking to their parents, have arrived at school with poor communication skills ... Head teachers had claimed that the behavioural and verbal skills of children starting school were at an all-time low, with some five-year-olds unable to speak properly.
>
> (BBC News, 4 November 2003, http://news.bbc.co.uk)

Not only has it been suggested that young children are linguistically deficient because of watching television, but it has also been claimed that playing computer games leads to increased violent behaviour (Wazir, 2001), obesity (*Guardian*, 17 September 2002) and even enlarged thumbs (Dunning, 2002). This is moral panic (Cohen, 1987) of the highest order. Needless to say, rigorous and convincing research evidence for this chain of events is difficult to identify. Nevertheless, this discourse needs to be challenged if early years educators are to arrive at reasoned conclusions about the role of new media in young children's lives.

Luke and Luke (2001) suggest that this fear of children's competences with new media technologies arises from a particular ideological stance in relation to childhood, a stance in which educators' own imagined (innocent) childhoods, when knowledge of such complex, multimodal texts was not necessary, are used as touchstones for practice. Certainly, anxiety around the use of media texts appears to relate to current educators' own nervousness towards the rapid changes taking place rather than any sustained evidence that children are disadvantaged by technological advances. However, the concerns surrounding young children's contemporary communicative practices reach far wider than educational contexts, as the media hype outlined previously indicates. Some might argue that this is a result of increased anxieties and risks in late modernity, as complex global shifts in social, economic and political fields have taken place (Beck, 1998), shifts which have moved the emphasis on the management of risk from governments to the individual. In this *Risikogesellschaft* or 'risk society', where the ability to control risks associated with the virtual world appears to be beyond the control of individual caregivers, it is assumed that all kinds of unimagined terrors may meet children. In addition, in such a world of uncertainty, traditional discourses are likely to be seized upon as a source of comfort and reassurance – in this case, the discourse of print-based early childhood literacy experiences. While there is no doubt that major transformations have taken place in the past 30 or 40 years with regards to globalized economies, transnational challenges to nation–state politics, new social conditions linked to post-Fordist employment patterns, increased migration across national boundaries and the social and cultural impact of new technologies, I would argue that the moral panic engendered by young children's engagement with media is, actually, nothing new. As Springhall (1998) notes, it was ever thus; older generations have always raised concerns about the cultural interests of the young. What is peculiar to such concerns in the twenty-first century is the way in which reactions to perceived threats now take place on a global, rather than a local scale. Thus, in recent years, the 'backlash blockbusters' (Mills, 2000) which have pervaded educational discourse (such as issues relating to boys and attainment) have included concerns regarding children and new technologies. These concerns have led to government intervention in educational agendas to an unprecedented extent, with the introduction of the National Literacy Strategy in England and the 'No Child Left Behind' policy in the USA as two major examples. In these cases, national interventions have sought to reinforce traditional, print-based literacy practices in the face of the rising tide of digital literacy practices (Luke and Luke, 2001). In the next section, I move on to examine one of these interventions in depth in order to illustrate key aspects of this phenomenon and explore the implications for early childhood education.

The Foundation Stage Profile: hyperprint?

The pervasiveness of print-based models of literacy in early childhood curricula can be demonstrated by a brief examination of a relatively recent development in England, the introduction of the Foundation Stage Profile (QCA, 2003). This profile is a baseline assessment tool, intended for use with children by the end of their Reception Year in school. The profile is related to the Curriculum Guidance for the Foundation Stage (QCA, 2000), which is the curriculum framework for 3- to 5-year-olds in England. The Curriculum Guidance for the Foundation Stage has been regarded as a positive development from earlier curriculum frameworks in that it incorporates a number of fundamental principles of early childhood education. These include learning through play (Miller, 2001) and certainly, the area of learning related to literacy is entitled 'Communication, language and literacy', which signals a broad conceptualization of early literacy practices. However, an examination of the guidance materials to be used with the Foundation Stage Profile narrows this conception somewhat. The *Foundation Stage Profile Handbook* contains exemplification materials which provide guidance for practitioners on assessing children's skills, knowledge and understanding in relation to communication, language and literacy. A close analysis of these exemplification materials indicates that the model of literacy on which they are based is very much related to print-based definitions. Table 12.1 presents an analysis of the inclusion of examples relating to ICT in the exemplar material.

As can be seen from Table 12.1, examples relating to the use of ICT are minimal (6 per cent of the total) and appear primarily in relation to oracy (the 'language for communication and thinking' strand), in which voice-related technology is featured (i.e. tape recorders and telephone). The use of ICT is non-existent in the reading and writing strands. Photographs illustrating these two strands feature children reading books and children using chalk and pens to write on paper and boards. Thus, this assessment tool is symptomatic of the over-emphasis in early childhood on print-based literacy practices. For example, in a review of the literature on emergent literacy, Whitehurst and Lonigan (2001) focus solely on research relating to reading and writing printed text. This position is severely limited in relation to the skills, knowledge and

Table 12.1 Analysis of Foundation Stage Profile exemplar material

	Number of exemplars	Number of exemplars featuring ICT
Language for communication and thinking	27	5 (3 × tape recorder; 1 × computer paint program; 1 × telephone)
Linking sounds and letters	25	1 (tape recorder)
Reading	28	0
Writing	24	0
Total	104	6

Source: QCA (2003).

understandings which young children are developing in their contemporary literacy practices for, as Carmen Luke suggests:

> These practices are increasingly less exclusively related to lexicosyntactic text and more to a foreground of complex iconography of pictures, symbols, moving images and sound embedded in a background environment (and complex cultural and political economy) of global connectivity.
>
> (2003, p. 400)

In the light of these changes, it can be seen that the emphasis on the written word in national curricula is short-sighted and has major implications for the development of skills which children and young people will need in a new media age. In addition, lack of attention to these multimodal practices means that the textual worlds of home and school remain distant for many children. In the next section, I move on to discuss data arising from two research projects which examined children's contemporary communicative practices in the home. There is very little empirical data on the use of new technologies and media in the lives of children under 4 years of age and, therefore, the conclusions to be drawn from these two relatively small-scale studies are limited but, nonetheless, interesting in terms of the wider issues that they raise.

Children's media use

In the studies reported in this chapter, parents and carers in two communities in the UK were asked to identify the media practices of their young children. Both communities consisted primarily of white, working-class families who lived in areas of high social and economic deprivation in the north of

England. In the first project, 18 parents of 3- and 4-year-olds maintained a literacy diary for four weeks, during which time they documented their children's practices across a range of media (see Marsh and Thompson, 2001). In the second project, 44 parents of children aged 2.5–3.11 years old completed questionnaires related to their children's media literacy practices and 26 of these parents were then interviewed at home. The questionnaire and interviews focused on children's literacy practices in the home in relation to a wide range of media such as books and comics, environmental print, television and film, computer games, mobile phones and music. Parents were asked about patterns of children's use across this media and then parents' attitudes towards this use were explored. Parents were also questioned about their own interaction with children as they used these media and their feelings about the use of such material in nurseries and schools were probed (see Marsh, 2004). Data from these two projects, with 62 families in total, have been used to inform the following analysis.

Across these two communities, parents recorded their children's interaction with a wealth of materials. Table 12.2 outlines this range according to the mode of the text used or produced.

These texts have been categorized according to whether they were print-based texts, moving image texts or other kinds of multimodal texts (containing a combination of print, still and/or moving image) and the following discussion focuses on each category in turn. Although this structure separates the strands out for analysis, it needs to be recognized that children crossed modal boundaries with ease, seamlessly navigating their multimodal worlds (see Robinson and Mackey, 2003, for a detailed discussion of this process).

Printed texts

Print-based texts featured largely in children's communicative practices and were embedded in children's interaction with the wider environment of home and community, a principle that has been well established in the work on the role of environmental print in early childhood (Hall, 1987; Weinberger, 1996). However, what was notable about the present studies was that the texts itemized by these families included many that were related to popular culture and media, for example, junk mail advertising toys, food labels related to popular characters (e.g. Barbie spaghetti), computer game magazines, computer game covers and instructions and CD/DVD covers. These texts were part of a complex semiotic system in which children were 'suspended in webs of significance' which they themselves had spun, to adapt Geertz's (1973, p. 5) metaphor. Texts were connected in a myriad of ways in children's lives and this intertextuality was central to literacy development in that it increased children's motivation to engage with them. Although issues relating to consumerism, commodification of culture and mass marketing of goods to

Table 12.2 Texts and artefacts related to popular culture (film and television narratives and characters, superheroes) which featured in the communicative practices of 2.5 to 4-year-olds

Literacy texts (Focused on lettered representation, some of which were multimodal in that they included visual elements.)	Moving image texts (Which were multimodal in that they included visual and oral elements. Some included lettered representation, but in a limited way.)	Multimodal texts (Which combined moving image – visual and oral elements – and lettered representation)	Toys	Artefacts
Books	Films	Computer games – on PC	Dolls	Clothes
Comics	Cartoons	and consoles	Trucks and vehicles	Shoes
Catalogues	Television programmes	Interactive games on	Figures and models	Body decoration
Magazines		satellite TV	Cuddly toys	Jewellery
Junk mail		Internet sites	Small-world play	Dressing-up clothes and
Environmental print			Construction toys	artefacts
Computer game covers and			Educational toys	Furniture
instructions			jigsaws	Bed linen
Video covers			Toys which replicated	Mobile phones
CD covers			adult cultural icons e.g.	Artefacts related to health
Cards			computers, mobile	and personal hygiene
Stickers			phones	(medicine and cosmetics)
Food labels			Games	Food
Posters				Drink
Writing and drawing				Sweets
materials (pens, pencils,				
paper)				

children are not to be dismissed, the relationship between consumerism, identity and social practices is complex (Humphery, 1998; Miller et al., 1998) and allows for readings in which children's agency facilitates consumptive practices which are transgressional and counter-hegemonic.

These data indicate that print-based literacy practices were still an important part of these children's early literacy practices. However, they were, in relation to other communicative practices, only a minor part of home-based practices. Far more potent for these 'toddler netizens' (Luke, 1999) were moving image texts. Moving image texts in this context refer to television programmes, live-action and animated films.

Moving image texts

For the young children in both projects, moving image media were accessed more often than other kinds of texts. This resonates with the research detailing the media use of older children (see Livingstone and Bovill, 1999). As research with older children indicates (Robinson, 1997), children were not 'couch potatoes' but a 'lively audience' (Palmer, 1986) who sang, danced, talked to characters, played and talked about the narratives they watched (see Marsh, 2004). Parents were, on the whole, unconcerned about their children's television viewing, outlining a wide range of skills and knowledge they felt their children had learned from watching TV, including recognition of letters, numbers, shapes, colours, nursery rhymes and various social skills. However, parents did encounter disapproval from educators for their television-related social practices in the home. For example, Sarah, mother of 3-year-old Tony, said that the teachers at Tony's nursery didn't like television:

Jackie: Oh, don't they?
Sarah: No.
Jackie: Why, what do they say then?
Sarah: They try to get you to go out more with them, and that . . . The teacher, like, said it's not very good for them. They learn more when you're teaching them than they learn off telly and stuff.

Despite this, the majority of parents were sceptical of media and educational discourse which suggested that children watch too much television:

Karen: Like some talk shows, and that, all say that about kids but, yeah, kids stuck in front of the television 24/7, I can understand it but what parent lets their kids sit there all day? There's not many is there?

This dissonance between the views of educators and parents with regard to popular culture, media and literacy has been noted elsewhere (Makin et al.,

1999) and, drawing on Bourdieu's work on judgements of taste (Bourdieu, 1984) is indicative of social class differences between the groups in these studies, as well as reflecting the doxic (Bourdieu, 1990) attitudes which exist in relation to new technologies in early childhood education. Bourdieu describes doxa as a pre-verbal taking for granted of certain principles, principles which are unquestioned because they are established as part of the hegemonic discourse of a field and these principles correlate with the habitus of individuals and groups engaging in that field. Thus, doxa 'goes without saying because it comes without saying' (Bourdieu, 1977, p. 167). Certainly, doxic attitudes towards media texts can be traced in studies of teachers' orientation to such material (Marsh, 2003). However, in the studies reported in this chapter, parents strongly resisted this negativity and persisted in their support for their young children's engagement in these practices.

The lack of attention paid to moving-image texts in young children's literacy development ignores a growing body of research which identifies the inter-relationship between skills and knowledge utilized across print-based and moving image modes (Mackey, 2002; Robinson and Mackey, 2003). For example, in Mackey's study of 16 teenagers who looked at texts in a range of media, she demonstrates how the students moved confidently across a range of diegetic boundaries and this fluidity enhanced their understanding of narrative structures, features of genre and the affordances of various modes.

Multimodal texts

As was the case with printed texts, many of the moving image texts accessed by children were part of a dynamic nexus in which narratives were pursued across various media. This was also the case with computer games. Children in both studies played computer games which related to their popular cultural interests, for example, *Rugrats*, *Pokémon* and *Super Mario*. The games played had been produced for an older age group, but these 2½ to 4-year-olds embraced them with eagerness. The majority of computer games played were console-based games (PlayStation, Dreamcast and Nintendo). Many parents reported that children had started to play PlayStation games as babies, usually while sitting in their fathers' laps:

> Marie: Well, he's always – his dad always had a PlayStation so he's also, like, had it from being a baby. His Dad would have him in his lap and Dan liked to sit and play, thinking he were playing it.

Families described how they colluded in constructing these young children as competent games players by handing them a disconnected set of controls which they could use at the same time as another relative:

Betty: Well, they got all sorts of different games and he just gets the control and says 'I want to play it'. So we give him the control that's not plugged in.

Jackie: And do his brothers play it?

Betty: Yeah. And that keeps him quiet.

Carol: She has watched her sister playing and she'd have a little dabble on the PlayStation. While Michelle's playing, she'll have the other control and pretend to play but she doesn't actually.

Jane: I think when our Steven's on his cars, he'll sit there with the control but it's not plugged in. Our Steven just tells him that he's crunching it and he's not.

This supportive scaffolding of children's early experiences with computer games was undertaken intuitively, with parents providing the kinds of experiences that would develop children's confidence as game-players, in much the same way that research has indicated parents intuitively support early reading (Hannon, 1995). Some of the children could play PlayStation games independently at the age of 3 and 4, but these were a minority. In the main, those children who did use these console games did so as part of a 'community of practice' (Lave and Wenger, 1991) and so were being apprenticed into the discourse by fathers and older siblings. The relationship between literacy learning and computer-game playing is complex, but nevertheless significant (Gee, 2003; Pahl, 2005) and it is therefore necessary to explore further the interface between them if the implications of a key aspect of children's early communicative practices are to be understood fully.

Toys

From an analysis of Table 12.2, it is clear that toys played a central role in the children's communicative practices. Inevitably, many of the toys children owned were related to their popular cultural interests and the effect of the adaptation of popular toys by the fast-food industry for commercial purposes was apparent:

Mary: He's got Bob the Builder, a writing thing, you know those magnetic things that you rub off, he's got one of those upstairs. And Bob the Builder hats and all the trucks and everything. All this is Bob the Builder. He's got, he loves fire engines . . . he pretends these two characters are Fireman Sam and his mate. He's always talking to them. He's got Tweeny figures, he's quite a few things really. Noddy, he's got Postman Pat – all that kind of thing. A lot due to McDonald's, I must admit. These are all McDonald's.

This McDonaldization (Ritzer, 1998) of children's toy play may be a contributing factor to the integration of narratives across media for young children as much as it is a result of the phenomenon. These integrated narratives are, as Fleming argues, 'links in the metonymic chains that make the toy figures meaningful by generating a semiotic space' (1996, p. 162). The toys were important to the development of early language and literacy practices; children played with them and related narratives they had encountered in print-based and moving-image media, they used them as imaginary audiences for re-telling of stories and they became the focus for extended imaginative play which involved other family members (see Marsh, 2004). Toys have been identified as important in relationship to book-related literacy learning (Rowe, 1998) and this analysis needs extending to non-book-based communicative practices. Toys enabled narratives to cross time–space configurations and undergo transmediation in the process (Pahl, 2003).

There were obvious gender patterns in the toys which children owned in that many of the girls' parents identified dolls and Barbie as key cultural artefacts for their children, whereas boys preferred male figures and vehicles. However, as Rand (1998) has indicated, just because girls play with Barbie dolls does not mean that they do so in ways which are compliant with stereotypical expectations:

> Jackie: How many Barbies has she got?
> June: Not many actually 'cause she keeps pulling the heads off them. She's a little boy at the end of the day, aren't you, sweetheart [to child]?

Similarly, discourses of masculinity were complex. Sandy, the mother of 3-year-old Carlos, commented:

> Sandy: Oh yeah, Power Rangers and what else does he play? Pokémon and, yeah, he's Pokémon mad, yeah, the fighting ones.
> Jackie: Which characters does he pretend to be?
> Sandy: Paul, yeah. He's mad on Paul. He's got a Paul teddy what he takes to bed with him.

So, from fighting Power Rangers to cuddling teddy bears and from playing with Barbie dolls to enacting decapitation, it was clear in these studies that children's engagement with popular cultural discourses was more complex than is often indicated and was part of a dynamic process in which cultural objects offered particular object–subject relationships in identity construction and performance. Some bemoan this integration of children's play with such commodification, but their criticism often reflects a romanticized view of childhood in the past when, 'Play as a cultural form was valued as an organic, imaginative, free-ranging, democratically rule-abiding social interaction' (Kline et al., 2003, p. 243). This view of play is a mythic invention which serves as a counter-image to the perceived constrained nature of children's play in an electronically mediated world (Levin and Rosenquest, 2001). In the studies reported in this chapter, play as a cultural form was embedded into familial practices and popular cultural worlds in a way which facilitated integration of communicative practices across media.

Artefacts

The final column in Table 12.2 outlines a range of artefacts which were identified as important in young children's communicative practices in this study. At times, these artefacts were the source of emotional security for children:

> Karen: . . . we've got a Barbie bedspread and some days she's got Winnie the Pooh in her bedroom and some days she'll go to bed and she will have a real fit because she doesn't want to sleep with Pooh Bear on her bed. She needs Barbie on her bed. And I'll have to change a complete bedspread just because of the point that she won't sleep in that bed if I don't. Or, if not, I end up with her in my bed.

At other times, children integrated these artefacts into their play and items of clothing or household objects were incorporated into their oral and embodied narratives. Some artefacts were produced for children; others were adult-orientated items which were embedded into children's daily communicative practices, such as mobile phones (see Marsh, 2004, for a discussion of mobile phones and text-messaging in pre-school children's lives). The materiality of children's culture is an important aspect of contemporary language and literacy practices for children in many societies. Material artefacts provide a bridge between 'real' and imagined worlds and are part of children's identity construction and performance (Marsh, 2005). Such artefacts connect children to cultural narratives which are shared by their peers and fostered by their families and become 'reified objects' (Paechter, 2003) which are markers of membership of a specific community of practice. Thus, the importance of such artefacts becomes clear when we consider their role in developing shared discourses in early childhood play and communicative practices. In this way, popular culture becomes the 'vernacular literacy' (Barton and Hamilton, 1998) of childhood worlds.

Conclusion

The data from the two studies discussed in this chapter would suggest that these children were saturated in various types of media worlds. This had a number of implications for the way in which popular and media texts informed their communicative practices. A number of purposes for communicative practices which involved popular cultural and media texts could be identified in these children's homes, an analysis which is based on Cairney and Ruge's (1998) typology of uses of literacy in homes. Cairney and Ruge, in a study of the home literacy practices of 27 families in Australia, identified the following four purposes for literacy in the domestic context: (1) to establish or maintain relationships; (2) to access or display information; (3) for pleasure and/or self-expression and; (4) for skills development. All of these categories were identified in the home communicative practices of the 62 families in the two studies reported here. In addition, a further category could be added: communicative practices for identity construction and performance. Table 12.3 provides examples of the practices occurring across the two studies in relation to these categories.

Table 12.3 Classifications of communicative practices related to popular culture and media and examples of home practices in each category

Communicative practices	Examples
to form social relationships	Playing console-based computer games with fathers and siblings
	Watching television and films with family members
	Reading print-based texts with family members, e.g. picture books related to television and popular culture, TV guides, catalogues, magazines
	Using toy mobile phones to talk to family members; watching family members send SMS text-messages
for identity construction and performance of self	Playing related to narratives accessed in a variety of modes
	Playing with toys and artefacts which were part of the narrativized semiotic system formed by popular cultural and media texts
for development of skills, knowledge and understating in relation to language and literacy	Developing vocabulary and phoneme–grapheme correspondence from watching television
	Developing skills in relation to (popular) computer-game playing e.g. hand-eye co-ordination, problem-solving, parallel-processing
	Developing specific skills related to educative PC computer games
	Developing oral language through media-related play

Table 12.3   *(continued)*

Communicative practices	Examples
	Interacting with comics and popular games focused on skills development
to access or display information	Reading junk mail/catalogues/computer game covers and magazines
	Reading teletext on satellite television
	Reading TV guide
	Accessing web sites on Internet (e.g. BBC children's site)
for pleasure and enjoyment	Watching television programmes, cartoons and films
	Playing computer games
	Playing with toys and artefacts related to popular cultural narratives

Source: Adapted from Cairney and Ruge (1998).

From this analysis, it can be seen that popular culture, media and new technologies are fundamental features of these young children's everyday lives. As such, they are integral to their language and literacy development and connect this learning to a complex nexus of social relationships and material cultural arefacts. These are not aspects of children's early development that can be marginalized or undervalued in early childhood education for much longer if we are to claim that we are successful in facilitating the development of the skills, knowledge and understanding children need to navigate the choppy waters of 'liquid modernity' (Bauman, 2000). In facing up to the challenges posed by the emergence of a digital generation whose skills in operating within contemporary 'economies of attention' (Bigum et al., 2003) far outweigh those of their parents, carers and teachers, we can ensure that early childhood education reflects the social, cultural and economic milieu of the early twenty-first century.

Note

1   The term 'communicative practices' (Street, 1997), rather than 'literacy practices' is used throughout to refer to children's engagement with a range of printed, visual and multimodal texts as this facilitates a broad analysis of children's meaning-making.

References

Barton, D. and Hamilton, M. (1998) *Local Literacies: Reading and Writing in One Community*. London: Routledge.

Bauman, Z. (2000) *Liquid Modernity*. Cambridge: Polity Press.

Beck, U. (1998) *Risk Society*. London: Sage.

Bigum, C., Knobel, M., Lankshear, C. and Rowan, L. (2003) Literacy, technology and the economics of attention, *L1-Educational Studies in Language and Literature*, 3(1/2): 95–122.

Bourdieu, P. (1977) *Outline of a Theory of Practice*. Cambridge: Cambridge University Press.

Bourdieu, P. (1984) *Distinction: A Social Critique of the Judgement of Taste*, trans R. Nice. London: Routledge and Kegan Paul.

Bourdieu, P. ([1980] 1990) *The Logic of Practice*, trans. R. Nice. Cambridge: Polity Press.

Buckingham, D. (1993) *Changing Literacies: Media Education and Modern Culture*. London: Tufnell.

Cairney, T.H. and Ruge, J. (1998) *Community Literacy Practices and Schooling: Towards Effective Support for Students*. Canberra: DEET.

Cohen, S. (1987) *Folk Devils and Moral Panics: The Creation of the Mods and Rockers* (2nd edn). Oxford: Blackwell.

Cope, B. and Kalantzis, M. (2000) *Multiliteracies: Literacy Learning and the Design of Social Futures*. London: Routledge.

Dunning, M. (2002) 'Thumbs', *Guardian*, 25 March.

Everett, A. (2003) 'Digitextuality and click theory: theses on convergence media in the digital age', in A. Everett and J.T. Caldwell (eds) *New Media: Theories and Practices of Digitextuality*. New York: Routledge.

Fleming, D. (1996) *Powerplay: Toys as Popular Culture*. Manchester: Manchester University Press.

Gee, J.P. (2003) *What Video Games Have to Teach Us about Learning and Literacy*. New York: Palgrave Macmillan.

Geertz, C. (1973) *Interpretation of Cultures*. New York: Basic Books.

Guardian (2002) Childhood obesity at 'epidemic' levels, 17 September.

Hall, N. (1987) *The Emergence of Literacy*. London: Hodder and Stoughton.

Hannon, P. (1995) *Literacy, Home and School: Research and Practice in Teaching Literacy with Parents*. London: Falmer Press.

Humphery, K. (1998) *Shelf Life: Supermarkets and the Changing Cultures of Consumption*. Cambridge: Cambridge University Press.

Kline, S., Dyer-Witheford, N. and De Peuter, G. (2003) *Digital Play: The Interaction of Technology, Culture and Marketing*. Montreal: McGill-Queen's University Press.

Kress, G. (2003) *Literacy in the New Media Age*. London: Routledge.

Lave, J. and Wenger, E. (1991) *Situated Learning: Legitimate Peripheral Participation*. Cambridge: Cambridge University Press.

Levin, D.E. and Rosenquest, B. (2001) The increasing role of electronic toys in the lives of infants and toddlers: should we be concerned? *Contemporary Issues in Early Childhood*, 2: 242–7.

Livingstone, S. and Bovill, M. (1999) *Young People, New Media*. London: London School of Economics.

Luke, A. and Luke, C. (2001) Adolescence lost/childhood regained: on early intervention and the emergence of the techno-subject, *Journal of Early Childhood Literacy*, 1(1): 91–120.

Luke, C. (1999) What next? Toddler netizens, PlayStation thumb, techno-literacies, *Contemporary Issues in Early Childhood*, 1(1): 95–100.

Luke, C. (2003) Pedagogy, connectivity, multimodality and interdisciplinarity, *Reading Research Quarterly*, 38(3): 387–403.

Mackey, M. (2002) *Literacies Across Media: Playing the Text*. London: RoutledgeFalmer.

Makin, L., Hayden, J., Holland, A., Arthur, L., Beecher, B., Jones Diaz, C. and McNaught, M. (1999) *Mapping Literacy Practices in Early Childhood Services*. Sydney: NSW Department of Education and Training and NSW Department of Community Services.

Marsh, J. (2003) Taboos, tightropes and trivial pursuits: pre-service and newly-qualified teachers' beliefs and practices in relation to popular culture and literacy. Paper presented at AERA Annual Meeting, Chicago, April.

Marsh, J. (2004) The techno-literacy practices of young children, *Journal of Early Childhood Research*, 2(1): 51–66.

Marsh, J. (2005) Ritual, performance and identity construction: young children's engagement with popular culture, in J. Marsh (ed.) *Popular Culture, New Media and Digital Literacy in Early Childhood*. London: RoutledgeFalmer.

Marsh, J. and Thompson, P. (2001) Parental involvement in literacy development: using media texts, *Journal of Research in Reading*, 24(3): 266–78.

Miller, D., Jackson, P., Thrift, N., Holbrook, B. and Rowlands, M. (1998) *Shopping, Place and Identity*. London: Routledge.

Miller, L. (2001) Shaping early childhood through the literacy curriculum, *Early Years*, 21(2): 107–16.

Mills, M. (2000) Shaping the boys' agenda: the backlash blockbusters. Paper presented at ECER Annual Conference, Edinburgh, September.

Paechter, C.F. (2003) Masculinities and femininities as communities of practice, *Women's Studies International Forum*, 26(1): 69–77.

Pahl, K. (2003) Artefacts, timescales and kinetic design: the semiotic affordances of popular culture for children's home communicative practices. Paper presented at ESRC Seminar on Children's Literacy and Popular Culture, University of Sheffield, November.

Pahl, K. (2005) Narrative spaces and multiple identities: children's textual explorations of console games in home settings, in J. Marsh (ed.) *Popular Culture, New Media and Digital Literacy in Early Childhood*. London: RoutledgeFalmer.

Palmer, P. (1986) *The Lively Audience: A Study of Children around the TV Set*. Sydney: Allen and Unwin.

QCA (2003) *Foundation Stage Profile Handbook*. London: HMSO.

Rand, E. (1998) Older heads on young bodies, in H. Jenkins (ed.) *The Children's Culture Reader*. New York: New York University Press.

Ritzer, G. (1998) *The McDonaldization Thesis: Explorations and Extensions*, London: Sage.

Robinson, M. (1997) *Children Reading Print and Television*. London: Falmer Press.

Robinson, M. and Mackey, M. (2003) 'Film and television,' in N. Hall, J. Larson and J. Marsh (eds) *Handbook of Early Childhood Literacy*. London: Sage.

Rowe, D.W. (1998) The literate potentials of book-related dramatic play. *Reading Research Quarterly*, 33: 10–35.

Springhall, J. (1998) *Youth, Popular Culture and Moral Panics: Penny Gaffs to Gangsta Rap*. Basingstoke: Macmillan.

Street, B. (1997) The implications of the new literacy studies for education, *English in Education*, 31(3): 45–59.

Wazir, B. (2001) Violence makes games 'unsuitable for children', *The Observer*, 16 December.

Weinberger, J. (1996) *Literacy Goes to School: The Parents' Role in Young Children's Literacy Learning*. London: Paul Chapman.

Whitehurst, G.J. and Lonigan, C.J. (2001) Emergent literacy: development from prereaders to readers, in S. Neuman and D.K. Dickinson (eds) *Handbook of Early Literacy Research*. New York: Guilford Press.

13 Literarily lost
The quest for quality literacy agendas in early childhood education

Leonie Rowan and Eileen Honan

While there is widespread agreement among educators, parents and members of the community that early childhood education plays a vital role in the consolidation of children's literacy skills, there is increasingly *less* agreement about what it is that the word 'literacy' actually means. Recent years have seen the emergence of a veritable 'literacy industry' within which the term has come to be associated not only with the traditional activities of reading and writing, but also with newer skills associated with contemporary life. Emphasis has increasingly been placed upon the importance of such things as media literacy, computer literacy, technological literacy, visual literacy, or emotional literacy, for example. This creates a challenging environment for early childhood educators who are expected to possess an increasingly wide range of operational, cultural and critical literacies, as well as skills in being able to map and monitor the progress of all their students in these areas.

While it is not difficult to understand the rationale behind the introduction of programmes designed to address ever-increasing forms of literacy, the plethora of literacies (coupled with increasingly public monitoring of literacy 'achievement' and regular declarations of literacy crises) create an environment that can be overwhelming, stressful, and ultimately unproductive for teachers and children. In this space it is easy for all educators to become both literally and literarily lost.

In response to these contexts, this chapter has the following aims. First, to provide a brief map of the current debates on literacy that impact on the fields of early childhood education and to identify some of the assumptions underpinning various literacy agendas; second, to explore an example of an early years programme currently operating in Australia, and to reflect upon the assumptions about contemporary literacy that underpin, and are constructed by, the implementation of this programme and finally, to identify some key ideas that may be useful in helping early childhood educators move positively through complex terrains in the pursuit of meaningful, defensible and achievable literacy goals.

The contemporary literary landscape

> It is a mistake to think that books have come to stay. The human race did without them for thousands of years and may decide to do without them again.
>
> (E.M. Forster)

Recent years have seen a vast amount of scholarship focused on the issues that surround the broad phenomenon of globalization. Arjun Appadurai (1990) has been particularly helpful in mapping the landscapes of globalization, writing of change across five key 'scapes': *finanscape, technoscape, mediascape, ethnoscape and ideoscape.*

Changes within and across each of these fields have raised a general consciousness about the 'new skills' or literacies required for active participation in contemporary society. Much is made of the ways in which changing information and communication technologies (ICT), coupled with reorganizations of industry and production, are combining to produce a 'knowledge economy'. Similar emphasis is placed upon the fact that to survive and, occasionally, to prosper in these 'new times', individuals will need skills associated not only with reading and writing and reckoning, but with creating, deconstructing and generally 'understanding' the diverse textual products of the new times.

In educational circles this has led to debate about the broad skill base that might be the most valuable for contemporary children. For those involved in literacy education, particular attention has been given to what are often conceptualized as the new literacies of the twenty-first century. These relate not only to the emergence or expansion of new textual products – such as those associated with various media texts (including TV shows, movies and advertisements), popular culture texts (e.g. bill boards, t-shirts, stickers, posters), information technology, mobile phones, various personal game stations and so on – and new textual practices (e.g. text-ing, web-logging, synchronous messaging) but also to new ways of thinking about the 'nature' of literacy itself.

Debates about what should be included in literacy programmes are not new. For many years, literacy educators have distinguished between different kinds of literacy and have argued for attention to what are sometimes described as different literacy domains. At the most basic level are 'operational' skills associated generally with the ability to encode or decode particular texts. The ability to read and write – to interpret and construct messages – is literacy at an operational level. In addition to this, the ability to construct certain kinds of texts in culturally appropriate fashions is recognized as cultural literacy. Beyond this, there is the ability to reflect upon, critique or analyse the ways in which literacy practices in various contexts reflect wider social patterns, and influence the operation of power, and norms of various cultures.

These three dimensions of literacy are often brought together within the framework known broadly as 'critical literacy' which has been conceptualized by Luke as:

> a rudimentary working definition of critical literacy entails three aspects. First, it involves a meta-knowledge of diverse meaning systems and the sociocultural contexts in which they are produced and embedded in everyday life. By meta-knowledge I mean having an understanding of how knowledge, ideas and information bits are structured in different media and genres, and how these structures affect people's readings and uses of that information. Second, it involves mastery of the technical and analytical skills with which to negotiate those systems in diverse contexts. This refers to how the pragmatics of use of literacy are translated into practice in different contexts. Third, it involves the capacity to understand how these systems and skills operate in relations and interests of power within and across social institutions. This means an understanding of how and why various social groups have different and unequal access to literacy (and knowledge), and how access and distribution work in the interests of some groups and can disadvantage others.
>
> (2000, p. 72)

It is, of course, possible for critical literacy education to focus on purely traditional texts. In recent years, however, many scholars have moved to emphasize the importance of both new literacies *and* new texts, by promoting the concept of new literacy studies: a framework that attends to most of the same questions as critical literacy, but which explicitly foregrounds 'new' literacy practices, and new (kinds of) texts.

A similar or related intent is captured by other authors who have focused on advancing the concept of 'Multiliteracies' as a new context for educators:

> The notion of Multiliteracies supplements traditional literacy pedagogy by addressing these two related aspects of textual multiplicity. What we might term 'mere literacy' remains centred on language only, and usually on a singular national form of language at that, being conceived as a stable system based on rules such as mastering sound–letter correspondence. This is based on the assumption that we can actually discern and describe correct usage. Such a view of language must characteristically translate into a more or less authoritarian kind of pedagogy. A pedagogy of Multiliteracies, by contrast, focuses on modes of representation much broader than

language alone. These differ according to culture and context, and have specific cognitive, cultural, and social effects. In some cultural contexts – in an aboriginal community or in a multimedia environment, for instance – the visual mode of representation may be much more powerful and closely related to language than mere literacy would ever be able to allow. Multiliteracies also create a different kind of pedagogy: one in which language and other modes of meaning are dynamic representational resources, constantly being remade by their users as they work to achieve their various cultural purposes.

(Cope and Luke, 2000, p. 3)

When an awareness of multiple texts is combined with an appreciation of the value of multiple levels of literacies, the end result is often a literacy agenda that challenges educators to broaden their understanding of what 'counts' as literacy, and to use an increasingly wide array of texts to engage their students in new forms.

It is important to acknowledge here, that this kind of work draws attention not only to textual practices, but also to cultural practices that are fundamentally interwoven with, and associated with, textual production and analysis. Specifically, it is important to acknowledge the fact that debates about Multiliteracies are emerging alongside debates about the best ways to educate 'productive citizens' and 'knowledge workers' in an era of uncertainty and change. In Australia, this debate is seen in the attempts by most state educational authorities to 'redefine' the kinds of knowledge that should be regarded as the 'core business' of education. In Queensland this has led to the emergence of a 'new basics' programme, which emphasizes the importance of Life pathways and social futures; multiliteracies and communications media; active citizenship and environments and technologies (see Yelland, Chapter 14, this volume). In Victoria, South Australia, and Tasmania, attention has been focused on the identification of 'essential learnings'.

In South Australia the essential learnings are defined as 'futures, identity, interdependence, thinking and communication'. In Tasmania, the designated essential learnings are 'thinking; communicating; personal futures; social responsibility; world futures'. In the Northern Territory, the term employed is EsseNTial Learnings, and the emphasis is on four knowledge domains 'the inner learner (Who am I and where am I going?), the creative learner (What is possible?), the collaborative learner (How do I connect with and relate to others?) and the constructive learner (How can I make a useful difference?)' (Australian Education Union, 2004). And soon another state, Victoria, will implement its own set of essential learnings.

Three points are particularly important to note. First, the general tenor of the 'Essential Learnings' frameworks indicates a move to prioritize the kinds of 'new' and emerging literacies that have been highlighted within literacy literature, particularly by those who are aligned with either the Multiliteracies framework, or the New Literacy Studies, over the past decade.

Second, these formalized quests to redefine and map what 'counts' as valued, valid, applicable, relevant, and responsible knowledge clearly impacts upon the world of literacy education, as teachers across all year levels are challenged to demonstrate the ways in which their literacy practices prepare kids in both technical and ideological ways for the world that is unfolding. Thus pressure is consistently placed on teachers to demonstrate that their students can perform basic tasks of encoding and decoding (i.e. 'old literacies'), *and* to illustrate the ways in which their literacy work helps to produce the kind of informed, reflective, tolerant citizens (with the 'new literacies') demanded in the age of diversity.

Third, the whole educational reform agenda (as illustrated here by the examples from the Australian context) is further complicated by the kinds of social and cultural anxiety that characterizes a world where terrorism is both a daily topic and a regular reality. At the time when educational policy places emphasis upon the celebration of new literacies, (and the development of skills that best prepare individuals to live in culturally diverse and rapidly changing societies), a whole range of cultural discourses are working to reinscribe divisions between the 'us' and the 'them' of terrorism.

Rowan has asserted that:

> at precisely the same historical period when concepts of difference, heterogeneity and multiplicity are prominent in critical discourse, mainstream media, political and popular culture texts are just as likely to insist upon the desirability of sameness, homogeneity and consistency.
>
> (2003, p. 6)

In this context, as Appadurai notes: 'minorities are the major site for displacing the anxieties of many states about their own minority or marginality (real or imagined) in a world of a few mega states, of unruly economic flows and compromised sovereignties' (2001, p. 6). In the year 2004, then, the average literacy educator is faced with at least four contextual debates; first, there is the academic literacy literature which emphasizes the importance of things such as Multiliteracies and critical thinking; second, the popular media promotes a literacy which insists on the value of the basic skills in reading and writing; third, there is educational policy which prioritizes, among other things, the kinds of multiple literacies that are considered to be the most likely to prepare the kind of 'good citizens' who can successfully negotiate complex, unstable and culturally diverse worlds but paradoxically wants or needs to take note of measures of basic skills; and finally there is a widespread set of anxieties about the ways in which cultural diversity should be most responsibly managed in a world where attention to difference seems less palatable to many community members, than an insistence of sameness.

The point we are trying to make here is that this average literacy educator is positioned in extremely complex terrain, trying to negotiate productive ways forward that will satisfy the diverse demands of all those involved in these debates including, of course, the heterogeneous community of parents, caregivers and students themselves.

If one accepts a literacy agenda that is focused on developing operational literacies and cultural literacies and critical literacies; and if one further accepts that these literacies relate to broad categories of text types, i.e. to print and spatial texts; to 'school' and not-school texts, then one could conceivably undertake a mapping of the terrain that might reveal where literacy activity was focused and productive. One could place text types, for instance, on an axis of a grid, and 'literacy' type on another, and then identify the extent to which any particular environment includes multiple text forms (visual, print; canon, popular culture, kid-centred, adult-centred, and so on) and various performances of literacy (reading, writing, analysing, making, critiquing texts, and so on). If the mapping was three-dimensional, it would be possible to add another aspect to the chart in order to reflect the ways these various literacies are assessed. The important point that emerges through the combination of these grids (which, we hasten to emphasize would be illustrative devices only, and not intended to be used as the sole criteria for analysing *any* literacy space) is that literacy programmes can be assessed in relation to the assumptions that they make about:

- literacy (and its most 'valuable' dimensions);
- texts (and the most 'significant' or important text 'types');
- learners (and their 'typical' or 'normal' behaviours);
- assessment (and its relationship to valuable literacy, significant texts and normal learners);
- the 'world' (and its contemporary challenges);
- education (and its fundamental purposes).

And, most importantly, by the inclusions and exclusions that they reproduce. For in a world where 'literacy' is an ever evolving term, this multiplicity is not automatically reflected in 'schooled' approaches to literacy education.

In the next section of this chapter we want to explore some of the ways in complex and competing discourses around literacy are reflected within one particular Early Years Literacy programme as it has been introduced in the state of Victoria in Australia. We will contrast this institutionalized response with a brief exploration of the different kinds of literacies likely to be found within the classrooms, and the homes occupied by some contemporary kids.

Contemporary literacy within 'old' classrooms and 'new' households: the possibilities and practices of different literacy environments

> Water water everywhere and still the boards did shrink
> Water water everywhere and not a drop to drink.
> (Samuel Taylor Coleridge, *The Rhyme of the Ancient Mariner*)

We turn now to an analysis of the Early Years Literacy Program in Victoria, Australia. Our primary goal is to identify the way this particular programme conceptualizes literacy and learners. It is necessary to begin with a description of what the programme involves and the resources that support it. It is hoped that this process will facilitate readers to critique their own contexts by illustrating the ways in which the techniques can uncover the uneasy tensions between policy and practice in contemporary educational settings.

Key features of the programme

The Early Years Literacy Program (EYLP) requires a whole-school approach to literacy teaching with the following features:

- a daily two-hour block of uninterrupted time for teaching literacy (called the literacy hour);
- a focus on 'data-driven instruction' (Hill and Crevola, 1999, p. 8) with regular and ongoing assessment and monitoring of students' progress throughout the year;
- the provision of support to the programme usually provided through the funding of Reading Recovery intervention programmes;
- funding for the appointment of a part-time Early Years Literacy Coordinator;
- professional development for teachers in the programme;
- 'strategically planned home/school liaison' (Alderson, 2000, p. 335).

These organizational features would be recognizable to teachers in the UK who are familiar with the National Literacy Strategy and the Literacy Hour (http://www.standards.dfes.gov.uk/literacy/).

There are three kits that are distributed to teachers implementing the EYLP: the Early Years Reading Resource Kit; the Early Years Writing Resource Kit; and the Early Years Speaking and Listening Resource Kit. Each kit contains resource books and videos. The books are Professional Development, a Teaching Guide (for example, Teaching Readers in the Early Years), and in the reading kit a book for parent helpers. There is also a substantial website with many of the materials available electronically (http://www.sofweb.vic.edu.au/eys/lit/index.htm).

Each Teaching Guide contains a diagram of the organizational framework (represented in Figure 13.1). Each Guide and Professional Development manual outlines the specific teaching strategies recommended for use in EYLP, and the Guides for Teaching reading and writing also include outcomes and indicators for each level of the 'six developmental stages' of reading or writing. The

TEACHING READERS
Whole class focus on reading
Reading to students, shared reading
Small group focus on reading

Reading to students	Learning Centres P-2	
Language experience	Learning Tasks 3-4	
Shared reading	Book Boxes	
Guided reading	easy familiar and unfamiliar	**TEACHING**
Guided reading- Reciprocal teaching	texts	

Whole class reading share time
Reflecting on and celebrating students learning

SPEAKERS

TEACHING WRITERS
Whole class focus on writing
Modelled writing
Shared writing
Small group focus on writing

AND

LISTENERS

Shared Writing	Independent writing tasks
Language experience	Teacher conducting roving
Interactive writing	conferences
Guided writing	Students working on various aspects of the writing process: planning composing recording revising publishing

Whole class writing share time
Reflecting on, sharing and celebrating students' writing

Figure 13.1   The structured classroom programme.

videos contained in each kit provide illustrative examples of each of the teaching strategies being used in classrooms.

The production of literacy within the EYLP

To come to some kind of understanding of the particular types of literacies that are conceptualized within the EYLP, we have analysed the texts described above to determine their discursive production of literacy. This of course is only one part of a discursive analytic framework – what is missing in this analysis is how teachers themselves take up positions within such discursive productions – how they make sense of the versions of literacy that are represented as normative in these texts. We are wary of falling into the trap so aptly described by Ball, of producing a policy textual analysis that ignores the 'secondary adjustments' (Ball, 1994) that teachers make as they work within and around the policies. In previous work, Honan has investigated this teachers' work through a rhizo-textual analysis of the 'provisional linkages' (Honan, 2001, 2004) that connect teachers' discursive practices and those discourses operating in policy texts. Making these connections is especially useful in discounting the privileging of the 'policymaker's reality' (Ball, 1994, p. 19) that is assumed in many descriptions of the relationship between teachers and policies. In what follows we use this rhizo-textual analytic method to explore how the discourses operating in the EYLP texts work together to produce a particular version of literacy teaching and learning.

Understanding both texts themselves, and the readings of these texts, as rhizomatic disrupts common assumptions about the relations between teachers and policy texts. In the introduction to *A Thousand Plateaus*, Deleuze and Guattari refer to their text as a rhizome and point out that:

> Any point of a rhizome can be connected to any other, and must be ... A rhizome ceaselessly establishes connections between semiotic chains, organizations of power, and circumstances relative to the arts, social sciences, and social struggles.
>
> (1987, p. 7)

This ceaselessness of the connections between rhizomes shifts attention away from the construction of a particular reading of any text towards a new careful attendance to the multiplicity of linkages that can be mapped between any text and other texts, other readings, other assemblages of meaning. A rhizo-textual analysis of the relation between texts and readers reveals a variety of 'scrupulous and plausible misreadings' (Spivak, 1996, p. 45). There is no one correct path to take through a rhizome, no one true way of reading rhizomatic texts. Grosz describes this understanding of texts as rhizomatic: 'A text is not a repository of knowledges or truths, the site for storage of information . . . so much as a process of scattering thoughts, scrambling terms, concepts and practices, forging linkages, becoming a form of action' (1995, p. 126).

Within the EYLP texts, this scrambling and scattered process establish connections between disparate discursive systems, about literacy, about texts, about students and how students learn, and about teaching, so that the version of literacy teaching that is produced seems to be normative, to be unquestionably rational, and therefore to be beyond critique. The nature of print-based texts in which this chapter is located necessitates a linear description of these different discursive systems that belies the complex interconnections between them as they play out in the EYLP texts. These 'discursive plateaus' (Honan, 2001, 2004) are like the roots of a rhizomatic plant in that they are always ceaselessly connected and interwoven within and around each other. But for the purposes of this chapter, we must lay them out separately, teasing apart each of the discourses in order to provide an artificial reading of their separate entities.

Assumptions about literacy education in the EYLP

The organizational framework, outlined in Figure 13.1, presupposes certain conditions of learning that are optimal for literacy teaching. These are:

- literacy is best taught in uninterrupted two-hour blocks of time;
- reading and writing are two distinct and separate components of literacy that should be taught separately;
- speaking and listening learning occurs as part of reading and writing while at the same time separated from the other modes;
- the organization of the class in the block is whole–small group–whole with emphasis on individual success and interactivity between groups of children and the teacher.

There are at least two different discourses on literacy teaching and learning operating within the texts of the organizational framework (not only the framework itself but the explanations of its operation contained in the professional development books, Teaching Guides and videos).

Back to basics and whole language
One of these discourses reflects a traditional skills-based approach to literacy teaching that resembles that found in syllabus and curriculum documents set in historical contexts as disparate as 1886 and 1941. In New South Wales in 1886 for example, Inspector Wilkins wrote: 'The first subject that strikes us as necessary for a primary school is Language, by which is to be understood a full knowledge of our mother tongue, including Reading, Writing, Grammar,

Analysis of Sentences, and Composition' (quoted in Green and Hodgens, 1996, p. 213).

And in 1941, again in New South Wales, the syllabus 'prescribed eight aspects of curriculum activity under the general auspices of "English"

> Reading (from the School Magazine and a large supply of supplementary readers from Third Class onwards)
> Poetry
> Oral Expression
> Written Expression
> Formal elements (phonics, punctuation, sentence and paragraph structure)
> Formal grammar
> Spelling
> Writing (handwriting)'
>> (1941 NSW curriculum quoted in Reid, 1996, p. 151)

This 'back to basics' discourse affirming the value of skills that can be separately defined and addressed connects closely with the discourses used in popular media accounts of what counts as literacy. Its presence within the EYLP could be seen as an attempt to assuage the anxieties and tensions that arise whenever debates about a 'literacy crisis' are mounted in popular media contexts (see Comber et al., 1998).

A second discursive system operating within the organizational framework could be seen to directly contradict this skills-based approach. There is an emphasis on individual responses, on small group work, and on interactions between groups of children. This emphasis reflects the whole language approach which, in Australia at least, was developed in a move to break free from the constrictions of 'the skill and sub-skills exercises that had been used to teach reading and writing. Using real books, as opposed to traditional "readers", and encouraging children to produce their own literature were highly emphasized' (Comber, 1992, p. 2). Whole language proponents would be pleased to recognize Cambourne's 'conditions of learning' (1988) and Graves' 'process writing' within the EYLP.

Those of us who believe that there have been significant developments in the teaching of literacy since 1886, and that, while the Dartmouth Seminar in 1966 was ground-breaking and innovative, considerable research into new approaches has taken place in the past 40 or so years, will look to other parts of the texts of the EYLP for validation.

From whole language to child development
The Teaching Guides and the professional development manuals explicitly and implicitly take up both the skills and whole language discourses while also

using at least two other discursive systems about literacy teaching and learning. The particular points made about literacy in these texts are:

- children learn how to read and write in developmental stages and achievement in these stages can be measured by normative standards achievable by all children;
- reading and writing are best taught through the use of particular and specific strategies;
- reading is 'primarily' about gaining meaning from texts;
- texts can be categorized as 'print' and 'non-print' or 'visual' texts;
- a range of 'text types' should be used in early years writing activities.

There is a close connection between the discourses of whole language and those surrounding child development that are reflected in the texts describing the 'developmental stages'. As Walkerdine has pointed out, there is an inextricable link between the ideas of 'individualized pedagogy' and Piaget's theory of child development:

> The new notion of an individualized pedagogy depended absolutely on the possibility of the observation and classification of normal development and the idea of spontaneous learning. It was the science of developmental psychology which provided the tools and in which the work of Piaget is particularly implicated.
>
> (1984: p. 177)

The EYLP, as do other policy documents in Australia and elsewhere, makes a seamless connection between this individualized pedagogy, the 'natural' progression of children through stages of development, and the measurement of this progression through normative standards. [In the EYLP children who do not meet this standard are routinely removed from the classroom that operates within the organizational framework and subjected to one-on-one tuition in Reading Recovery programmes.] So, on the one hand, there is a discourse operating that claims individual children naturally progress through sequential stages of learning how to read and write, while on the other hand, children who are seen not to be progressing at the same pace as a significant number of their peers, do not meet the standards required, and are diverted from the natural progression. (See Nichols, 2004, and others in the *Australian Journal of Language and Literacy* special issue on 'Questioning literacy development').

Sociolinguist approaches to literacy

The (relatively) recent development of sociolinguistic approaches to literacy teaching and learning is also taken up in the EYLP within the discourses related to texts. In the late 1980s a group of linguists and educators working at the University of Sydney, drawing on the linguistic theories of Halliday, and theories of semiotics developed by Kress, constructed a pedagogy known as the 'genre approach' (Martin, 1991; Halliday and Martin, 1993). This approach requires explicit teaching and modelling of the linguistic features and textual structures of a particular genre. In the EYLP (and in the NSW policy documents as well) genres are now known as 'text types', drawing on what McWilliam (1994) calls 'folkloric assumptions' about teachers' inabilities to engage with 'difficult' concepts (such as 'genre'). As well there is a clear indication that only a certain number of these text types are suitable for children in the early years of school. While a 'range' is suggested, this does not include expositions, arguments or discussions.

Sociolinguistic accounts of the multiplicity of texts are reflected in the discourse describing the categories of texts. It is acknowledged that texts are not only print-based, and 'visual' texts are referred to. However, the primacy of print is explicated clearly: 'Teaching Readers in the Classroom is primarily about assisting students to gain meaning from print text' (Victorian Department of Education, 1997, EYLPa, p. 3). There is no mention of the use of digital texts.

Assumptions about teachers' work in the EYLP

As we have pointed out earlier, these discursive systems on the purpose of literacy education interweave and connect to produce persuasively 'reasonable' versions of what counts as literacy. Crossing over and interconnecting with these discourses is the thread of another discourse about the nature of teachers' work. This is especially evident in the texts concerning the recommended teaching strategies for teaching reading and writing. For reading, these strategies are named as: reading to, shared reading, language experience, and guided reading. For writing, the strategies are named as: modelled writing, shared writing, language experience, interactive writing, and guided writing. While all these strategies would be part of an effective teacher's repertoire of practices, the texts take up a narrowly defined view of these strategies. Each strategy is carefully explained in the Guides, with clear descriptions of how teachers should use the strategies, including a series of steps, and examples of questions to ask children in each step. Here, the texts take up new managerialist discourses about teachers' work, where they are constructed as bureaucrats, as 'capitalism's "soft cops" '(Lather, 1994, p. 245). In these discourses the teacher is seen to be technician, 'a routinized and trivialized deliverer of a pre-designed package' (Goodson, 1997, p. 137; see also Apple and Jungck, 1990, and Robertson, 1996). The ideal automated technician of the new managerialist discourses is atheoretical and practical, is profoundly interested in the ways in which practice can transform lives, work and society, and is not so interested in the reflexivity that is needed if one is to question the transforming work being done.

The binary of theory–practice permeates teaching, teacher training, and theories of pedagogy to such an extent that it is often taken for granted. The implicitness of the theory–practice binary allows Connell to disavow teachers' abilities to theorize their work: 'In place of theories of education these teachers have what might be called operating principles about how to be a teacher: something between a rule of conduct and a style of approaching the world' (Connell, 1985, p. 179). Connell's statement itself constructs a binary between theories and operating principles, as if one's style of approaching the world cannot be called theoretical. This construction has much to do with the structuralist construction of knowledge, with the Cartesian split between the mind and body, and with the common-sense view that theory is somehow aesthetic and esoteric (the thinking), while practice is pragmatic, embodied actions (the doing). Construction of this binary denies the realities of the ways in which theoretical propositions inform embodied realities. This in turn denies the realities of teachers' work; classroom practice is always pragmatic, embodied, and is always informed by some kind of thinking.

The discourses that construct teachers as atheoretical and practical permeate not only the texts of the EYLP, but also the practices and processes that have developed around the implementation of the programme in Victoria. For example, the Department of Education in Victoria funds a regular Early Years Conference. The focus of these conferences is exemplary stories of 'good practice'. The conferences are not open to everyone – academics must be invited to participate either as participants or presenters. Most presentations are by teachers who report on success stories related to the implementation of EYLP. We are not refuting here the validity of teachers acclaiming their best practice, but pointing out that these kinds of conferences continue to maintain the binary between theory and practice.

The EYLP proponents could probably counter this criticism with the often quoted claim that the programme is 'research-driven' which allows a further claim that it is theoretically justified. The research was conducted by Hill and Crevola. The Early Literacy Research Project was a large-scale longitudinal study with the aim to 'refine, implement and evaluate a whole-school, design approach to improving early literacy outcomes' (Hill and Crevola, 1999, p. 1). The study created a link between whole-school organization, the improvement of student learning outcomes and the equivalent increase in 'standards'. This link may be empirically valid, and this is not the place to delve into the research that supports or contradicts this claim. What has happened in Victoria, though, is that this research has become not only accepted as empirically valid, but it holds a uniquely esteemed place in educational circles. Other equally important longitudinal studies such as those undertaken by Susan Hill and her colleagues (1998, 2002) are ignored and, of particular concern, the Hill and Crevola study appears to be above critique as it is accepted in as equally normative terms as the accounts of literacy it describes.

Provisional linkages between discourses

These quite disparate discourses about literacy, the teaching of literacy, and about children's learning of literacy are connected, and interconnected, by 'provisional linkages'. These linkages are commonalities and taken-for-granted assumptions that seem reasonable and unquestionable. These discursive linkages are like the lumpy nodes that can appear within a rhizomatic root system, or like the coupling bands that connect varied systems of pipes in some underground water systems. The first of these linkages is provided by the notion of the individual child, a creature of progressivist discourses that has become a common assumption in many policy documents related to schools and teaching:

> 'The child' in western liberal democratic societies is positioned as a special category of person who lacks, for a time, the complete range of capacities necessary for full functioning as a citizen. 'The child' is understood to acquire those capacities by progressing steadily along a universal path of development to emerge as a self-regulating, autonomous individual, the possessor of a range of attributes.
>
> (Tyler, 1993, p. 35)

There is a dichotomy here that allows this developing child to be described in terms of individual characteristics, while at the same time she is representative of the whole of society. This dichotomy underlies one of the fundamental tensions in teaching today, especially in early years classrooms: the tension between paying attention to each child's unique and individual differences while at the same time teaching that child using homogeneous practices in small group or whole-class situations. As Davies and Hunt explain:

> The concerted nature of students' work to achieve a reading group . . . reveals the common-sense knowledge we have of classrooms, that they must work in a collective way if learning is to take place. At the same time, in the attitude of teaching-as-usual, we think of learning as an individual activity. We assess individual performances and take ourselves to be legitimately doing so.
>
> (2000, p. 113)

The second of these provisional linkages connecting different discursive systems in the EYLP is the assumption that literacy is best learned in classrooms. Fundamental to the educational project, and drawing on historical versions of pedagogy based on the child's mind as a *tabula rasa*, this assumption denies the postmodern realities of children's lives today as they interact and engage with varieties of textual representations almost from birth. There are clear indications in the EYLP texts that textual interactions, occurring in the home, playground, and in other social contexts outside of the classroom, are to be ignored. The use of 'book boxes' and 'take home readers' is illustrative of this assumption. Book boxes contain sets of 'levelled readers', usually readers drawn from a variety of reading schemes produced by commercial educational publishers. These readers provide a connection between the school and home. Each child takes home one of these readers and parents are required to read this text with their child and sign a sheet that indicates their compliance. The parent guide and video that are included in the Reading Kit outline the process for parents to use in this reading time. Here, school reading practices and processes are taken into homes while the home literacy practices are ignored, as is the significant and sustained research that reports on the importance of making home/school connections (see, for example, Heath, 1983; Moll, 1992; Freebody et al., 1995).

It is the gap between the discursive construction of 'students', 'literacy' and 'learning' within classrooms endorsed by the EYLP, and some of the kinds of home environments currently occupied by contemporary children that is illustrated in the hypothetical graphing investigation of literacy types and text types explored above. A different representation of this gap is provided by two brief descriptions of the competing 'worlds' of classrooms and homes. The snapshots that follow demonstrate the ways in which the discursive systems surrounding students, teachers, teaching and literacy (and the linkages that connect them) work to produce a normative view of literacy teaching and learning.

A classroom snapshot

The snapshot described below is an amalgam of the observations that Honan has made during her visits to classrooms, the written and verbal observations that her students share with her after their school practicum experiences, and descriptions of the models for the teaching strategies included in the EYLP videos. The snapshot is therefore not meant to provide empirical evidence of what is occurring in Victorian EYLP schools, but is intended to provide an illustration of the types of practices that are occurring. The snapshot is not intended to be embedded within any 'cinéma veritas' tradition of ethnographic analysis (see for e.g. Knobel, 1999), but in a more postmodern sense is an image that has been verbally enhanced in ways that are similar to the digital enhancement of glossy magazine photos.

> *The classroom wall clock reads 9.10am. There are about 22 small children sitting cross-legged on a large square of carpet at one end of the classroom. Their posture is largely determined by their distance from the teacher, who sits on an upright chair in front of the group. So those directly under her gaze*

sit straight-backed, hands neatly folded in their laps. As the distance grows, so the posture deteriorates until you find, hidden from the teacher's gaze by the bodies of the rest of the class, two small boys lying on their backs. One is quietly humming to himself and rocking his lower body and legs from side to side, almost as an adult does in a physiotherapy exercise. The other boy is wriggling his whole body in a snakelike attempt to move closer to his neighbour. His arm is outstretched, at the point of grabbing the other boy's hair.

The teacher's chair is located close to a blackboard that stretches the width of the classroom. On one part of the board is a brightly coloured chart, with the heading Task Board, and a table of five columns and four rows. The days of the week form the headings for the columns. At the beginning of each row is a pictograph, a symbolized representation of one of the teaching strategies from the EYLP. For example, guided reading is represented by an image of four heads and a book. There are four small cards attached to the chart with velcro, and each card holds the image of an Australian animal, platypus, wombat, kangaroo, echidna.

On the other side of the teacher's chair is an easel, on which are pinned some large pieces of blank paper. Leaning against this paper is a large 'big book'. The teacher is reading the big book to the class. The class all seem familiar with the text, with some children reading loudly along with her. Two children talk loudly to each other about what is coming up, describing in some detail to each other the contents of the following pages. As with the posture of the children, their attention to the book reading seems to be directly related to their proximity to the teacher. The teacher's gaze seems to be divided between the pages of the book she is reading, and those children who sit close to her. There is an invisible circle of literary appreciation drawn around the teacher and those eight or so children who appear to be enjoying the reading.

The teacher finishes the reading of the big book and draws the children's attention to the Task Board. She elicits group and individual responses to her questions from the class. To the two wriggling boys at the back, she asks: 'What group are you in Troy and Toby?' The boys sit up and call back, 'Wombats miss!!' 'And what will the Wombats be doing this morning?' After a few seconds of silence, she asks, 'Can one of the Kangaroos help the Wombats – what will the Wombats be doing this morning, Sarah?' Sarah, one of the girls sitting directly at the teacher's feet replies, 'Reading with you miss.' 'Good girl, Sarah. And what will the Kangaroos be doing?' There is a choral response as many of the class shout, 'Sheets!!!!' 'That's right, Kangaroos will be working on their worksheets at their desks.' The other two groups of children are reminded of their activities (reading from the Book Boxes, and reading with a parent helper, who is sitting quietly at the back of the classroom, close to the door). The teacher reminds the class of the rules for the morning: 'What happens when I'm working with the Wombats, girls *and boys? – What do you have to remember – Echidnas?' The Echidnas' responses are varied: 'Don't talk to you'; 'Stay away!', 'Sit in our seats til we've finished.' 'That's right, good girls, when I'm working with the Wombats I don't want to be interrupted, so you read your book quietly, and if you finish reading your book, what do you do?' 'Read it again!', the Echidnas reply in unison.*

The signal to move is almost invisible to the outsider. The teacher merely says, 'Right, off we go' and many of the children stand immediately and walk purposefully around the room. One girl goes to a corner and pulls out a large plastic crate filled with 'levelled readers'. Another girl goes to the teacher's desk and collects a cardboard folder with a Kangaroo drawn on the cover. Five children cluster around the parent helper, who appears not to notice them, as she is bent over her own daughter who is whispering in her ear. The Wombat group, four boys and two girls remain on the carpet. Some children sit at desks and pull out pencil cases containing pencils and coloured markers. Within a few minutes all children seem to be 'on task', reading quietly or aloud, writing on worksheets, or responding to questions from the teacher. There is a 'working buzz' in the room. Gradually though the buzz is subsumed by the sounds of giggles and loud conversations.

The Echidnas have all read their Book Box readers, and have obeyed the instruction to read them again. All five children have now read their texts twice, and now discard the books. They are giggling, telling stories, there is the occasional pinch or tweak of an arm or leg.

The Platypus group with the parent helper are taking turns to read aloud from a reader. They too have finished this 'round robin' once, but the parent has begun the reading again. The children who are waiting for their turn do not follow the text, but whisper to each other.

The Wombats are still working with the teacher, but she seems to find it difficult to hold all their attention at once – so when she asks one girl a question about the text they are reading, the other five children appear to be daydreaming.

The Kangaroo group seems to be the quietest, and seem to still all be on task. However, they have all finished answering the questions on their worksheets, and are quietly and carefully colouring in the illustrations that border the sheets.

Occasionally the teacher looks up from her reading and questioning and glances at the wall clock. At exactly 9.40am, she stands up and claps her hands in a short rhythmic pattern. The children all fall quiet, some instantly while others are nudged into silence by their neighbours or by a certain look from the teacher.

'Right, thank you Grade 1s, onto the carpet please', the teacher commands. While most children scamper and scramble to reach the carpet square, some detour to return books to the crate, and a small group cluster

around the teacher, eager to inform her of exciting developments during the 20-minute activity time. She hushes some, listens carefully to a couple, and gives permission for two to go to the toilet. She then resumes her straight-backed chair at the front of the class – this again seems to be an invisible signal to the class, many of whom begin to try to catch her attention – hands waving frantically in the air, calling out, 'Miss, Miss, me please, me!!' The teacher selects one child, 'Tanah, your turn I think today.' The small girl clambers through the group and stands beside the teacher. The teacher asks, 'What did you do today Tanah?' Tanah replies looking directly at the teacher. During her reply the teacher gently holds her shoulders in an attempt to direct her gaze towards the class, but Tanah's body resists the gentle pushes and swivels around again to look at the teacher. Tanah's reply seems well rehearsed, there are phrases within her reply that the teacher mouths silently along with Tanah. 'This morning, the Kangaroos wrote a lot of B words. Then we wrote our words in sentences. Then we coloured in our pictures of balls, and baskets and biscuits. Then we packed up our sheets.' The teacher asks three other children, representing each of the four groups, to come to the front one at a time. They each describe the activity engaged with, each using similar words and phrases. The other children sit on the carpet in much the same positions and postures as they had taken at the beginning of the morning. The same children sit upright and cross-legged close to the teacher and the same two boys lie on their backs on the edge of the carpet square, hidden from the teachers' gaze by the other children.

When Honan's preservice students return from their school practicum experiences in early years classrooms, she asks them to describe the literacy activities occurring, and to answer the question: What are children learning about reading during this activity? If we apply this question to the snapshot above, the answers could be:

- Reading involves being organized into small groups.
- Teachers read to the whole class, children read aloud in small groups.
- Reading is writing words beginning with the same consonant.
- Reading is colouring in pictures of words beginning with the same consonant.
- There is a connection between ability to read, and ability to listen to instructions, recall previous activities, and sit with straight backs and crossed legs (see Kamler et al., 1992).
- Reading is about reading the same text repeatedly until you are completely familiar with the text.
- Reading is about gaining operational skills, or being able to draw on codebreaking resources to make meaning from a text (Freebody and Luke, 2003).

- When we talk about reading, we talk about what we do with texts, rather than our feelings or understandings of the content of the texts.

A family snapshot

We now attempt to enter into the world of young children at home, through the writing of a snapshot that produces one version of the literacy practices engaged in by a (non)representative family. This snapshot draws on our combined experiences with young children in family homes, particularly Rowan's as a mother, and Honan's as a long-term visitor in her family and friends' homes. In this snapshot we have not deliberately set out to be as contradictory as possible to the classroom snapshot, but have attempted to describe what we observe as commonplace and unremarkable in these homes in which young children we know live.

> *The living area is open plan. The kitchen is bounded by a high bench that serves as a place to eat breakfast, talk on the wall-mounted telephone, talk to people working in the kitchen preparing food, serving drinks, stacking the dishwasher. It is cluttered with school notices, mail including junk mail catalogues, take-away food flyers, bills and other textual features of a busy family. A computer is set up on a desk in a corner of the living area, with an internet connection and colour printer attached. A large carpet square delineates a television viewing area, with two couches and a low table organized around a large screen television with DVD player attached. 'Surround sound' speakers and amplifier are also connected to a CD player. An adult visitor has brought her laptop computer which is open on the low table, with The Sims loaded and temporarily paused. A sliding glass door leads to an outside area: there are external speakers mounted to the outside wall here, a large wooden table and chairs, a barbecue, and bar fridge.*
>
> *There are three bedrooms in the house. There is a television with gaming machine attached in one bedroom. On the floor of this bedroom is an assortment of figurines, trading cards and magazines related to Pokémon and Digimon cartoon series. Electronic games for the gaming machine are stacked on top of the television. There is another television with VCR attached in the second bedroom. In this bedroom there are large posters of pop-stars, soapie actors, and football players adorning the walls. A bookshelf and study desk are stacked with various types of texts: Total Girl and Girlfriend magazines; copies of fictional texts written as series (as diverse as Goosebumps series by R. L. Stine, the Famous Five series by Enid Blyton, and the Just . . . series by Andy Griffith; a copy of Lord of the Rings is also on the bed); and school artefacts such as report cards, certificates of achievement, exercise books and folders filled with worksheets.*
>
> *There are four adults and six children in the house, although only two adults and six children actually live here. The father is in the kitchen,*

talking on the phone and stacking the dishwasher. The mother and two adult visitors are sitting in the outside area talking and listening to a CD that is broadcast through the outside speakers.

Two girls sit at the computer using the internet connection and instant messaging software to chat online with school friends. A younger girl is sitting on a small chair in front of the television in the living area, watching a DVD of The Lion King. There are two boys in one bedroom playing an electronic game.

One girl leaves the online chat to resume playing The Sims on the laptop. She provides a running commentary on the onscreen actions of the characters for the girl who remains at the computer desk, who offers suggestions for movements of the characters ('get them to dance', 'she needs to go to bed') while at the same time reading aloud some of the online chat to her friend who is playing The Sims ('he says he likes Tam!'). The younger girl uses the indexing feature of the DVD remote control to find and replay one scene of The Lion King, reviewing this scene three times. She sings loudly and stands up to dance along with the music from this scene. In the middle of dancing for the third time, she moves out into the outside seating area and switches to singing and dancing along with the music of The Beatles coming from the outside speakers.

One of the boys from the bedroom appears in the outside area and describes to no one in particular the actions of one of the characters in the electronic game (he slayed the dragon, I slayed the dragon and now he's, we've only got one more level and we've won!!). He moves into the living area and sits in front of the television for a few minutes, watching The Lion King.

If we sent the preservice students to observe this family home, what kinds of responses would we get to the question, what are children learning about reading in this space? Some possible answers might include:

- Reading is about gaining information, following instructions, and sharing with friends.
- Reading involves making meaning from texts displayed on screens.
- There are many types of text that we read onscreen – instructions for video games, online chat, digital 'menus' for DVDs, text boxes within simulation games.
- There are also many types of print texts that we read – children's series books, catalogues and newspapers, take-away menus, handwritten notes, school artefacts.
- Reading is not a static activity – reading can be undertaken simultaneously with other activities, reading can be undertaken while moving around a room.
- Reading does not usually involve adults and children reading together.

- Reading texts are closely related to television, movie and computer game texts with the same topic, similar content, and sometimes the same structural layout.

The different sets of assumptions that underpin the classroom and household snapshots clearly signal some difficult terrain for educators. Those who wish to reflect the 'real world' in their teaching will inevitably struggle to negotiate the versions of 'real literacy' that are endorsed within the discourses underpinning the EYLP. Certain texts are routinely excluded. Certain forms of literacy are privileged over others. Certain kinds of relationships between students and teachers are more consistently endorsed than others. And what is most interesting is that the texts, practices, relationships most likely to be excluded are precisely those central to the 'new times' discussed at the start of this chapter. So while educators are constantly reminded of the need to teach in ways that respond to contemporary times, formal literacy programmes are increasingly narrowing down (rather than widening out) understandings of literacy (and the ways this can be assessed).

And yet it is entirely possible that the outcomes measured within schools actively pursuing EYLP goals will be met with positive responses. In the final section of this chapter, then, we'd like to put forward some of the questions we believe should be asked before any conclusions are drawn about the success, failure, value or relevance of any early childhood literacy programme.

Questions for moving forward

> Henceforth, it is the map that proceeds the territory.
>
> (Jean Baudrillard, *Simulations*)

If we begin from the premise – outlined in the first half of this chapter – that contemporary educators have a responsibility to respond in systemic, persistent and meaningful ways to the contemporary world of children, certain kinds of questions must be asked of any literacy programme. These questions do not exclude attention to the extent to which children are encouraged or supported to develop operational skills associated with encoding and decoding 'traditional' literacy texts. But this is not the only criteria. Other questions must be asked. We are particularly interested in the extent to which the EYLP and similar contemporary literacy projects respond to the following challenges:

- What kinds of literacies are acknowledged, included/excluded and valued in the programme goals? Are operational, cultural and critical literacies accommodated?

- What kinds of texts are seen as legitimate classroom texts?
- To what extent, and in what kinds of ways, are texts chosen by children welcomed in the classroom?
- In what ways are children encouraged to look at the meanings naturalized within diverse texts?
- To what extent are social and cultural literacy agendas engaged with in the programme?
- To what extent is the diversity of the student population reflected in the content of texts?
- To what extent is the diversity of the student population reflected in the 'teaching' about/around certain texts, and text types?
- In what ways are teachers supported to develop their own literacies, and to enable them to incorporate a broader, more 'challenging' set of materials?
- In what ways are children's networks (of caregivers and families) legitimated within the chosen texts?
- In what ways does classroom practice support or complement out-of-school practice?
- In what ways does classroom practice constrain or devalue student enactments of 'out-of-school' literacies?

While this list is in no sense exhaustive, our main intention is to indicate the kinds of questions most likely to draw attention to the gaps and the silences within any literacy project. This is more than an academic exercise since the extent to which any programme includes or excludes diverse texts/points of views and people directly impacts upon the quality of the educational experience that children enjoy. And in a world that is characterized as much by persistently uneven educational outcomes as it is by anxieties over identity, citizenship and community, it seems to us absolutely vital that every discipline area, at every educational level, works to create links between diverse students and educational success.

And there is one final question that needs to be raised. This concerns the extent to which literacy programmes or frameworks designed to respond to 'new times' recognize and respond to the real capacities of teachers they involve. Narrow, prescriptive, overly structured programmes not only have little chance of engaging the full range of students, they also show little faith in the skills and abilities of classroom educators. To put it simply, teachers are not stupid. Nor are they characterized by a lack of vision, foresight, creativity or imagination. This is not to suggest that teachers are not in need of support (be it in the form of professional development opportunities, or personnel assistance, or the provision of resources) to respond to the complex terrain of literacy education. But it is absolutely vital that literacy programmes designed to respond to the 'real world' recognize and build upon the existing interests and skills of students, teachers and community members. It is this combination, this particular mindset, will help us navigate the complex terrain, and minimize the chance that we lose sight of the people who must remain always at the centre of our enquiries: contemporary children. Many years ago, French philosopher Michel de Certeau made the powerful point that:

> Finally, beyond the question of methods and contents, beyond what it says, the measure of a work is what it keeps silent. And we must say that the scientific studies – and undoubtedly the works they highlight – include vast and strange expanses of silence. These blank spots outline a geography of the *forgotten*.
>
> (de Certeau, 1986, p. 131)

The key challenge for literacy educators is to embrace the challenge of mapping out their past, present and future work patterns to examine not only what they include, but also, and most importantly, those people, ideas and perspectives who are silenced and forgotten. With this in mind, we have a much better chance of creating the kind of literacy futures that can genuinely claim to respond to the demands of these complex, changing times.

References

Alderson, A. (2000) Early years literacy policy and practice, in Research Evaluation Programme, Higher Education Division, Department of Education, Training and Youth Affairs, *The Impact of Educational Research*. http://www.detya.gov.au/highered/respubs/impact/splitpdf_default.htm (accessed 20 May 2004).

Appadurai, A. (1990) Disjuncture and difference in global cultural economy, in M. Featherstone (ed.) *Global Culture: Nationalism, Globalization and Modernity* (pp. 295–310). London: Sage.

Appadurai, A. (2001) New logics of violence. http://www.india-seminar.com/2001/503/503%20arjun%20apadurai.htm (accessed 14 May 2004).

Apple, M. and Jungck, S. (1990) 'You don't have to be a teacher to teach this unit': teaching, technology, and gender in the classroom, *American Educational Research Journal*, 27(2): 227–51.

Australian Education Union (2004) Essential learnings. http://www.aeuvic.asn.au/professional/papers/Essential_Learnings/ (accessed 10 June 2004).

Ball, S.J. (1994) *Education Reform: A Critical and Post-Structural Approach*. Buckingham: Open University Press.

Baudrillard, J. (1983) *Simulations*. New York: Semiotext(e).

Cambourne, B. (1988) *The Whole Story: Natural Learning and the Acquisition of Literacy in the Classroom*. Auckland: Ashton Scholastic.

Comber, B. (1992) Critical literacy: a selective review and discussion of recent literature, *South Australian Educational Leader*, 3(1): 1–10.

Comber, B., Green, B., Lingard, B. and Luke, A. (1998) Literacy debates and public education: a question of 'crisis'? In A. Reid (ed.) *Going Public: Education Policy and Public Education in Australia*. Deakin West, AC: Australian Curriculum Studies Association.

Connell, R.W. (1985) *Teachers' Work*. Sydney: George Allen and Unwin.

Cope, B. and Luke, C. (2000) Introduction: Multiliteracies: the beginnings of an idea, in B. Cope and M. Kalntzis (eds) *Multiliteracies: Literacy Learning and the Design of Social Futures* (pp. 3–8). South Yarra: Macmillan.

Davies, B. and Hunt, R. (2000) Classroom competencies and marginal positionings, in B. Davies, *A Body of Writing, 1990–1999*. Walnut Creek, CA: Alta Mira Press.

de Certeau, M. (1986) *Heterologies*. Minneapolis: University of Minnesota Press.

Deleuze, G. and Guattari, F. (1987) *A Thousand Plateaus: Capitalism and Schizophrenia*. London: The Athlone Press.

Freebody, P., Ludwig, C. and Gunn, S. (1995) Everyday literacy practices in and out of schools in low socio-economic urban communities, a project funded by the Commonwealth Department of Employment, Education and Training, as part of the National Equity Program for Schools, National Priorities, Literacy and Learning Component and administered by the Curriculum Corporation, Commonwealth of Australia, Canberra.

Freebody, P. and Luke, A. (2003) Literacy as engaging with new forms of life: the 'four roles' model, in G. Bull and M. Anstey (eds) *The Literacy Lexicon* (2nd edn). Frenchs Forest: NSW Pearson Education.

Goodson, I. (1997) The life and work of teachers, in B.J. Biddle, T.L. Good and I.F. Goodson (eds) *International Handbook of Teachers and Teaching*, Vol. 1, Dordrecht: Kluwer Academic Publishers.

Green, B. and Hodgens, J. (1996) Manners, morals, meanings: English teaching, language education and the subject of 'Grammar', in B. Green and C. Beavis (eds) *Teaching the English Subjects: Essays on English Curriculum History and Australian Schooling*. Geelong: Deakin University Press.

Grosz, E. (1995) *Space, Time and Perversion*. Sydney: Allen and Unwin.

Halliday, M.A.K and Martin, J.R. (1993) *Writing Science: Literacy and Discursive Power*. London: Falmer Press.

Heath, S.B. (1983) *Ways with Words: Language, Life and Work in Communities and Classrooms*. Cambridge: Cambridge University Press.

Hill, P.W. and Crevola, C.A. (1999) Key features of a whole-school, design approach to literacy teaching in schools. Paper presented at ACER Research Conference October 1999: Improving Literacy Learning, Melbourne, Victoria.

Hill, S., Comber, B., Louden, W., Reid, J. and Rivalland, J. (2002) *100 Children Turn 10: A Longitudinal Study of Literacy Development from the Year Prior to School to the First Four Years of School*. Canberra, ACT: Department of Education, Science and Training.

Hill, S., Comber, B., Louden, W., Rivalland, J. and Reid, J. (1998) *100 Children Go to School: Connections and Disconnections in Literacy Development in the Year Prior to School and the First Year of School*. Canberra, ACT: Department of Employment, Education, Training and Youth Affairs.

Honan, E. (2001) (Im)plausibilities: a rhizo-textual analysis of the Queensland English Syllabus. Unpublished doctoral thesis, James Cook University, Townsville.

Honan, E. (2004) (Im)plausibilities: a rhizo-textual analysis of policy texts and teachers' work, *Educational Philosophy and Theory*, 36(3): 267–81.

Kamler, B., Maclean, R., Reid, J. and Simpson, A. (1992) *Shaping up Nicely: The Formation of Schoolgirls and Schoolboys in the First Month of School*. Canberra, ACT: Department of Employment, Education, and Training.

Knobel, M. (1999) *Everyday Literacies: Students, Discourse, and Social Practice*. New York: Peter Lang.

Lather, P. (1994) The absent presence: patriarchy, capitalism and the nature of teacher work, in L. Stone (ed.) *The Education Feminism Reader*. New York: Routledge.

Luke, C. (2000) Cyber-schooling and technological change: multiliteracies for new times, in B. Cope and M. Kalantzis (eds) *Multiliteracies: Literacy Learning and the Design of Social Futures* (pp. 69–91). South Yarra: Macmillan.

McWilliam, E. (1994) *In Broken Images: Feminist Tales for a Different Teacher Education*. New York: Teachers College Press.

Martin, J.R. (1991) Critical literacy: the role of a functional model of language. *Australian Journal of Reading*, 14(2): 117–32.

Moll, L.C. (1992) Literacy research in community and classrooms: a sociocultural approach, in R. Beach, J.L Green, M.L Kamil and T. Shanahan (eds) *Multidisciplinary Perspectives on Literacy Research*. Urbana, IL: Illinois NCTE.

Nichols, S. (2004) Questioning development: introduction to Special Issue, *Australian Journal of Language and Literacy*, 27(2): 90–8.

Reid, J. (1996) Working out one's own salvation: programming primary English teaching, in B. Green and C. Beavis (eds) *Teaching the English Subjects: Essays on English Curriculum History and Australian Schooling*. Geelong: Deakin University Press.

Robertson, S.L. (1996) 'Teachers' work, restructuring and post-Fordism: constructing the new 'professionalism', in I.F. Goodson and A. Hargreaves (eds) *Teachers' Professional Lives*. London: Falmer Press.

Rowan, L. (2003) Back from the brink: reclaiming 'quality' in the pursuit of a transformative education agenda. Geelong, Quality Learning Research Priority Area, Faculty of Education, Deakin University. http://www.deakin.edu.au/education/quality_learning (accessed 5 June 2004).

Spivak, G. (1996) Explanation and culture marginalia, in D. Landry and G. MacLean (eds) *The Spivak Reader. Selected Works of Gayatri Chakravorty Spivak*. New York: Routledge.

Tyler, D. (1993) Making better children, in D. Meredyth and D. Tyler (eds) *Child and Citizen: Genealogies of Schooling and Subjectivity*. Brisbane: Qld Institute for Cultural Policy Studies, Faculty of Humanities, Griffith University.

Victorian Department of Education (1997) *Early Years Literacy Program*. South Melbourne, Vic: Addison-Wesley Longman.

Walkerdine, V. (1984) Developmental psychology and the child-centred pedagogy: the insertion of Piaget into early education, in J. Henriques, W. Hollway, C. Urwin, C. Venn and V. Walkerdine (eds) *Changing the Subject: Psychology, Social Regulation and Subjectivity*. London: Methuen.

14 Curriculum, pedagogies and practice with ICT in the information age

Nicola Yelland

Introduction

Information and communication technologies (ICT) have fundamentally changed the ways in which we carry out everyday and academic tasks and in doing so have permeated every aspect of our lives in a myriad of ways. However, even though this is apparent in personal and social lifeworlds from the local to the global, the use of computers in educational contexts is still not fully integrated into learning, despite the infusion of policy and hardware into our schools and the fact that new technologies are an important part of children's lives (CEO, 1999; Kaiser Family Foundation, 1999). In fact there are still those who question government spending on ICT (e.g. Healy, 1999; Alliance for Childhood, 2000; Armstrong and Casement, 2000) in an age in which nothing remains untouched by new technologies.

Twenty years ago there was a vigorous debate about the role of technology in early childhood curriculum (e.g. Barnes and Hill, 1983; Cuffaro, 1984). It was contended that young children should not use computers because the representational medium was too complex for their levels of understanding according to developmental theory (e.g. Piaget, 1953). Additionally, it was also considered that once children were 'hooked' on computers, they would become transfixed by them and the activities inherent to their use and would then cease to play in their 'real-life' environments with three-dimensional materials. It was then suggested that young children's learning and development would be negatively affected by this and that they would become socially inept and isolated.

Certainly current arguments which call for a suspension of funds to support the purchase of computer hardware and software in schools (e.g. Armstrong and Casement, 2000) and a moratorium on the use of computers in American schools (Alliance for Childhood, 2000) receive good media coverage. They are supported by misleading arguments and anecdotal stories of wary parents, like one who 'called upon his school board to eliminate all computer use in kindergarten through fifth grade and to use computers in middle school for library searches only' (quoted in Armstrong and Casement, 2000, p. 199). No reason was given how or why this person had formed this opinion, yet it was represented as a commonly held view. The arguments against the use of computers by children are often framed in budgetary terms. That is, the money spent on computers could be better spent elsewhere on traditional educational materials. For example, Armstrong and Casement argued: 'While we were spending a bundle on computers, our library needed books, magazines, and atlases, and many classes were short on math textbooks' (2000, p. x). The statement privileges old technologies but does not provide a rationale to support the assertions made. It is evident that publishers of all the text materials cited above have to ensure that their product is marketable, and they are not all subject to quality controls. It is interesting to ask, for example, when is the quality of books, from an educational perspective, discussed and how long is it before the information in a particular book is outdated, or even, obsolete? In relation to the contention that the library needs magazines, it is not clear why schools would in fact allocate funds to these when many are on line and not only easily accessible, but available at no cost. The inclusion of atlases in this example is particularly surprising. Here is a wonderful example of when the Internet is advantageous over books. If you go to a search engine and enter 'atlas' or 'world atlas' or any permutation on those words, or use a specific country as a request, you will acquire a myriad of maps (e.g. www.mapresources.com) and associated resources which are current because they are regularly updated, and far beyond what a traditional print-based atlas can provide. Finally, the authors mention the much-needed 'math text books'. There is a certain irony here. Mathematics texts often emulate those features of bad software that such authors as Armstrong and Casement, and Healy, constantly criticize. That is, they drill basic facts, contain disembedded and abstract tasks and rarely engage children in authentic problem solving or problem posing in relevant contexts. They are selected by State departments and uniformly administered into the school system with little consultation and much expense either to the district (local education authority), or indirectly, to parents. Attendance at any of the national conferences for teachers reveals the extent of this lucrative industry. It has now branched out into producing companion books and associated exercises for the various National and State tests, again with the aim of drilling the basic facts into as many young minds as possible. Given the nature of expenditure on implementing texts for each of the subject areas in schools, it is surprising that there is not a call for a moratorium on the use of textbooks in which the same questions are posed as with the use of computers: that is: do Math/English texts improve the quality of instruction in schools? (Armstrong and Casement, 2000, p. xi).

There seems to exist a great deal of concern about the amount of time that children spend using computers which the data shows is unwarranted. For example, Shields and Behrman (2000) cited the results of national survey data which revealed that children from 2 to 17 years of age spend approximately '34 minutes per day, on average, using computers at home, with use increasing with age. (Preschoolers ages 2 to 5 averaged 27 minutes per day ...) ... exposure in the early primary grades, at least, is relatively modest' (ibid., p. 6) They also found that use of computers in the home context was associated with 'slightly better' (ibid., p. 9) academic use. Other studies of achievement have reported gains in reading, mathematics, computer knowledge and grammar for children with extensive experience with computers in an after-school program called the *5th Dimension* (Blanton, Moorman, Hayes and Warner, 2000). This group achieved better test scores, and were also more proficient in following adult direction than a group that did not participate in the programme.

It is interesting to note that after reading this particular section of Armstrong and Casement's book, I entered the keywords *math texts, math activities, math experiences* in a well-known search engine, and found an extensive range of resources that were readily available and more learner-centred than the usual text series. One that was of interest (www.project-approach.com/examples/previous/cafe.htm) discussed an integrated approach via the use of a cafeteria project. There were other examples available to peruse in linked sites. The range of authentic activities that were provided supported the acquisition of numeracy in a much more meaningful way than the completion of a series of algorithms with the goal of obtaining a right answer, to prove you could execute an operation, as commonly found in math texts. Even when the texts attempt to link the process of calculating to an everyday activity like shopping, it is often rendered useless by asking learners to work with fictitious products in mythical shops with unrealistic prices. They then compound the problem by requiring the use of a process to determine the amount of change required which is often the complete opposite of what actually happens in authentic shopping contexts. That is, using subtraction to find the difference between amounts rather than counting on to find the amount of change.

The focus of the debate on the use of computers in schools so often gets bogged down around denouncing their use because of inadequate software, violent video games and the possibility of children accessing pornography on the Internet if unsupervised. They are clouded with irrelevant questions like 'Why should children be exposed to computer technology from an early age? Are computers and computer software so essential to children's education? What can we expect them to gain?' (Armstrong and Casement, 2000). Children are exposed to computers and a vast range of new technologies in every aspect of their lives. It is impossible for any of us to avoid technologies since they are integral to everything we do. If schools ignore this, they cease to be relevant to life in the twenty-first century. Children need to be able to choose to use technology for their activities in school when they need to. They should be able to engage with ideas in new and dynamic ways because of the new technologies and become creative, collaborative problem solvers and problem posers because of these experiences.

New curriculum for the twenty-first century

One of the basic problems associated with the use of computers in schools is that their use has been mapped onto existing curricula which were created in a non-computer age. Thus, it is difficult for teachers to create opportunities for new explorations and understandings with ICT since the content of curricula and the assessment of outcomes inhibit this. Research has shown (e.g. Tinker, 1999; Yelland, 1999; Yelland, 2002c) that we have a great deal of information about the ways in which new technologies are able to transform learning but the school curriculum essentially remains the same as it was in the last century. Resnick (1998, 2000) has urged us to regard the use of computers like that of any other materials that we might find in early childhood settings, like finger paints, blocks and beads, since they are all useful for active learning, inquiry and problem solving. He suggested, like others, that computers afford the opportunity for new types of explorations as well as for possibilities of sharing the strategies and findings with a wider community. Such a perspective, of course, requires a radical rethinking of the curriculum that encapsulates contemporary notions about creativity, imagination and design that provide opportunities for children to explore and investigate in ways that were not possible without the new technologies. It means that they will be able to generate new knowledge as well as learn about existing knowledge bases. Such an approach has already been suggested since 'Studies overwhelmingly suggest that computer-based technology is only one element in what must be a coordinated approach to improving curriculum, pedagogy, assessment and teacher development, and other aspects of school structure' (Rochelle et al., 2000, p. 78).

In rethinking the structure of new curriculum, there has been an increasing recognition that curriculum decision-making needs to take note of children's out-of-school experiences and build upon them. Dede, for example, has called on educators to 'reshape children's learning experiences in and out of school to prepare them for a future quite different from the immediate past. Meeting this challenge involves teaching new skills, not simply teaching old skills better' (2002, p. 178).

The Australian Council of Deans of Education put forward a charter for education that focused on *new learning* in the twenty-first century (2001). New learning was conceptualized around eight propositions:

1   Education has a much larger role to play in creating society.
2   Learning will be lifelong and lifewide.

3   Education is one of the main ways to deliver the promise of democracy.
4   A new basics is emerging.
5   Technology will become central to all learning.
6   The work of educators will be transformed.
7   The place of the public and private in education will be redefined.
8   The focus of education policy must change from public cost to public investment.

For the purposes of this chapter, propositions 4 and 5 are most relevant to our rethinking of new curricula and the contributions that ICT can make to the learning processes of children in our schools.

In the context of the charter the 'new basics' is a very different way of organizing knowledge (Table 14.1). For example: Mathematics is not viewed as 'a set of correct answers but a method of reasoning, a way of figuring out a certain kind of system and structure in the world' (2001, p. 89). The new learning curriculum is based on three learning areas which are mapped onto three domains of social action which 'define the new person'. New technologies underpin the creation of a new basics curriculum in schools and have become important in the transformation of learning relationships both in school and out of school.

There have also been a number of other initiatives to address a new way of thinking about curriculum in our schools. In Queensland, Australia, for example, a 'new basics' curriculum has been identified which is supported by a productive pedagogies framework and rich task assessment. The new basic curriculum does not consider knowledge as residing in the traditional disciplines but rather has four organizational components:

1   *Life pathways and social futures*: *Who am I and where am I going?*
2   *Multiliteracies and communications media*: *How do I make sense and communicate with the world?*
3   *Active citizenship*: *What are my rights and responsibilities in communities, cultures and economies?*
4   *Environments and technologies*: *How do I describe, analyse and shape the world around me?*

Alongside the Queensland new basics curriculum, a productive pedagogies framework has been conceptualized in four basic areas (see Department of Education Queensland, 2001, p. 7):

1   *Intellectual quality*: to ensure that students have opportunities to acquire and manipulate information and ideas in ways which transform their meaning and implications, understand that knowledge is

Table 14.1 The new basics: new worker, new citizen, new person

	Work	Civics	Identity
Techne Technology, and more – the capacity to use various tools and instruments to get things done, technique, method, practical reasoning and science, human impacts on the environment.	Scanning Discovery Innovation	Agency Selection Advocacy	Navigation Discernment Appropriation
Oeconomia Commerce, business, economics and more – frameworks for getting things done in the social world, for being productive and effective, including work in the home and community as well as paid work.	Calculation Entrepreneurship Innovation	Complexity Motivation Mediation	Negotiation Reflexivity Application
Humanitas Understanding one's own culture and the cultures of others, acting sociably, boundary crossing and working with diversity.	Investigation Cooperation Reflection	Communication Ambiguity Compromise	Multiplicity Recognition Transformation

Source: ACDE (2001, p. 92).

not a fixed body of information, and can coherently communicate ideas, concepts, arguments and explanations with rich detail.

2 *Connectedness*: to ensure that students have experiences in which they can engage with real, practical or hypothetical problems which connect to the world beyond the classroom, which are not restricted by subject boundaries and which are linked to their prior knowledge.

3 *Supportive classroom environment*: to ensure that students influence the nature of the activities they undertake, engage seriously in their study, regulate their behaviour, and know of the explicit criteria and high expectations of what they are to achieve.

4 *Recognition of difference*: to ensure that students know about and value a range of cultures, create positive human relationships, respect individuals, and help to create a sense of community.

Further, rich task assessments (Dept. of Education, Queensland, 2001) engage children in authentic activities that may involve the use of new technologies, or not. What distinguishes them from traditional assessment is that they are multifaceted and require an integration of knowledge and skills which is well beyond the simplistic type of knowledge and skill use that is assessed in computer marked multiple choice tests. Further, they do not have one right answer in the traditional sense, and might require working and collaborations in groups. For example, a rich task for Years 1 to 3 (age 6 to 8 years) level might be to create an itinerary for a visitor to the local town or school. Or students can investigate an endangered plant or animal and present a case regarding the extent to which it is at risk. They may then use this investigation to take constructive action and create a persuasive argument for action and present their case to an audience using multimedia of their choice.

The assessment debate is one that is often used to dismiss the investment or funds that have been spent on providing computers in schools today. Governments want to know that their investment has 'paid off' while critics state 'if computers make a difference . . . it has yet to show up in achievement' (Salva, cited in Armstrong and Casement, 2000, p. 197). The arguments are interesting from many perspectives, apart from the fact that this question is never asked of other educational materials. One wonders why anyone would think that the 'old learning' measured in tests would be influenced by computer use. Yet, the same question is never asked about textbooks, which tend to focus on teaching facts that are often included as test items. Additionally, it would be useful to see the *empirical* data to show that young children learn best via play, and the precise ways in which playing with materials such as blocks, play dough, and jigsaws – all materials found extensively in preschools, specifically *improve cognitive outcomes* and *educational achievement* for children. The benefits of such materials are taken for granted but rarely scrutinized to the same extent that computers are.

Dede (2000) recognized that fluency in higher-order thinking skills is an essential component of living effectively in the twenty-first century. He suggested that a particular important skill is the ability to 'thrive on fluency', which he defined as the ability to make quick decisions based on incomplete information in new situations. He also indicated that other skills are needed in this new era. These included being able to collaborate with others and the ability to navigate and select information that is relevant to a problem-solving process.

In their arguments against the use of computers, Armstrong and Casement (2000) finally state that 'Good teachers convey their own interests and excitement in learning.' This should also be the case with their enthusiasm for using new technologies to advance learning. Advocates of the use of computers in educational contexts have always had, as their central interest, new ways of learning and as we are now living in the twenty-first century, it is even more essential to incorporate the use of ICT into school learning environments. This view is supported by Rochelle et al. who concluded that studies have revealed that:

> a teacher's ability to help students depends on a mastery of the structure of the knowledge in the domain taught. Teaching with technology is no different in this regard. Numerous literature surveys link student technology achievement to teachers' opportunities to develop their own computer skills.
>
> (2000, p. 90)

In summary, Dede puts forward a challenge that

> we have the technical and economic capacity to develop technologically rich learning environments for children to prepare them for life as adults in a world very different from the one we have known. Whether we have the political and cultural will to accomplish innovative uses of media for learning and empowerment across all segments of society remains to be seen.
>
> (2000, p. 180)

In this chapter I look at three different ways that schools and teachers have incorporated the use of ICT into learning experiences with children in their classes. These schools and teachers did not begin the change process by mapping the new technologies onto their existing curriculum. Instead they had the courage to take a whole-school approach to rethinking their pedagogy within the confines of a state education system with a stringent accountability framework in place, which included State and National mandatory testing. This chapter will provide examples of the ways in which numeracy has been reconceptualized in light of this process – so that it becomes relevant to children's present and, hopefully, their future lives. Next, we explore examples of rich tasks within the context of an integrated curriculum approach. Finally, we examine the ways in which learners may keep a record of their learning processes so that they are able to reflect on the strategies deployed as well as consider the knowledge-building process inherent to the tasks that they have completed.

Innovative teaching and learning with ICT

Forman and Steen (1999) have characterized the times we live in as being a data-drenched society. By this they mean that we are surrounded by numbers and the need to process, interpret and use them in a large variety of ways. They suggested that the need to become quantitatively literate or numerate has indeed become an important imperative for citizens. Life in the twenty-first century also requires that we feel confident and competent with the use of ICT and the development of what we call higher-order thinking skills (i.e. being able to think creatively and in divergent ways, analysing contexts and making plans to solve problems, posing problems, collaborating effectively in teams, monitoring progress, responding to feedback, synthesizing ideas and re-evaluating new plans where necessary) which should now be included as essential elements or skills inherent to the 'new' basics need for living effectively in the present day.

Around the world there has been recognition by educators that it is imperative that education should have as one of its goals the preparation of numerate citizens who can apply practical mathematical skills and knowledge to their everyday life (e.g., Australian Council for Educational Research, 1990; Her Majesty's Inspectorate, 1998; National Council of Teachers of Mathematics [NCTM], 1998, 2000; Department of Education Training and Youth Affairs [DETYA], 1999, 2000). Further, new demands in high performance workplaces (Maughan and Prince Ball, 1999) mean that a traditional view of mathematics which focused on memorization, rote learning and knowing facts devoid of context and application has been replaced with one in which mathematics has some purpose and application, and where becoming numerate is regarded as an essential component of schooling (e.g. DETYA, 2000). Such a vision considers mathematics and becoming numerate in the context of societal and individual expectations. This vision has been accompanied by a shift in pedagogy which now emphasizes the use of both whole class and small group teaching, active exploration, inquiry and problem solving, engagement with mathematical ideas via collaborations and creative explorations, mathematical representations incorporating a variety of media which include the use of ICT and the communication of findings with peers and authentic audiences.

In a project[1] that aimed to explore the concept of numeracy in light of such changes, the research team worked with teachers documenting the ways in which mathematics is used specifically as a skills base for numeracy and the ways in which children, in the school context, use skills and knowledge from mathematics across the curriculum. For the purposes of the project mathematics was regarded as the 'school subject' in which the children experience the skills and knowledge base, and numeracy was conceptualized as the application of these in a variety of formal and informal contexts. This occurred within the subject called Mathematics, across the curriculum in other subject areas, as well as in extra-curricula activities such as school excursions and in the children's homes.

In observations of Mathematics lessons and those of other subject areas it soon became apparent that each 'subject' had its own content, but that it was not always exclusive to that subject. The deployment of processes, such as those of active inquiry, problem solving, problem posing, exploration and communication of ideas was in evidence across the curriculum depending on the philosophy of the teacher. Further, it was evident that there was a need to make explicit the connections between the various activities and ideas that children experienced in the course of their 'school work', so that children were able to think about them from different viewpoints or perspectives.

Teachers' comments and observations of classrooms confirmed that 'old learning' was about knowledge as content and the acquisition of skills, often in a vacuum. In this way teachers constantly felt the pressure to 'cover' content, traditionally organized in 'key learning areas' and to test what students 'know'. In contrast, 'new learning' was concerned with knowledge-building communities, the acquisition and refining of skills and processes (which included skills regarding the use of ICT) via active exploration, inquiry, problem solving and posing and communication of ideas using multiple modes of representations to illustrate a variety of ways of understanding. In exploring the Mathematics curriculum and plans of the teachers, it was evident that there existed various forms of activity that made up the curriculum, that ranged on a continuum from being uni-dimensional to multi-dimensional. Basically, uni-dimensional activities were simple sequences of activity that usually had a single outcome, and they were often used as an introduction to concepts and processes. The pace of activity was then largely determined by the collective yet the tasks were carried out individually by each child in the class. Multi-dimensional activities generally built on or followed these basic tasks and were integrated investigations in which skills and concepts were used in innovative ways to solve authentic problems which often could not be categorized into traditional subject areas. This is shown in more detail schematically in Figure 14.1.

It was also evident that ICT had a vital role to play in learning experiences, both as one way of acquiring knowledge about content and as a vehicle for communicating ideas in effective ways (e.g. Kilderry, Yelland, Laziridis and Dragicevic, 2003). Thus, traditional conceptualizations of numeracy based on the effective application of number in everyday, or supposed 'real-world' contexts, were limiting the type of activities that were encountered in these contexts. The types of numeracies observed in the classrooms were dynamic and multi-dimensional, and could not be separated from the methods of inquiry used (e.g. problem solving and problem posing) and the sharing and communication of new ideas with audiences. They were also experienced in a variety of modes that were related to the use of various forms of new technologies. This then called for a reconceptualization of numeracy in the plural, since it was apparent that there was not a singular element but rather a range of multi-modal activities and applications in diverse contexts that were in evidence. The dimensions of these are illustrated in Figure 14.2.

In the model, the basic tenet of numeracy, that is to know, and be able to

Uni-dimensional ◄————————► Multi-dimensional

1. Using mathematical concepts and processes

Structured use	Open-ended use
• The task requires a single outcome and usually only one way is accepted to achieve it • The teacher has structured the task for learner to use and practise a particular process or concept • The children complete the task requirement(s) and do not deviate from set goal(s) • Children are not challenged to go beyond the single outcome or level achieved • Traditional media used (pencil, paper)	• The task allows for problem solving and problem posing opportunities in open-ended investigations • The children share strategies and have input into the direction of their learning • Children are motivated and inspired to investigate and trial ideas • There are opportunities for the children to experience challenges • The children and teacher integrate various media, including ICT

2. Applying mathematical knowledge

Focused application	Extended application
• Specific mathematical concepts and processes are introduced via structured tasks • The application/use is not integrated with other knowledge • There are few connections made between the task and the children's prior understandings	• A range of mathematical concepts and processes are applied by the children • Application of knowledge is integrated • Connections are made and encouraged between the task and the children's prior understandings • The children use their own initiative and draw on a broad range of knowledge and processes to complete the task

3. Opportunities for exploration

Minimal opportunities	Multiple opportunities
• Children are mostly taught in large groups (whole class instruction) • The task is mostly teacher-directed and completed individually • The children are encouraged not to deviate from predetermined instructional plan • Children respond with yes/no answers or closed/fixed answers • The child mainly learns process/concept in isolation • The children may not show interest in the task if the concept is already known and the solution is mechanical application of skill	• Children have ample time in large and small groups and on their own to conceptualize, plan and reflect • The children engage and lead discussion about their learning • Tasks are initiated and/or extended by the child • The structure of the session is flexible • Children can approach the task in different ways • The children can learn additional and complementary processes and mathematical concepts in task solution • Collaborative and cooperative learning is encouraged • The children find the task meaningful and are interested

4. Learning outcomes

Limited learning outcome(s)	Varied learning outcomes
• The children's work looks the same • The learning processes are specific to the task • There are right and wrong answers and particular processes to follow • Opportunity to use initiative is limited • The children's own interpretations and learning extensions are not recognized as valid • Communication of findings is not valued as a learning outcome	• The children choose different media to represent and communicate their ideas and knowledge • The children's learning processes are varied • There are multiple solutions and outcome levels • The children develop confidence in their own learning initiatives • The children's additional learning is recognized as valid or important • The children communicate their findings to others

Figure 14.1   Mathematical tasks continuum.

apply/use mathematical concepts, in a variety of contexts, is adhered to. However, traditionally, this has been related to the use of number. This has led to a narrow definition of numeracy which is no longer appropriate. More detailed and relevant understandings are derived from also considering the

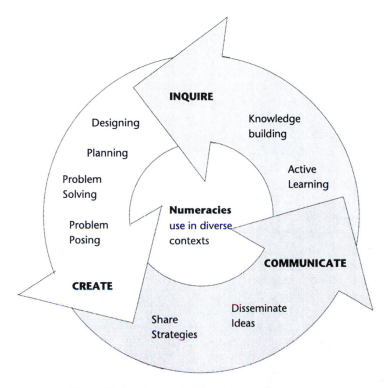

Figure 14.2 Numeracies for the twenty-first century.

different ways in which applications and contexts impact on learning processes. Additionally, there is recognition that numeracies involve opportunities for learners to inquire, create and communicate their ideas in various and appropriate modes of representation. It has been helpful to use this model to consider not only the types of learning and examples of numeracies that children have been engaged in, both individually and collectively, but also as a frame for planning learning opportunities to assist children to become numerate. Many of these opportunities incorporate the use of ICT as a natural choice for investigations and employ them to represent their ideas as well as for sharing and communicating the findings of their explorations.

Individual tasks, both uni- and multi-dimensional, need to provide contexts in which children can use ICT, or not, as part of the learning process. In one example, with a preparatory class with children of 5 years of age, a series of uni-dimensional tasks were used to introduce and use the operation of division, and link it to other mathematics concepts.

The lesson began with the children all seated together in front of the teacher who asked them about songs and rhymes that they knew which incorporated mathematical ideas or operations. They started with counting and the children enthusiastically sang, '1–2–3–4–5 once I caught a fish alive!' The children then went through various songs and activities before singing 'BaBa Black sheep!' at the request of Paul. When the teacher asked Paul what mathematical operation was used in the song, Paul explained that it was division since: 'Well, there are three bags of wool and they are divided up between the master, dame and the little boy who lives down the lane.' After the 'whole class' time the children worked in their groups on various activities about division which required them to use the operation in different ways. One task was based on the computer with the *Kidpix* software (Figure 14.3).

The task instructions were: 'Laura, Dean and Harrison wanted to buy all the goldfish in the Aquarium. Share the goldfish equally between them and record your findings.' When the children came to do the task they had a basic template of a large aquarium and three small bowls labelled with the names of the children who were getting the goldfish on the screen. The children could choose the number that they wanted to start with and create their own fish. In this way, the context became more meaningful for them rather than just completing pre-designed algorithms, with or without pictures, and entering the numbers in a number sentence on a sheet of paper. Not only that, but the children were then able to use the features of the environment to allocate the fish one by one to the individual tanks and if there were any left over,

Let's Divide

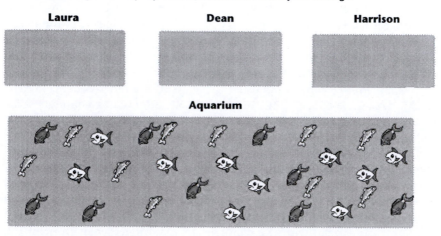

Laura, Dean and Harrison wanted to buy all the goldfish in the Aquarium. Share the goldfish equally between them and record your findings.

Laura   **Dean**   **Harrison**

Aquarium

Figure 14.3   The aquarium.

they were able to delete them and in doing so have their first experience of remainders, but not how to accommodate them!

This uni-dimensional task reinforced the concept in such a way as to give the children choice and ownership and afforded them the opportunity to work both individually and collaboratively so that they were able to talk about the actions and mathematical operations that they were using. In this way the experience, together with the others in the mathematics rotation that day helped to enrich their idea of the concept of division since it allowed for choice and control of one's own learning and thus went beyond being a simple uni-dimensional task.

Multi-dimensional tasks are characterized by their integrated nature and complexity, in that they consist of a series of tasks that may or may not result in a final product that is shared with an audience in their chosen media. The tasks that exemplify this way of thinking about numeracy were in evidence throughout the school in the study. Children were engaged in a myriad of projects ranging from *Energy* to preserving our national parks and made choices about the ways in which they want to conduct the investigation, about the medium to represent their ideas and additionally selected how they would record the information acquired and share it with their peers. In developing their *imovie* on the topic of *Energy*, one group of children took an historical approach. They considered how people in the past used machines in their everyday lives and then compared this to their own lives today. In doing this they not only increased their knowledge base but also used a number of skills and processes in unique ways. In terms of numeracy these were related to, for example:

- looking at chronological order in sequences of *time*;
- incorporating *time* and *measurement* concepts into editing features of *imovie*;
- exploring *capacity* in science experiments with water to find out more about consumption and conserving water;
- *counting, ordering, using the operations to calculate* ways in which they could organize their information for presentation to the group;
- investigations on *money* in order to discover more effective ways to use energy such as electricity and gas;
- discussions of concepts of *space and shape* in their consideration of, for example, storage of petroleum and transmission of electricity and the structure and shape of electricity pylons.

The children stated that they enjoyed being engaged in such project work. They were able to articulate this in a variety of ways but the general sense of what they were saying was that they liked working with their friends, choosing what to do and they liked using computers to find out 'stuff' on the

Internet and for making (PowerPoint) presentations and movies. It was interesting to note that the boys especially liked writing on computers (the information that they had collected and synthesized) whereas they had previously
indicated that they avoided writing much as they 'hated' it so much. What
was also interesting was that the children were also able to summarize what
they had learnt at the end of the presentation to the whole class as well as
what they would do differently next time if they wanted to change something.

In another project[2] one of the teachers in the study discussed with her
class of Reception children (age 5 years) not only what they had learnt from a
content and process perspective, but also to articulate their feelings about their
learning and what they felt worked best for them. In creating their own port-
folios of learning with PowerPoint they worked in collaboration with the
teacher and some older students in Year 6 to become familiar with the software
and for assistance in preparing the oral and written language components of
the portfolio. In one example, Sean created a portfolio of his learning
throughout his first year of school. Sean's portfolio represents the culmination
of his work over the time period and it was saved on a CD-ROM so that his
parents have a permanent record of the major events, according to Sean, that
constituted his first year at school. The topics included in the 'My Learning'
portfolio by Sean included headings such as;

- I am a reader, a writer, a mathematician.
- I speak and listen.
- I am an artist.
- Playing helps me to learn.
- I am fit and healthy.
- I choose my learning.
- I think about my learning.

It was evident that in his first year of school Sean had had a variety of experiences that increased his knowledge base and extended his learning. The portfolio consists of samples of work that had been scanned, as well as digital
photographs and movies. In the process of creating the portfolio Sean had
opportunities to reflect on his learning and in doing so think about what he
might do next. An important element for him was his statement that he 'liked
to choose my own learning . . . and I chose to learn about lifeguards!'

The examples provided exemplify an approach to pedagogy that promotes
the achievement of numeracy from the perspective that has been outlined
in the model (shown in Figure 14.2). The diverse and complex nature of lives
in the twenty-first century requires that numeracies be considered in new and
dynamic ways that go beyond just being viewed as the application of mathematical skills and processes in everyday life. This requires a consideration of
the ways in which individuals can build knowledge via active exploration in

areas or with issues that children have defined themselves, as well as responding to the needs of others in problem-solving contexts. Further, numeracies involve notions inherent to the pedagogy of multiliteracies (New London Group, 1996) which incorporates the variations of the design process. In this way children, as learners, are engaged in *using existing designs, building on existing designs* and *creating new designs* for specific purposes. Finally, it is essential that learners be provided with opportunities within the framework to communicate and disseminate their ideas. This is important for the creation of knowledge-building communities, and because we can learn a great deal from each other about the varied processes and strategies used, in order to evaluate their effectiveness. It is increasingly evident that ICT plays an important role in becoming numerate since it has the potential to extend each of the facets outlined in the model in new and dynamic ways that were not possible without the technology. The ramifications of such extensions have not been fully realized in school activities which are contained and justified in industrial models of curriculum which place limits on what learners are able to achieve in year-level 'quotas'. With new technologies in learning environments there is potential for teachers of young children to create opportunities for explorations that extend their knowledge and create a skills base that can be built on in the years to come. This can only be achieved with a clear articulation about the goals of the educative process and a realization that we need to reconceptualize curriculum to make them appropriate for life in the information age.

Notes

1   ARC Discovery Project (DP0211777) Becoming Numerate with ICT (2001–2004).
2   ARC Linkage project (LP 0215770) Kids of the New Millennium (2001–2002).

References

Alliance for Childhood (2000) Fool's Gold: A Critical Look at Computers in Childhood. Alliance for Childhood. www.allianceforchildhood.org

Armstrong, A. and Casement, C. (2000) *The Child and the Machine: How Computers Put Our Children's Education at Risk*. Beltsville, MD: Robins Lane Press.

Australian Council of Deans of Education (2001) *New Learning: A Charter for Australian Education*. www.acde.org

Australian Council for Educational Research (1990) *Being numerate: What counts?* Victoria: ACER.

Barnes, B.J. and Hill, S. (1983) Should young children work with microcomputers?: Logo before Lego? *The Computing Teacher*, May: 11–14.

Blanton, W.E., Moorman, G.B., Hayes, B.A. and Warner, M. (2000) Effects of participation in the Fifth Dimension on far transfer. http://129.171.53.1/blantonw/5dClhse/publications/tech/effects/effects.html

CEO Forum (1999) The power of digital learning: integrating digital content. CEO Forum on Education and Technology. http://www.ceoforum.org

Clements, D.H. (1999) Concrete manipulatives, concrete ideas. *Contemporary Issues in Early Childhood*, 1(1): 45–60.

Cope, B. and Kalantzis, M. (eds) (2000) *Multiliteracies: Literacy, Learning and the Design of Social Futures*. Melbourne: Macmillan.

Cuffaro, H.M. (1984) Microcomputers in education: why is earlier better? *Teachers College Record*, 85: 559–68.

Dede, C. (2000) Commentary: looking to the future. *The Future of Children*, 10(2): 178–80.

Department of Education, Queensland (2001) *New Basics: The Why. What, How and When of Rich Tasks*. Brisbane: Access Education.

Department of Education, Tasmania (2003) Essential learnings framework. http://www.education.tas.gov.au/ocll/publications/default.htm

Department of Education and Community Services (South Australia) Early Years (2003) Essential learnings framework. http://www.decs.sa.gov.au/earlyyears/pages/151/7226/

Department of Education, Training and Youth Affairs (1999) The Adelaide declaration on national goals for schooling in the twenty-first century. http://www.deet.gov.au/schools/adelaide/text.htm

Department of Education, Training and Youth Affairs (2000) *Numeracy: A Priority for All: Challenges for Australian Schools*. Canberra, ACT: DETYA.

Department of Further Education and Employment (1998) The implementation of the national numeracy strategy: the final report of the numeracy task force. http://www.dfee.gov.uk/numeracy/index.htm

Education Queensland (1999) *The Next Decade: A Discussion about the Future of Queensland State Schools*. Brisbane, Qld: Education Queensland.

Forman, S.L. and Steen, L.A. (1999) *Beyond Eighth Grade: Functional Mathematics for Life and Work*. Berkeley, CA: National Center for Research in Vocational Education.

Healy, J. (1999) *Failure to Connect: How Computers Affect our Children's Minds and What We Can Do about it*. New York: Simon and Schuster.

Her Majesty's Inspectorate (1998) *The National Numeracy Project: An HMI Evaluation. A Report from the Office of Her Majesty's Chief Inspector of Schools*. London: OFSTED.

Kaiser Family Foundation (1999) Kids and media and the new millennium. The Kaiser Family foundation. http://www.kff/content/1999/1535/

Kilderry, A., Yelland, N.J., Lazaridis, V. and Dragicevic, S. (2003) ICT and numeracy in the knowledge era: creating contexts for new understandings. *Childhood Education*, 79(5): 293–8.

Mathematical Sciences Education Board (1995) *Mathematical Preparation of the Technical Workforce*. Washington, DC: National Research Council.

Maughan, G.R. and Prince Ball, K.S. (1999) Synergistic curriculum for the high performance workplace, *The Technology Teacher*, April: 28–30.

National Association for the Education of Young Children (NAEYC) (1996) Position statement: technology and young children. www.naeyc.org/resources/position_statement/pstech98.htm

National Council of Teachers of Mathematics (1998) *Principles and Standards for School Mathematics: Discussion Draft*. Reston, VA: NCTM.

National Council of Teachers of Mathematics (2000) *Principles and Standards for School Mathematics*. Reston, VA: NCTM.

New London Group (1996) A pedagogy of multiliteracies, *Harvard Educational Review*, 60(1): 66–92.

Papert, S. (1996) The Connected Family: Bridging the Digital Generation Gap. Atlanta, GA: Longstreet Press.

Parette, H. and Murdick, N. (1998) Assisstive technology and IEPs for young children with disabilities, *Early Childhood Education Journal*, 25(3): 193–8.

Piaget, J. (1953) *The Origins of Intellect in the Child*. London: RKP Press.

Resnick, M. (1998) Technologies for lifelong kindergarten, *Educational Technology Research and Development*, 46(4): 43–55.

Resnick, M. (2000) Commentary: looking to the future, *The Future of Children*, 10(2): 173–5.

Rochelle, J., Pea, R., Hoadley, C., Gordin, D. and Means, B. (2000) Changing how and what children learn in school with computer-based technologies, *The Future of Children*, 10(2): 76–101.

Scardamalia, M. and Bereiter, C. (1994) Computer support in knowledge building communities, *The Journal of the Learning Sciences*, 3: 265–83.

Scardamalia, M. and Bereiter, C. (1993) Technologies for knowledge building discourse, *Communication of the ACM*, 36: 37–41.

Shields, M.K. and Behrman, R.E. (2000) Children and computer technology: analysis and recommendations, *The Future of Children*, 10(2): 4–30.

Tinker, R. (1999) New technology bumps into an old curriculum: does the traditional course sequence need an overhaul? http://www.concord.org./library/1999winter/newtechnology.html

Yelland, N.J. (1998a) Empowerment and control with technology for young children, *Educational Theory and Practice*, 20(2), 45–55.

Yelland, N.J. (1998b) Making sense of gender in mathematics and technology, in N.J. Yelland (ed.) *Gender in Early Childhood* (pp. 249–73). London: Routledge.

Yelland, N.J. (1999) Reconceptualizing schooling with technology for the 21st century: images and reflections, in D.D. Shade (ed.) *Information Technology in Childhood Education Annual* (pp. 39–59). Virginia: AACE.

Yelland, N.J. (2001) Girls, mathematics and technology, in W. Atweh, H. Forgasz and B. Nebrez (eds) *Socio-Cultural Foundations of Mathematics* (pp. 393–409). Hillsdale, NJ: Lawrence Erlbaum.

Yelland, N.J. (2002a) Shades of grey: creating a vision of girls and computers, in N. Yelland and A. Rubin (eds) *Ghosts in the Machine: Women's Voices in Research with Technology* (pp. 139–66). New York: Peter Lang.

Yelland, N.J. (2002b) Creating microworlds for exploring mathematical under-standings in the early years of school, *Journal of Educational Computing Research*, 27(1and2): 77–92.

Yelland, N.J. (2002c) Asdf;lkj: Challenges to early childhood curriculum and peda-gogy in the information age, in A. Loveless and B. Dore (eds) *Information and Communication Technologies in the Primary School: Changes and Challenges* (pp. 85–101). Milton Keynes: Open University Press.

15 Postmodernism, passion and potential for future childhoods

Nicola Yelland and Anna Kilderry

The Enlightenment is dead, Marxism is dead, the working class movement is dead . . . and the author does not feel very well either.

(Smith, cited in Harvey, 1989, p. 325, describing the condition of postmodernity)

The postmodern context

We live in a postmodern world and the ideas and techniques of postmodernism are connected to our lives in dynamic and pluralistic ways. Some of these ways have been illustrated in the chapters in this book. Teaching in the postmodern era is characterized by change and uncertainty. Hargreaves, in fact, believes that 'We are living in a defining moment of educational history, when the world in which teachers do their work is changing profoundly, and the demographic composition of teaching is turning over dramatically' (2003, p. 2). We have attempted to outline some of the critical issues that are facing educators in the twenty-first century and illustrate the ways in which we might be able to deal with them from alternative frames and perspectives.

Although postmodernism and its supporters are often critiqued on the basis that they are 'Obsessed with deconstructing and de-legitimating every form of argument they encounter, they can end only in condemning their own validity claims to the point where nothing remains of any basis for reasoned action' (Harvey, 1989, p. 116), the perspective can also be considered as being vital for pulling apart, and perhaps rejecting the meta-narratives or dominant discourses that currently operate within education. Postmodernism with its versatile manifestations, and reactionary forms (or *antiform* as claimed by Hassan, cited in Harvey, 1989), enables educators to view their students and children, their teaching, the educational setting, and the greater social and cultural context in ways that they may not have considered before. Applying the same teaching techniques, and delivering or providing the same content that was considered to be relevant in society and in education in previous times, is not sufficient in the current educational climate where educational goals and needs are rapidly shifting. This does *not* mean that all current and past pedagogy and content must be disbanded and disregarded, but rather that we should now be open to the changing social and cultural contexts that we find ourselves in (Hall and Gieben, 1992) and rethink our pedagogies and content of curricula accordingly to suit the demands of contemporary life.

The authors in this book have started the discussion by critiquing educational practice using postmodern thinking and contemporary frames to disrupt some of the accepted 'truisms' of early childhood education. They have put forward different conceptualizations of early childhood practices and proposed perspectives that are relevant to consider as we move further into the millennium. The authors have argued for the need for multiple and critical views in early childhood education and have suggested ways in which we might rethink a variety of critical issues. These perspectives, practical examples and future visions have added to the repertoire of new theoretical platforms now available in early childhood education (for example, see Dahlberg et al., 1999; Soto and Swadener, 2002; Cannella and Viruru, 2004). The process of articulating and detailing the critical issues found in this book, assist in the authentication process and legitimate different perspectives in early childhood education that are 'essential to the pluralistic stance of postmodernism' (Harvey, 1989, p. 48). The approaches can assist by helping us to frame investigations in ways that facilitate the viewing of issues from new perspectives. They are not meant to just be 'critical' via the disapproval of certain issues; but instead are able to distill the historical processes that perpetuate dominant discourses and maintain the status quo (Carr and Kemmis, 1986). This is particularly important in education which should be at the forefront of preparing citizens for changing times, since it has been suggested that: 'Education is an example of the way patterns of modern societies are collapsing. It's not enough to adapt within the norms of the past. We need to discover profoundly new ways of perceiving the world in which we live' (Theobold, cited in Deveson, 2003).

The authors in this book have considered and critiqued issues in the field of early childhood that have included ideological and political beliefs, cultural understandings, dominant pedagogical beliefs and they have foregrounded social justice and equity issues. By interrogating situations and incidents, the authors have opened up further educational thinking and practice spaces that might enable educators to reconsider their educational priorities and the ways in which they interact on a daily basis with young children. Whether this takes the form of a practical example, a theoretical perspective or gaze, or just a good idea, such critical teaching 'leads' can provide opportunities for early childhood teachers to revitalize their practice and enrich lives. They have taken up the challenge to discover new ways of regarding and enacting early childhood education, especially in the postmodern context. We have argued that early childhood programmes require new theoretical foundations that are flexible and responsive enough to update and sustain the field in the new millennium. Critical examples of practice and theory have the ability to shift pedagogical ideas by illustrating real-life teaching scenarios and educational passion in practice to propel teachers into new educational realms. Postmodernism, and the critical standpoint associated with it, assists in the re-envisioning of early childhood education in much-needed 'other ways' (Soto, 2000).

Inspired educators: the passion

> Think back to your best teachers. If you are a teacher, think of your best students. Or consider your most admired engineer, scientist, or artist – living or dead. What do they all have in common? Passion. Passion expresses itself in many forms of excitement and curiosity, it is frequently playful, and it is always consuming.
>
> (Negroponte, 1994, p. 1)

In each of the chapters that comprise this book, the authors have provided examples of what it means to be an *inspired educator*. Inspired educators confront difficult issues and situations, challenge the status quo, and take the lead, following their passion. They act as *agents of change* by re-envisioning early childhood issues and discourses and thereby hope to influence changing practices. Another way that inspired educators have the potential to move us forward with our thinking is via their critical reflection on situations and their viewing of issues from different standpoints without losing their essential educational commitment. This then leads us to further understandings about issues such as:

1 How the dynamics of power and knowledge can affect the educational process.
2 How hegemonic assumptions can maintain the status quo (Brookfield, 1995) in early childhood education.
3 What it takes to bring about change in the educational context.

Via ideological critiques, interrogating social and political environments, pulling apart familiar teaching practices, the authors in this volume have highlighted and brought to our attention many critical issues and incidents that constitute the important and varied role that early childhood educators play. Educational priorities vary across the disciplines and perspectives, but all the authors in this book have noted what they believe to be critical in early childhood education; critical in nature, and critical for young children. The authors have demonstrated the ability to see familiar situations in new ways and display the insight and courage to try new ways in practice. The chapters represent an attempt to breathe life back into the practices of early childhood educators. They provide inspiration, possibilities, and hope for the field as we realize that we are all agents of change. Each reader will connect differently with the pivotal concepts and issues raised in this book. However, in an attempt to capture some of these critical issues we offer the following questions to stimulate discussions and perhaps initiate change:

- How can we act as a *critical advocate* for early childhood education?
- Is the *over-emphasis of developmental theory* in early childhood education a problem? In what ways is it or is it not?
- Is there a place and time for *risky teaching*?
- How do we create *spaces for children's views*?
- In what ways do we negate *silence* in early childhood education?
- Why do we seem to yearn after notions of the '*ideal child*' or '*normal child*' in early childhood settings? What are the consequences for the child who is not considered to be 'ideal' for the programme?
- What does the term *critical diversity* mean? How is diversity conceptualized and manifested in your educational setting?
- Should *child-centred pedagogy* be disrupted? And in what ways would it affect your practice?
- How can we enact *socially-just teaching*?
- What is the value of disrupting the way that we *view play materials* that are commonly found in early childhood settings?
- How do *popular culture and new technologies* impact on the lives of young children and how are they relevant to early childhood programmes?
- What is your vision of *literacies or multiliteracies* in early childhood education?
- What do *innovative teaching incorporating ICT* look like in practice?

After considering such critical questions regarding early childhood theory and practice, it might be relevant to consider what issues stand out for you as a reader of the text. These issues and critical questions have the potential to make us think about our educational goals, passions and priorities in early childhood education in new and dynamic ways. For example, how can we organize the content of our programmes or develop teaching styles that are relevant and meaningful? This leads us to the question of, What makes issues 'critical'? We suggest that it is possible to *think* critically, *practise* critically, *reflect* critically and *examine* issues in a critical way. This usually involves identifying the situation, uncovering the power relationships, and highlighting the hegemonic discourses in operation with the goal of having the potential to transform the situation. In considering what actions we can initiate in order to practise critically, it becomes evident that there is a great deal of potential, including:

1   Reorganizing educational priorities, and articulating 'What are the specific educational priorities that should be focused on, especially priorities that are relevant for the children in my care?'
2   Highlighting the salient issues that are critical in your educational environment and becoming critically focused on their interrogation in both theory and practice.
3   Being cognizant of the significant role that early childhood educators play in young children's lives and the far-reaching effects that education can have.
4   Being aware that knowledge informs practice, and thus it is essential to read (critically), think (critically) and interrogate practice (critically).
5   Approaching issues in diverse ways. Considering the implications of research for one's own specific educational contexts and discussing the ramifications with stakeholders.
6   Articulating what inspires us as early childhood educators. And creating contexts in which we are able to make a contribution and difference to the lives of young children.

The potential to make a difference

The authors in this book have not attempted to provide comprehensive solutions, or even definite answers, to all the issues that have been raised. Instead, they have created thought-provoking contexts in which we might interrogate such critical issues. The chapters in this book represent attempts to reconceptualize early childhood knowledge and ways to create new knowledge from which we are able to theorize. According to Edwards and Usher, 'Any reconceptualization of pedagogy must go hand-in-hand with a reconceptualization of knowledge' (2000, p. 154) especially if it is dominant knowledge that is taken for granted. In this way, educators 'should examine knowledge both for the way it misrepresents or marginalizes particular views of the world' (McLaren, 2003, p. 85) in order to realize their own unique educational commitments and priorities that they live by.

In this volume we have advocated that there must be recognition of the impact that our role has on the lives of young children and their families as well as the need to celebrate diversity and promote the principles of equity and social justice. How we do this will not only vary across contexts but will need to be considered as individual events. We hope that this book has provided its readers with new conceptual and educational pathways on which to travel.

References

Brookfield, S. (1995) *Becoming a Critically Reflective Teacher*. San Francisco: Jossey-Bass.

Cannella, G.S. and Viruru, R. (2004) *Childhood and Postcolonization: Power, Education, and Contemporary Practice*. New York: RoutledgeFalmer.

Carr, W. and Kemmis, S. (1986) *Becoming Critical: Education, Knowledge and Action Research*. Victoria: Deakin University.

Dahlberg, G., Moss, P. and Pence, A. (1999) *Beyond Quality in Early Childhood Education and Care: Postmodern Perspectives*. London: RoutledgeFalmer.

Deveson, A. (2003) *Resilience*. Sydney: Allen and Unwin.

Edwards, R. and Usher, R. (2000) *Globalisation and Pedagogy: Space, Place and Identity*. London: Routledge.

Hall, S. and Gieben, B. (eds) (1992) *Formations of Modernity*. Cambridge: Polity Press in association with Open University.

Hargreaves, A. (2003) *Teaching in the Knowledge Society: Education in the Age of Insecurity*. New York: Teachers College Press.

Harvey, D. (1989) *The Condition of Postmodernity: An Enquiry into the Origins of Cultural Change*. Oxford: Basil Blackwell.

McLaren, P. (2003) Critical pedagogy: a look at the major concepts, in A. Darder, M. Baltodano and R. Torres (eds) *The Critical Pedagogy Reader* (pp. 69–96). New York: RoutledgeFalmer.

Negroponte, N. (1994) Learning by doing: Don't dissect the frog, build it. http://archives.obs-us.com/obs/english/books/nn/bd2079.htm (accessed 16 June 2004).

Soto, L.D. (2000) An early childhood dreamspace of social justice and equity, in L. D. Soto (ed.) *The Politics of Early Childhood Education* (pp. 197–208). New York: Peter Lang.

Soto, L.D. and Swadener, B.B. (2002) Toward liberatory early childhood theory, research and praxis: decolonializing a field, *Contemporary Issues in Early Childhood*, 3(1): 38–66.

Index